D0883491

Gottfried Keller and His Critics

Studies in German Literature, Linguistics, and Culture
Literary Criticism in Perspective

Editorial Board

Literary Criticism in Perspective

James Hardin (*South Carolina*), General Editor

Steve Dowden (*Brandeis*), German Literature

Reingard M. Nischik (*Constance*), Comparative Literature

About *Literary Criticism in Perspective*

Books in the series *Literary Criticism in Perspective* trace literary scholarship and criticism on major and neglected writers alike, or on a single major work, a group of writers, a literary school or movement. In so doing the authors — authorities on the topic in question who are also well-versed in the principles and history of literary criticism — address a readership consisting of scholars, students of literature at the graduate and undergraduate level, and the general reader. One of the primary purposes of the series is to illuminate the nature of literary criticism itself, to gauge the influence of social and historic currents on aesthetic judgements once thought objective and normative. Another purpose is to show how literary criticism has enhanced our appreciation of literary works by revealing their underlying structures and themes.

Richard R. Ruppel

Gottfried Keller and His Critics

A Case Study in
Scholarly Criticism

CAMDEN HOUSE

PT2374
Z5R84

Copyright © 1998 Richard R. Ruppel

All Rights Reserved. Except as permitted under current legislation,
no part of this work may be photocopied, stored in a retrieval system,
published, performed in public, adapted, broadcast, transmitted,
recorded, or reproduced in any form or by any means,
without the prior permission of the copyright owner.

First published 1998
Camden House
Drawer 2025
Columbia, SC 29202–2025 USA

Camden House is an imprint of Boydell & Brewer Inc.
PO Box 41026, Rochester, NY 14604–4126 USA
and of Boydell & Brewer Limited
PO Box 9, Woodbridge, Suffolk IP12 3DF, UK

ISBN: 1–57113–055–1

Library of Congress Cataloging-in-Publication Data

Ruppel, Richard R., 1953-
    Gottfried Keller and his critics : a case study in scholarly
criticism / Richard R. Ruppel.
        p.   cm. – (Studies in German literature, linguistics, and
culture. Literary criticism in perspective)
    Includes bibliographical references and index.
    ISBN 1-57113-055-1 (alk. paper)
    1. Keller, Gottfried, 1819-1890 –Criticism and interpretation.
I. Title. II. Series: Studies in German literature, linguistics,
and culture (Unnumbered). Literary criticism in perspective.
PT2374.Z5R84 1998
838'.809—dc21   98-20320
                                                          CIP

For Hans Wysling

Contents

Preface

GOTTFRIED KELLER'S FICTION AND POETRY grew in popularity in the final decade of his life. While his books never did achieve the broad best-seller status of some of his contemporaries, his works became part of the nineteenth-century canon of German literature we still read today, which cannot be said of those best-selling authors who were his contemporaries. Thus Keller, who did not write for the general public, has become a Swiss classic in the canon of nineteenth-century German letters; one that warrants our discussion today. Over the last decade at least one new volume has been published each year on Keller or his fiction. The proliferation of new approaches and interpretations of Keller's works in recent decades is a perennial tribute to the ability of Keller's fiction to engage the modern reader by addressing issues that are as prevalent today as they were in Keller's time. The decision of the Bibliothek der deutschen Klassiker to publish a new historical-critical edition of Keller's works in seven volumes must be joyfully greeted and must be viewed as a manifestation of Keller's enduring popularity.

Why, one may ask, do we need yet another book on Keller, much less a volume that discusses the critical scholarly literature devoted to him? The explosion of scholarly writing on Keller and his works which spans a century and a half offers the modern lay reader and literary scholar alike a plethora of approaches, interpretations, and assessments of Keller's oeuvre. In writing this book I have sought to offer the general reader and the scholar an orientation in Keller scholarship and have done so by selecting and briefly discussing those representative scholarly works that have contributed to our understanding of Keller's writing. I have attempted to tell the story of Keller scholarship which fortuitously parallels the development of literary scholarship in the German-Swiss tradition from its youthful stage as journalistic criticism in the middle of the nineteenth century to literary scholarship as we know it today.

This study opens with an introduction to Gottfried Keller and to the literary industry in the nineteenth century that discusses both the plight of authors and the rigors of the publishing industry. The second chapter provides a representative sampling of the journalistic criticism in Keller's day and allows Keller through his essays and correspondence to enter into dialogue with his early critics. The study then shifts in the third chapter to the transitional years as literary scholarship and German Studies emerge and distinguish themselves from earlier journalistic criticism; likewise Keller scholarship in the years following his death emerges from a circle of friends such as Jakob Baechtold and Adolf Frey, and eventually achieves distance and hence greater objectivity and depth in the works of Emil Ermatinger, Hans Dünnebier and Hans Max Kriesi. The next chapter traces the most significant trends in Keller scholarship in the decades following the anniversary of his birth in 1919, in which Keller scholarship enjoyed an unprecedented proliferation in both volume and diversity. Those years saw the establishment of the Gottfried Keller Society, which supported the first comprehensive critical edition of his works and correspondence. A separate extensive chapter is dedicated to the representative Keller scholarship in the Anglo-American tradition. The study concludes with a discussion of those milestone publications of the past few decades that have breathed new life and given new direction to our understanding of Keller and his works.

This study presumes a knowledge of Keller's fiction. It should serve both scholars and readers less familiar with Keller's works by enabling them to orient themselves in the most significant criticism on Keller's works. In writing this volume in the Camden House series on Literary Criticism in Perspective, it has been my task to assess some one hundred and fifty years of Gottfried Keller scholarship. Apportioning space to all those fine contributions, which have broadened and deepened our understanding of Keller, his fiction and poetry, has left me with the difficult task of deciding what to include and exclude. Any such undertaking is fraught with subjectivity despite the most open-minded intentions. The selection of critical texts can best be termed representational. The primary goal of this book is to discuss the heights of scholarly prowess, so of necessity I have omitted most dissertations, many articles and most *Herbstboten* (annual published lectures of the Gottfried Keller Society). However, despite awareness of the difficulty, there is still the danger of stressing some aspects too much and others too little, as well as the constant potential for grievous omission. Therefore, in keeping with the intention of the Literary Criticism in Perspective series I have chosen to write at length about certain texts that I consider representative of a general trend or period in Keller scholarship, which have over the decades broadened and deepened our understanding of Keller and his works.

Throughout Keller scholarship, scholars have referred to the Jonas Fränkel and Carl Helbling critical edition of Keller's works, the *Sämtliche Werke,* which I have cited with the abbreviation *S.W.* and volume and page numbers. Likewise, they have referred to Carl Helbling's critical edition of Keller's collected letters, the *Gesammelte Briefe,* which I have cited with the abbreviation *G.B.* and volume and page numbers. Finally, I have abbreviated all references to the *Jahrbuch der Gottfried Keller-Gesellschaft,* the official publication for the proceedings of the Gottfried Keller Society, as *Jb. GKG.*

Acknowledgments

MY ACKNOWLEDGMENTS AND OBLIGATIONS are many. I extend my special thanks and friendship to the scholars, past and present, referred to in this book for their fine contributions to our knowledge and understanding of Meister Gottfried and his works. This book is dedicated to the late Hans Wysling a dear friend and mentor; Wysling was for many years a professor at the University of Zurich, Director of the Thomas Mann Archive, and President of the Gottfried Keller Society. Wysling accomplished much over the years in his ever gracious and tireless manner to further discussions of Keller through seminars, colloquia, books, articles, and exhibitions.

It is in sincere gratitude that I turn to the Gottfried Keller Archive in the Zentralbibliothek in Zurich, in particular to Martin Germann and to M. Kotrba who made it possible for me to locate and access the Keller materials despite the fact that they were then being relocated in the renovated Central Library in Zurich. In the same breath I also wish to extend particular thanks to the University Personnel Development Committee at the University of Wisconsin in Stevens Point, whose gracious travel stipend made it possible to carry out on-site research in Zurich, and to Claudia and Huib Ernste, whose kind hospitality made our stay in Zurich all the more enjoyable. Heartfelt thanks are also extended to Hajo Romahn for his willingness to facilitate my research in the library of the Ruhr University of Bochum. I want to express my gratitude to all those who provided assistance in the library at the University of Wisconsin in Stevens Point, in Memorial Library at University of Wisconsin in Madison, and in Olin Library at Cornell. Sincere thanks to Jan and Mark Seiler and to Suzanne Lewis, my colleagues in German at the University of Wisconsin in Stevens Point, whose willingness to cover courses while I was on sabbatical, contributed to making this project a reality. Special thanks to Steve Dowden, Jim Hardin, Jim Walker, and Eitel Timm, whose editorial services, patience, and encouragement were invaluable to all that is good in this book. I wish to express my thanks to Doris and Roland Brendel, my in-laws, whose gracious home and hospitality over three summers provided the peace of mind and the congenial atmosphere that helped me to prepare this manuscript. Lastly, I am ever grateful to my loving wife Jutta, whose unfailing support, understanding, and patience enabled me to see this project through to completion.

R. R. R.
Stevens Point, Wisconsin
March 1998

1: The Literary Industry of Keller's Day

GOTTFRIED KELLER (1819–1890) IS RESPECTED today as a novelist and as a master of the novella. He is arguably the most prominent author to hail from German-speaking Switzerland. Keller was also a good poet, a moderately respected painter, and an erudite critic. He aspired at first to become a landscape painter, but he lacked the training and sufficient talent to become financially successful in that artistic medium. In the 1840s he abandoned the canvas and brush for paper and quill, and eventually made the written word his own. During those early years as a poet, he composed a slim volume of nature and political poetry before focusing his talent on prose fiction. It was in the medium of prose that he would excel, establishing himself as a Swiss author of prominence within the canon of nineteenth-century German literature. Keller's oeuvre includes works that have come to embody the literary epoch of German poetic realism (1850–1890). In recent decades, literary historians have begun to view Keller's fiction in the context of European Realism; his fiction has been compared to that of Balzac, Dickens, and Tolstoy.

Keller's themes are universal and far-ranging, yet they are indelibly connected to his own experiences, to Switzerland, and to the times in which he lived. Central to his fiction is the concern for the development of individuals into responsible citizens. Keller believed the childhood experience to be central to the well-rounded development of the whole individual; indeed this belief constitutes the central theme of his greatest novel, *Der grüne Heinrich,* (Green Henry, 1855), a blend between a self-reflective novel and an educational novel (Bildungsroman) in the tradition of Goethe's *Wilhelm Meister.* Keller's enlightened and progressive father died when he was five. The author, raised by his mother, was unfairly punished with expulsion from trade school because of a childhood prank. This single event forced young Keller to became an autodidact. His expulsion from school was simultaneously an expulsion from Swiss middle-class society, because to deny a young child an education was in Keller's own words to "decapitate" him, to deny him any hope of securing a position in society. As if to provide some compensation to Keller for his unwarranted expulsion from school, the cantonal government of Zürich granted him what became a renewable scholarship to study drama in Heidelberg (1848–49) and in Berlin (1849–55). His first novel, *Der grüne Heinrich,* and his first collection of novellas, *Die Leute von Seldwyla,* were composed in Berlin. With these publications Keller became a respected author. Unable, however, to live on the proceeds from his fiction, Keller assumed the highly respected position of cantonal clerk in Zurich when he was 41, and held it for some fifteen years before retiring to pursue his calling as an author.

In his bent for employing fiction as a medium for educating his readers, Keller furthered a long-standing Swiss tradition of educating through fiction, which had been pursued by Jean-Jacques Rousseau, Heinrich Pestalozzi, and Jeremias Gotthelf, among others. Keller, however, achieved a far greater degree of integration between his fiction and its moral, social, and didactic mission than did his predecessors. Whereas the others have a tendency to tell and explain, even to preach, Keller shows; he paints a picture that conveys his message to the observant reader; his message remains buried beneath an artistic veneer of exquisite prose and subtle irony.

Keller's fiction contain a plethora of misguided souls, dreamers who stumble into confrontations with reality that force them to examine their ways and to make decisions. Poetic justice prevails. There are those characters who make the correct decisions, who embrace reality: for example, Pankraz, who overcomes his sulking to become a responsible citizen; Fritz Amrain, who matures under his mother's guiding hand to become a responsible businessman and citizen, and Wenzel Strapinski, who learns to accept his station in life and become a loving husband and a successful tailor. There are also those characters who fail to bring their subjective views of life into alignment with objective reality. Heinrich Lee, the protagonist of Keller's first novel, is just such a dreamer; he is modelled on the author's own experience. Lee's extensive education leads to a premature death because he fails to become a supportive son and thereby fails to become a productive member of society. Individual greed drives the three combmakers into a frenzied competition, in which they are all losers. The conflict between the subjective individual character's self-interests and the inevitable confrontation of those interests with a greater objective reality places Keller's fiction at the heart of discussions of Realism. How does a character — or an author — objectify his own subjectivity?

Keller captures in his fiction many questions and topics of his day that remain prevalent in our own time. Recent literary scholars have uncovered Keller's subtle criticism of the middle-class social fabric in his *Romeo und Julia auf dem Dorfe* (1856, *A Village Romeo and Juliet*) and in the Seldwyla novellas. Others cite his acute critical observations of the transition from family oriented businesses to the cottage industry, and on to urban industrialization with all its ramifications for family, society, and tradition as they are clearly depicted in *Das verlorene Lachen* (1874, *The Lost Smile*). Still others point to his ever-evolving religious and ethical views. Keller's philosophy of life — and consequently his fiction and his poetry — were influenced by the philosopher Ludwig Feuerbach, who believed that God was a mere projection of man's own virtues, that eternal life is nothing more than man's attempt to overcome death. Feuerbach espoused a worldly religion and advocated that his followers seek fulfillment in the material world. Keller's fiction is suffused with debates on and discussions of Christianity, the church, and God in an increasingly secular world. Keller's *Sieben Legenden* (1872, *Seven Legends*) exemplify this transformation of Christian legends into secular stories of humane actions that further humanity.

The range of Keller's abilities might be summed up by the juxtaposition of his last two works, *Das Sinngedicht* (1883, *The Epigram*) and *Martin Salander* (1886). *Das Sinngedicht* is the most aesthetically pleasing and artistically perfect of Keller's novella cycles. It has been heralded as the most integrated novella cycle in European literature. In this work, the estranged scientist Reinhart sets off into the world armed with an epigram, through which he hopes to find the perfect bride. He eventually encounters Lucie, a highly intelligent woman. Through the story-telling duel that ensues and in which they each narrate a novella, Reinhard and Lucie each reveal themselves to the other developing a growing affection for one another, until they join hands in marriage. In sharp contrast, in *Martin Salander*, Keller's last novel, the author turns his full attention to social themes, to the moral, political, and social decay brought on by industrialization. This last novel is linked to earlier works through the illusionary dreams of the main protagonist, but the novel itself exhibits none of the artistic beauty and little of the humor for which Keller's fiction is known. The fine line between showing and telling becomes transparent. Keller had become disillusioned with the cultural ramifications of Swiss industrialization. What we find in *Martin Salander* could well be said to anticipate the next literary epoch of German naturalism.

Keller lived to begin the arrangements for the publication of a ten-volume edition of his collected works. The publication of a collected edition during the author's lifetime demonstrates the tremendous success his fiction had attained. Keller's critical essays on Jeremias Gotthelf are as respected today as they were in his own time. His critical dialogues with the literary historians and authors of his day, which are contained in his correspondence, constitute a body of critical thought. Keller could be paternally supportive of those burgeoning young authors who sought his assistance and explosively cruel to those who sought to use his good name as a bridge to success, particularly when they lacked sufficient talent. His novella *Die Mißbrauchten Liebesbriefe* is a literary satire of would-be authors who feign talent. The impact of Keller's fiction on German authors has been profound. Thomas Mann, Gerhard Hauptmann, Hugo von Hofmannsthal, Carl Spitteler, Ricarda Huch, Hermann Hesse, and such cultural sages as Walter Benjamin have all sung Keller's praises.

Keller's themes are both universal and contemporary. The social, economic, religious, and ethical questions Keller raises are imbued with foresight. His depiction of women, exemplified in the strength of his many female characters, can in many respects be considered modern. Keller's interest in the scientific revolution of his day, and particularly his interest in ecology, was well in advance of its time. Certainly the process by which one overcomes individual subjective preoccupation with the self to become a productive, critical, contributing member of an ever-changing society is no less quintessential today than it was in Keller's time. It should therefore not be of surprise to anyone that the vast majority of undergraduates studying German have been assigned to read either *Romeo und Julia auf dem Dorfe* or *Kleider Machen Leute* (*Clothes Make the Man*) for the timeless universal truths these stories contain.

With the publication of his first novel, *Der grüne Heinrich*, in 1855, Gottfried Keller immediately distinguished himself as an author of purport. Keller's novel initially enjoyed the praise of a small readership and gradually garnered the respect of his artistically gifted contemporaries such as C. F. Meyer (1825–1898), Paul Heyse (1830–1914), and Theodor Storm (1817–1888), among others. However, this is not to suggest that he was always lauded for his literary efforts, nor that he was in agreement with his critics — whether friend or foe. Keller's relationship to his craft might best be described as a lifelong struggle to coordinate the independent will of his muse with the rigors and demands of the publishing industry of his day. He wrote when he felt inspired to write; his muse was not one to be harnessed to the treadmill of literary production. His free-spirited muse drove publishers such as Eduard Vieweg (1796–1869) to despair and severely tried the generous patience of such editors and good friends as Julius Rodenberg (1831–1914). That the serialized segments of novels such as *Martin Salander* were written under the duress of meeting deadlines distressed both Keller and his editors. His correspondence is peppered with apologies to publishers, and with rage to friends over unpolished works of fiction that were put to press before they had been given sufficient time to mature.

The journalistic critics and literary historians of the day often took Keller to task for not having refined and polished his prose pieces. His novellas, such as the Seldwyla collection, were initially accessible to a general reading public through such literary journals as *Die Rundschau*, and were later published as books and made available through the commercial lending libraries. But the journals and lending libraries, while securing a broader readership, reduced the number of books sold, and thus profits. To compound these difficulties, books were expensive, and the average family in Germany in the nineteenth century, in spite of the industrial revolution, did not have the surplus income to purchase them. Furthermore, in addition to the fiscal realities only seventy percent of the public was literate by 1860; literate in the sense that seventy percent of all Germans could read a newspaper or a pamphlet. Literacy does not assume the ability to comprehend a literary text such as a novella, much less a sophisticated and complex four volume novel such as *Der grüne Heinrich*.

German literary criticism was itself in its infantile stages in those days and was mostly found in journals and in so-called literary essays (*Besprechungen*) in newspapers, the forerunner to the modern *feuilleton*. *Die Deutsche Literaturzei-*

tung featured a special column for new publications in which many students of the prominent nineteenth-century literary historians such as Wilhelm Scherer published their critiques. The critical journal the *Grenzboten* (1848–1857), edited by Gustav Freytag and Julian Schmidt included a column that discussed recently published novels. German literary history evolved into a discipline during Keller's lifetime. Even the then newly founded Swiss Federal Technical University (ETH) in Zurich saw fit in the 1850s to establish a chair in literary history. The contemporary reader can obtain much useful information on Keller criticism through his ambitious correspondence with critics, literary historians, fellow authors, publishers, and friends; this correspondence constitutes an extensive discourse unique to Keller, and we shall turn to it in the next chapter.

Keller was well aware of the critical discourse, the aesthetic and academic discussions of his time. He was perhaps his own most aggressive and relentless critic. His critical essays on the nineteenth-century Swiss author Jeremias Gotthelf (1797–1854) and the German Romantic writer Jean Paul Richter (1763–1825) as well as on the criticism of the prominent nineteenth-century critic Friedrich Theodor Vischer (1807–1887) are well known. Before turning to Keller and his critics, it is necessary to understand Keller's relationship to his craft and to the creative process, in order to comprehend his often strained relationship with the literary industry of his day.

Keller's mode of composition was not well suited for the inflexible deadlines of the publishing world. In his early correspondence with Vieweg in 1850 he vowed that he would never again sign a contract without having a manuscript in hand (*G.B.* III/2, 30). In a letter to Paul Heyse, Keller expressed similar sentiments: "The real evil is to have to write down within set deadlines that which one has peripatetically dreamed up; this pressure has plagued me since last December, even if I was usually able to complete the amount of writing required for the month within eight days, I was forced to put all correspondence aside. At long last I have completed my contract with the *Rundschau* and can think of other things" (*G.B.* III/1, 51). Adolf Frey (1855–1920), who knew him personally, writes that it remained incomprehensible to Keller that other authors were masters of their own time, that they followed a strict daily schedule and could sit down at their desks at a regularly appointed time and put a sufficient quota of words on paper. According to Frey, Keller waited for the muse to smile benevolently, and then grasped his pen in the wee hours of the morning when no author or scribe of a more disciplined nature would have considered working (Frey, 41). Frey saw Keller often during the last fifteen years of the poet's life, but only chanced to stop by once when Keller was composing a poem. He offered to leave rather than to disturb the creative spirit, to which Keller is reported to have replied, "Please stay. I am not working on a production line and will simply continue writing tomorrow from that point where I left off today" (41). Whether Keller picked up the quill the next morning or ten months later was a matter of destiny, a matter of the muse speaking. We know from his correspondence with Hermann Hettner (1821–1882) and Vieweg that while he was struggling to complete *Der grüne Heinrich* Keller was fashioning in his head what became *Die Leute von Seldwyla* (*People of Seldwyla*) and the *Sieben Legenden*. His promise to his publisher not to work on anything until the novel was done, could only be kept in this manner. We know from his correspondence with Storm and Heyse that Keller carried around the plans for his last novel, *Martin Salander*, for years before he actually put it down on paper. Mozart supposedly created entire symphonies in his head and then wrote them down in a flowing manner without correction, erasure or rewriting; likewise, Keller allowed novellas to mature in his head, and then wrote them down, although unlike Mozart he never remained bound to any plan, and was open to whatever changes the muse dictated. Writing to Storm in June 1882, Keller apologized for his long silence and blamed his overly active muse for keeping him away from their pressing correspondence (*G.B.* III/1, 475). Likewise, in a letter to the Viennese literary historian Emil Kuh (1828–1876), Keller discussed his intense periods of creative productivity interspersed by long periods of procrastination (*G.B.* III/1, 183). Adolf Frey asserts that Keller would on occasion write something straight through to completion. Other works he would begin somewhere and see how the work progressed (Frey 42). Meister Gottfried was his own scribe: he could not compose when other people were present, and never resorted to dictation. If the first attempt did not please him, he did not hesitate to set the work aside, often for months or years. Likewise, in his correspondence there are letters that were begun and then discontinued until weeks, even months later. The spontaneity and elasticity of Keller's language, which reflects the author's many moods, may be attributed in part to his peculiar relationship to his craft. Keller wrote when the spirit moved him; he wrote when the muses spoke to him. His primary concern was to write well, to achieve literary artistry. In the late 1850s Keller emerged after the publication of *Der grüne Heinrich* and *Die Leute von Seldwyla* as a respected, if relatively new and little-known author. The years in Berlin that were fraught with financial misery had proven to be a wellspring of industrious artistic endeavor from which Keller would draw for the rest of his life. On the completion of *Der grüne Heinrich*, Keller wrote to Vieweg of his plans to become an author of consequence (*G.B.* III/2, 102). Promoting his own artistic career, Keller instructed his publisher to send review copies of the novel to Fanny Lewald (1811–1889) and to Hermann Hettner (*G.B.* III/2, 79). Keller seemed satisfied with the reviews of his novel, commenting that such established literary critics as Varnhagen von Ense (1785–1858) had appraised his novel as no worse than most; moreover, the many acquaintances who had borrowed the novel had good things to say about it; Keller mentions that many lending libraries in Berlin had even purchased two copies of it (*G.B.* III/2, 105).

Keller, promoting his interests abroad, requested that Vieweg send his friend Ferdinand Freiligrath (1810–1876) a review copy of the novel to pass along to friends in London who were interested in German literature (*G.B.* III/2, 11). In a letter to Hettner, Keller harbored some naive hope of living as a financially independent author, suggesting, before the completion of *Der grüne Heinrich*, that once this novel was done and he had written some dramas, he would return to Switzerland with a financially secure future and a changed outlook on life (*G.B.* I, 368). This optimism was already tempered eight months after the publication of his novel, as we see in Keller's letter to his publisher Vieweg, in which he disclosed his plan to return to Zurich, where an easy position in the cantonal government had been promised to him; this position would provide financial stability and would not consume too much of the time and energy needed to write (*G.B.* III/2, 123). Clearly Keller had learned firsthand how difficult it was to establish himself as a financially self-sustaining author. Although he wrote to others of his plans to live from his writing, his own financial situation and the literary industry of the day made it impossible for him to do so. The need for financial security forced him to seek gainful employment elsewhere, and Keller assumed the position of cantonal clerk in Zurich, a position he held for some fifteen years.

Keller's decision to seek the position of cantonal clerk was founded on the realization that he could not expect during the 1850s to live from revenues generated by his publications, a realization born of experience. His predicament was shared by other German writers. Joseph Eichendorff (1788–1857) was an Austrian civil servant. Authors such as C. F. Meyer and Paul Heyse were independently wealthy. Wilhelm Raabe (1831–1910) stubbornly refused to accept any form of work that was not associated with his artistic aspirations. Theodor Storm was a district magistrate; the Austrian author Adalbert Stifter (1805–1861) had been a teacher. For his own part, only during the last decade and a half of his life could Keller afford to live on the royalties from his literary endeavors.

The plight of the nineteenth-century author urges one to examine the literary marketplace of Keller's epoch. The literary salon of the late eighteenth century presents itself as a magnificent if antiquated model of literary discourse enjoyed by a literate elite. As Peter Hohendahl has shown, one can hypothesize that 25% of the German population was literate in 1800, 40% in 1830, 75% in 1870 and as many as 90% by 1900 (1985, 309). These figures seem to indicate a vast market of readers, but they must be seen for what they are: literacy statistics. It would be presumptuous to assume that the ability to read a newspaper also implies ability to read a literary text. It is necessary to distinguish between popular literature and canonized literary texts that presume a certain level of education. In Prussia in 1864 fewer than six percent of secondary school students received an education that would enable them to read the classical canon of German; if the criteria for sufficient education are tightened, this figure is reduced to approximately three percent. By 1878 this situation had hardly changed at all. Thus an author in the mid-nineteenth century could hardly expect to live on the royalties earned from publications.

The literary marketplace played an equally important role in the ability of an author to live from the sales of his books. The publishing industry had improved its technology and was capable even before 1848 of mass producing books, journals, and newspapers quickly and less expensively. The efficiency of the publishing industry was well ahead of its ability to market its literary products, due in part to limited literacy. Industrialization led to urbanization, to a movement into the cities, thereby stimulating increased awareness of publications as well as the desire to own them or at least to have access to them. However, very few readers could afford to purchase their own books, because books were expensive despite innovations in publishing. Research has shown that as late as 1900 only fifteen percent of the typical worker's wage was disposable income (Hohendahl, 1985, 314). Publishers could not hope to sell many books to individuals. Thus, during the 1850s and 1860s most publishers such as Vieweg aimed to sell their publications to the lending libraries. While sales to lending libraries initially increased the sales for the publisher, it ultimately reduced the number of individual copies that might have otherwise been sold. Moreover, rise of literary journals, such as the *Gartenlaube* and the *Rundschau*, in which many authors, including Keller, serialized their works, became very popular and reached a circulation of over a million by the end of the 1860s (Hohendahl, 1985, 312). These journals would eventually replace the lending libraries in the early twentieth century as the reading public grew. The serialization of novels in the journals reduced the sales of books over the long term. The literary journals, which required authors to produce their creations according to deadlines, played a significant role in making the novella the preferred genre of many nineteenth-century German authors, because the shorter novella form was more realistically deliverable under a deadline.

The publishing industry of Keller's day was of course interested in what its readership wanted to read. E. Last provides us with a glimpse of what readers of diverse social classes read, based upon subscriptions to the Vienna Public Library in 1876. Approximately 85 percent of the subscribers read novels, not only German ones, but English and French as well, as compared with 67 percent of the subscribers, who read dramas and 38 percent who read poetry. The preference for prose, if we can take this example to be representative of a broader spectrum, would certainly encourage publishers to publish prose. However, as has been shown, the libraries and their reading public demonstrated a universal need for entertainment; authors such as Fontane, Keller, Raabe, and Storm, who were later canonized, were acquired and read alongside Auerbach, Freytag, and Marlitt, authors who are considered of secondary or trivial rank today.[1]

Literary Criticism in Keller's Day

Literary criticism in the latter half of the nineteenth century, not unlike the literary industry of the time, was a predecessor of the modern *feuilleton* and at best a forerunner to the literary scholarship we know today. The English term "literary criticism" encompasses the interpretation of literature in the broadest sense, including an aesthetic, intellectual, and scholarly examination. Of the two German terms that correspond to the one English term, *Literaturkritik* is associated with journalism, and carries with it the connotation of shallowness and temporality, whereas *Literaturwissenschaft* is associated with the academic or scholarly interpretation of literature. What we understand the term *Literaturwissenschaft* to mean has evolved over the ages. Certainly Hettner's comments, raised in the spirit of intellectual inquiry, followed by Emil Kuh's and Friedrich Theodor Vischer's essays on Keller, raised criticism to a higher intellectual level, later pursued by Otto Brahm (1856–1912) and Jakob Baechtold (1848–1897), who were by nineteenth-century standards of criticism considered scholars; nevertheless, their conception of literary analysis is quite different from what we assume literary scholarship to be today. Theirs was a form of criticism less interested in the spirit of inquiry than in rendering judgment according to the standards of the day:

> "Criticism assumes the task of regulating literature both in its production and in its reception. Thus the treatment in reviews always involves a decision as to whether an individual work should be accepted within the canon of literature or excluded from it, ... " (Hohendahl, 1988, 269).

Keller wrote and published in an age in which literary criticism evolved from journalistic critiques into the literary scholarship we know today; *Germanistik*, or German Studies began to evolve in Keller's time. The academics who established what has become the canon of German literature were not literary historians by trade; rather, they came to literature from other disciplines. Some were independent authors in their own right. Georg Gottfried Gervinus (1805–71) had a substantial role in shaping what became the canon of classical German literature; he was by trade and by education a historian. A disciple of Hegel, Gervinus held a chair in European history even after the publication in 1853 of his seminal five volume *Literaturgeschichte* (History of Literature). Other promi-

---

[1] Hohendahl, 1985, p. 319. I recommend that readers interested in the literary public of Keller's day read Hohendahl's chapter on "Das literarische Publikum," to which I am indebted for these statistics. Alberto Martino's article "Die deutsche Leihbibliothek und ihr Publikum" in *Aufsätze und Forschungsberichte zum 19. Jahrhundert*, (ed. Alberto Martino, Günter Häntzschel, and Georg Jäger [Tübingen: Niemeyer, 1977], 1–26) is also recommended reading.

nent literary historians, such as Robert Prutz, came to literary history from classical philology; Rudolf Haym hailed from philosophy, and even Wilhelm Dilthey, representing the youngest generation, began his academic career as a student of theology. Those friends and critical promoters of Keller's earlier publications, such as Hermann Hettner, Emil Kuh, and Julian Schmidt, were not schooled in literary history. Hettner held a professorship in aesthetics and art history in Heidelberg. Emil Kuh was an art historian. Julian Schmidt, together with Gustav Freytag, became co-editors of the *Grenzboten*, a leading literary journal of the day. History of literature as an academic discipline came into its own only after 1850. In 1853 Keller was offered a newly established professorship for modern literature in the recently established Polytechnikum in Zurich, which he declined, and indeed even sought to persuade Hermann Hettner to apply for(*G.B.* I, 386). Friedrich Theodor Vischer held perhaps the earliest academic appointment of its kind, insofar as he was professor of aesthetics and German literature as early as 1835. This is not to suggest that Keller's evolving oeuvre was misjudged or misplaced in what became the established canon of German literature in the nineteenth century, but rather to reveal that Keller was writing in an era in which the very concept of a German literary history was still being fashioned: the critical methodology was still being honed. Furthermore, all of this must be measured against the economic and political backdrop of central Europe, namely industrialization, the establishment of what became the modern Swiss Federation, and the unification of Germany under Bismarck.

It is not within the scope of this study to undertake an extensive examination of the formation of the canon of nineteenth-century German literature. However, a brief digression into the problems and evolving methodologies of Keller's day may help us to understand Keller's critics and his place in the canon, and in German literary history. The task of the literary historian lay in the reconstruction of the development of past literary epochs in order to make those authors and their works accessible to a modern audience by providing extensive biographical and historical detail pertaining to the work. Naturally this historical interpretation of earlier authors and their works involves not only the description and cataloguing of such works, but must of necessity also include their evaluation. The educated modern reader thinks of Fontane, Keller, Raabe, and Storm as German authors writing in the tradition of German Realism, and is probably not as familiar with Auerbach, Freytag, Heyse, and Marlitt, although all of these writers were published side-by-side in the journals of the day, and were widely read. Thus, German literary historians in the nineteenth century not only sorted through historical literary works to determine what should belong in the canon, but also, through their criticism, assumed an active role in the ongoing creative process of contemporary authors. Some of these early literary critics, such as Auerbach, Freytag, and Gutzkow, were themselves authors. Some were editors of their own literary journals: Freytag published the *Grenzboten*, Robert Prutz edited the *Deutsche Museum*, and Rudolf Gottshall published the *Blätter für literarische Unterhaltung*. Both Freytag and Gottshall, who wrote the two most important literary histories, wrote for the general reading public, rather than for academic circles. Rudolf Haym, perhaps the most "modern" of the literary historians of that era, was editor of the *Preußischen Jahrbücher*. These literary scholars wrote not for those well versed in literary scholarship as is often the case today, but for the general reading public. They were deeply involved in the literary and political discourse of their day. The *Besprechung*, or literary essay, was their genre of choice. Their literary histories were far more akin to the historical novel than to contemporary academic scholarship. They wove together a patchwork of biographical and historical facts pertaining to a particular work and its author, which provided background information, but little interpretation. The unique blend of literary scholarship and active literary discourse with contemporary authors that these earliest literary historians embodied lasted approximately until 1900, when literary scholarship became too scholarly esoteric to be of interest to the general reader, who found the impressions of the daily *feuilleton* much more accessible (Hohendahl, 1985, 266).

The European historian Georg Gervinus became perhaps the most important German literary historian of the the the *Vormärz*, the period prior to the revolutions of 1848. His achievement, no matter how much disputed in the latter half of the nineteenth century, was the canonization of Weimar Classicism, which he touted as the pinnacle of German literary achievement. Gervinus, while thoroughly acknowledging Goethe and Schiller's literary achievements, was more critical toward their political orientations. Gervinus's five volume *Geschichte der deutschen Dichtung* suggests that German literature, having attained its apogee, was in decline. How then were critics to assess the authors of future generations, who must of necessity live in the shadow of Weimar Classicism? Keller became acquainted with Gervinus in Heidelberg, where Gervinus was the chief editor of the *Deutsche Zeitung* (1847–50). Hettner refers to this publication as a scholastically eloquent academic newspaper that excluded bourgeois and liberal tendencies; very pleasant for the learned, but completely unsuited for the general reading public (Luck, 1970, 87). Keller, in a letter to his friend Wilhelm Barmgartner (1820–1867) refers to Gervinus and his ilk as crass, uncultivated rogues (*G.B.* I, 276). Hettner's first volume of his *Literaturgeschichte des 18. Jahrhunderts* was criticized by Friedrich Theodor Vischer for its light style, with which Hettner sought to reach a broader reading public. With this observation one stands at the heart of the nineteenth-century literary discussion: Namely, for whom did these latter-day literary historians write their criticism and their literary histories? For fellow academicians or for a broader reading public?

The split between *feuilleton*-style criticism and academic literary history did not occur until around 1900. The so-called positivist literary historians of Keller's day sought to interpret literary works through biographical facts about the author (Luck, 88). The goal was to fashion a complete image of what the author intended, founded upon psychological insights, previously published works, fragments, and authentic documents from the author's life. The modern literary historians, in contrast to Gervinus, did not restrict their methodology to past monuments of German and classical literary history, but applied this methodology to living authors as well. This raises two obvious questions: First, can a literary historian analyze a contemporary novel without overstepping his own literary competence? And second, are the strategies used to analyze the historical phenomenon of literature applicable to contemporary authors whose work is not yet complete? Keller discouraged both Emil Kuh and Jacob Baechtold from writing a critical biography or attempting a comprehensive interpretation of his works before they were completed, that is to say before his death. Although grudgingly flattered, Keller remained annoyed by Vischer's critical attempts to assess his oeuvre, and looked askance on Otto Brahm's lengthy 1883 essay on his fiction.

Gervinus had created a dilemma for all future literary scholars and authors. If they accepted his assertion that Weimar Classicism was the apex of German literature, it must be deduced that all authors who follow this high point of culture must be seen in its shadow, or even as contributors to its decline. Various literary scholars of Keller's day sought solutions to this unsettling problem. The literary historian Rudolf Gottschall believed that the classicists had created their works in the tradition of the ancients, but with humane spirit; the Romantics had turned away from the classical forms of antiquity in order to liberate their creativity and fantasy from past traditions, so as to produce poetry that was more *Volksthümlich* (folkloristic). The efforts of the Romantics dissipated into a chaotic *Urpoesie* and became dependent upon medieval and folk poetic forms. It was Gottschall's contention that contemporary writers should take up the well-intended aspirations of the Romantics by attempting to write for the present while striving to achieve the perfection of the Weimar Classicists. Seen from this perspective the classical age of German literature becomes not the conclusion, but rather the foundation for modern literature, which may be interpreted as a synthesis of classical and Romantic elements (Hohendahl, 1985, 181). Hettner, writing in 1850, believed that the national unification of Germany would naturally lead to a higher level of cultural advancement, which would in turn make possible a new age of German classicism.

After 1850, many literary historians developed an increasing dislike for Gervinus's five volume history of German literature. They questioned his aesthetic sensitivity as a historian and his ability to assess the canon-worthiness of a given work, questioned his methodological approach, and questioned his assertion that Weimar Classicism was destined to remain the pinnacle of German literature. Thus methodology and purpose became increasingly important. Karl Hillebrand's argument against Gervinus, published in 1873 in the *Preußischen*

Jahrbücher, provides some insight into literary debates of that time. Hillebrand asserts that it was puzzling to the critics of the day how an author without style, an academic without methodology, a thinker without depth, a politician without vision, a human being without any outstanding attributes could have made such an impact upon the spiritual, moral and political history of Germany (Hillebrand, 379). Julian Schmidt, the most prominent literary historian of the *Nachmärz,* the period from 1848 to 1890 was critical of Gervinus, but he was also influenced by him, and was more willing to accept Gervinus's *Geschichte der deutschen Dichtung* as one of the classical documents of the German nation.

One of Peter Uwe Hohendahl's central theses demonstrates how the canon as it evolved came to be identified by the literary historians of the 1850s and 1860s as a pan-German political cultural heritage that served as a unifying force for German culture and was not unimportant to German unification under Bismarck. Gervinus's analytical methodology distinguishes between historical significance of a work and its aesthetic contribution or relevance. Gervinus wrote in his first critique in 1833 that the literary historian is not interested in aesthetics. Aesthetics serves only as a medium, much like the political serves as a useful medium for the writer of history. Gervinus interpreted literature by its historical significance, its ability to capture the political and historical happenings of its day: an approach to literature that should hardly prove surprising when one recalls that Gervinus was a historian by trade. In this tradition the biography of the author would become truly historical when it came to embody the history of the age in which the author lived.

The evolving methods of literary interpretation also raised questions concerning two important literary terms, namely Realism and humor, that would undergo numerous transformations in meaning before the industry of criticism matured into the discipline of *Literaturwissenschaft.* Certainly the term "realism" in the European context has endured many diverse interpretations over the past century. German Realism came into being in the mid-nineteenth century; however the discussion of realism can be traced back to antiquity, specifically to Plato and Aristotle, who centered the discussion around the term mimesis, defined as an imitation (or reproduction) of reality. The discussion of mimesis has been carried forth into our own day by such notable scholars as Erich Auerbach, Georg Lukàcs, and Fritz Martini. A discussion of Keller's realism in its modern context will be taken up under the rubric of realism in chapter 4, but for the present we are concerned with realism as it was conceived by nineteenth century literary criticism.

The literary epoch of Realism (1850–1890) emerged as a reaction to historical happenings (the revolutions of 1848, the Sonderbundkrieg in Switzerland in 1847, industrialization, etc.) and was strictly speaking a reaction to classical idealism and Romanticism. The German realist, rather than to portray the world as it ought to be, sought to portray the world as it was. German Realism, after flourishing in the latter half of the nineteenth century, dissipated toward the close of the century into two distinct movements: an intensified version that gave birth to naturalism, and another that evolved into symbolism and impressionism and ultimately into a return to aesthetic ideals.

German Realism corresponds to the historical, political, and economic developments of the nineteenth century. At the conclusion of the Napoleonic Wars, the Congress of Vienna returned the German-speaking Europeans to an apolitical, provincial, pre-French-Revolution lifestyle embodied by the Biedermeier era, with its concentration on family, nature, and culture. The failed revolutions of 1848 and increasing industrialization transformed the antiquated class structure so that it now manifested itself in a new reality. The yearning for the Romantic unattainable, symbolized by the *blaue Blume* (the blue flower), which so characterized much of German Romanticism, was out of step with the grey, empirical reality of industrialization. Realism, which better reflected the social, political, and economic turmoil of the era, had come into its own time.

The author Otto Ludwig (1813–1865) is generally given credit for having coined the term "poetischer Realismus" (poetic realism), which he understood to include the pursuit of realistic ambitions and the expression of social reality.[2] The goal of the realist author is not to establish a cold objective tone, but rather to transfigure reality. According to Ludwig it is the task of the author to portray or to recreate the world again, not a fantastic world, but rather an all-inclusive environment, a world in which the connections between fantasy and reality, between fiction and fact, between the banal and the significant, are more transparent than in the real world.

Keller's prose, as various literary scholars of his day recognized, began with a blend of Romantic elements in a realistic landscape. The literary historian Otto Brahm recognized the influence of Jean Paul Richter upon Keller, particularly in *Der grüne Heinrich*. But Brahm also acknowledged what he called the "Swissness" in Keller's prose, which he associated with Keller's realism. He portrays the Germanic elements as synonymous with the Romantic, the poetic, the dreamy, and the fantastic. The unification of realistic and fantastic elements constitutes the outstanding hallmark of Keller's prose (Brahm, 16). Brahm divides Keller's work into three distinct creative periods that move from subjectivity in the earlier works to objectivity in the later ones; this is best exemplified by the two versions of *Der grüne Heinrich*. This question of subjectivity and objectivity was even in Keller's day at the center of the discussion of realism: Did Aristotle understand realism to mean mimesis, the objective reproduction of happenings, events, and people? Ludwig's understanding of poetic realism was that the author must pro-

---

[2] The main discussion of Realism in this book takes place in the fourth chapter, "Keller Scholarship 1920–1969" beginning on page 84f. There the reader can pursue the realist debate as explored by Aristotle, O. Ludwig, and Keller as well as by such twentiety-century scholars as Auerbach, Lukács and Martini.

ceed one step further than the historian; it is the task of the author not merely to record historical events as objectively as possible, but rather to make the reader, through his prose, more aware, more cognizant of the event than is implied by a knowledge of the facts of the event itself. The author must enable the reader to achieve a higher form of consciousness, enable him to acknowledge the significance of an event for the first time, an event that would otherwise not have made a great impression. Keller's own reflections on the matter were very much in line with Ludwig's.

Eventually, Keller was to develop his own conception of the task of the realistic writer, which he coined in a letter to Heyse on July 27, 1881, as the "Reichsunmittelbarkeit der Poesie" (*G.B.* III/1, 57). With this expression Keller asserts the right of the Realist poet to immerse himself in a world of dreams which may or may not have been generated by real events. The author as artist possesses the poetic license to embellish real happenings with the natural endowment of his own fantasy. The only restriction that holds the poet's imagination in reign is the obligation to make his characters believable and to make their actions credible. The challenge of the author is to embroider the banal event with his own fantasy, until the resulting interwoven patchwork of fiction and reality reveals something far deeper than the original event could ever convey.

The critics of Keller's day were obsessed by what Sammons calls "an idealistic transcendental dimension in realism," which gave vent to ethical purpose, toward which all good realist writing should strive (Sammons,10). Keller came to view writing as an influential force that embellished real events in order to stimulate the reader's conscience and make him cognizant of the world around him. Thus, like most authors, Keller sought to influence society through his writing, and in so doing was very much part of the Swiss tradition that preceded him, from Rousseau's *Emil* to the highly didactic overtones of Pestalozzi's *Lienhard und Gertrud* to the fiction of Jeremias Gotthelf, whose wonderful ability to spin a tale often succeeded in enshrouding the underlying didactic tendencies. Keller's poetic genius, suffused with his unique humor, was far more successful than were Gotthelf and Pestalozzi at subsuming the pedagogical message beneath a veneer of well-wrought prose; rarely does he allow the ethical purport to surface as it does in *Das verlorene Lachen* and in *Martin Salander.*[3]

The German term *Humor* was imbued with multiple definitions for the authors as well as for the critics and literary historians of Keller's day; moreover, *Humor* in German possessed a different meaning from the corresponding English term. Certainly no single term could subsume the humor of such diverse in-

---

[3] For a more extensive overview of the relationship between the ethical and the aesthetic aspects of Keller's artistry, see my essay entitled "Gottfried Kellers Ethik im Zusammenhang mit ästhetischen, religiösen und historischen Aspekten seiner Kunst," in *Gottfried Keller, Elf Essays zu seinem Werk*, (ed. Hans Wysling, [Zürich: Verlag neue Zurcher Zeitung, 1990], 61–76).

dividuals as Shakespeare, Cervantes, Moliere, Sterne, Jean Paul Richter, and Gottfried Keller. The humor of Shakespeare and Cervantes is considered outstanding because both authors captured the timeless fates of the individual, both tragic and comic, for all eternity; their humor is not caught up in or limited to bourgeois sentimentality. Furthermore, their humor reveals empathy with the rest of the world, but that they also find the world endearing in an affirmative way. Likewise, the German term *Humor* is an idealistic one and tends to describe a euphoric condition, a harmonious whole that soars above the fray of everyday life. It is perhaps most typically exemplified by Jean Paul Richter, who referred to it as "sich selber belächelnde Hausväterlichkeit." Richter's humor is empirically based and tends to be more realistic than Romantic. This down-to-earth quality is also a noteworthy trait of Keller's humor, which is firmly rooted in this world as opposed to the more ethereal aspects of German Romantic humor. The metaphysically-laden humor of German Idealism gave way to a new epoch in which a worldly humor would embrace life. Humor is the new force with which the authors of Realism bridge the eternal chasm between spirit and material, between freedom and necessity. In contrast to Romantic irony, which supposedly uplifts the reader, the humorist of German Realism reaffirms the reality that he is poeticizing; rather than falling prey to poetic fantasy and passionate yearning; he attempts to reconcile the worlds of fantasy and reality with his humor. Humor rescues him from two dangers: from Romantic extravagance on the one hand and from bourgeois provinciality on the other. He loves the infinite diversity of life, whose weakness he can laugh away, because in spite of all life's shortcomings, life itself remains self-affirming and worth living. Whereas the writer of tragedies exposes hopelessly unbridgeable chasms, the humorist attempts to overcome irrefutable dualism with laughter. Both share an impassioned earnestness in their search for meaning in life.

With this brief introduction to the literary industry in the nineteenth century and with these literary expressions defined in the context of the nineteenth century, we are prepared to turn to Keller scholarship and criticism during the author's lifetime.

Works Cited

Keller, Gottfried. *Sämtliche Werke*. Ed. Jonas Fränkel and Carl Helbling. 24 vols. 1926–1948. (Vols. 3–8 and 16–19 published by Eugen Rentsch in Zurich; vols 1, 2, 9–15 and 20–22 were published by Benteli in Bern.) Cited in text as *S.W.*

Keller, Gottfried. *Gesammelte Briefe*. 4 vols. Ed. Carl Helbling. Bern: Benteli, 1950–54. Cited in text as *G.B.*

Brahm, Otto. *Gottfried Keller. Ein literarisches Essay*. Berlin: Auerbach, 1883.

Demeter, Hildegard. *Gottfried Kellers Humor*. Berlin: Ebering, 1938.

Frey, Adolf. *Erinnerungen an Gottfried Keller*. Leipzig: Haessel, 1892; rpt. 1893, 1919.

Gervinus, Georg Gottfried. *Geschichte der Deutschen Dichtung*. 4th rev. ed., 5 vols. Leipzig: W. Engelmann, 1853.

Haym, Rudolf. *Gesammelte Aufsätze von Rudolf Haym*. Ed. Wilhelm Schrader. Berlin: Weidmann, 1903.

Hillebrand, Karl. "G. G. Gervinus." *Preußische Jahrbücher* 32 (1873): 379–428.

Hohendahl, Peter Uwe. "Literary Criticism in the Epoch of Liberalism." In *A History of German Literary Criticism. 1830–1980*. 177–276. Lincoln: U of Nebraska P, 1988.

——. *Literarische Kultur im Zeitalter des Liberalismus 1830–1870*. Munich: C. H. Beck, 1985.

Jäger, Georg and Jörg Schönert, eds. *Die Leihbibliothek als Institution des literarischen Lebens im 18. und 19. Jahrhundert. Organisationsformen, Bestände, und Publikum*. Hamburg: Hauswedell, 1980.

Luck, Rätus. *Gottfried Keller als Literaturkritiker*. Bern: Francke, 1970.

Albert Martino, Günter Häntzel, & Georg Jäger, eds. "Die deutsche Leihbibliothek und ihr Publikum." In: *Aufsätze und Forschungsberichte zum 19. Jahrhundert*. Tübingen: Niemeyer, 1977. 1–26.

Prutz, Robert. *Die deutsche Literatur der Gegenwart 1848–1858*. Leipzig: Voigt & Günther, 1859.

Sammons, Jeffrey L. *The Shifting Fortunes of Wilhelm Raabe*. Columbia, SC: Camden House, 1992.

Scherer, Wilhelm. *A History of German Literature*. Trans. F. C. Conybeare, ed. F. Max Müller. New York: Haskell House, 1971.

Schmidt, Julian. "Rezension der Newcomers." *Grenzboten* 15, 1 (1856): 405–409.

Vischer, Friedrich Theodor. "Gottfried Keller, eine Studie." In *Friedrich Theodor von Vischer: Altes und Neues*, vol. 2. 135–216. Stuttgart: Bonz & Co., 1881.

2: Keller and His Contemporaries: Critical Discourse in an Epistolary Mode

KELLER'S CORRESPONDENCE WITH FELLOW authors, literary historians, critics, and friends offers the modern reader extraordinary insight into criticism and scholarship in his century. It is not feasible within the scope of this study to conduct a comprehensive examination of the reception of Keller's texts by critics and literary historians in the nineteenth century. Rather, an attempt has been made to select the most important and representative reviews by the best-known nineteenth-century literary critics, scholars, and authors, in order to provide a sampling of how Keller was received by critics and friends during his lifetime. Understandably, only the most prevalent themes, concerns, and concepts that interested the literary historians and critics as they pertain to Keller can be presented here; among them are: discussions of literary genres, the effort to define good realistic writing, the question of what realism is and ought to be, and finally, the assessment of whether the works in question were worthy of inclusion in the canon of German literature.

Keller's critical audience can be divided into groups. There were his publishers such as Eduard Vieweg, Julius Rodenberg, and Wilhelm Hertz, who were primarily concerned with deadlines, the details of publication, and marketing. Fortunately, Keller could count among his friends several literary historians and critics such as Josef Widmann (1842–1911), Friedrich Theodor Vischer, and Emil Kuh. Then there were the Germanists or literary scholars such as Adolf Frey and Jacob Baechtold, who courted Keller's favor. Perhaps most important to Keller personally, as revealed in his correspondence, were his friendships with contemporary authors such as Theodor Storm and Paul Heyse, with whom he openly discussed ideas and freely exchanged criticism. Finally, there was the circle of friends and correspondents that included the intellectual Hermann Hettner and the widely- and well-read government council of Schleswig, Wilhelm Petersen (1835–1900). In this chapter a representative sampling of discussions and criticism of Keller's major works will be provided, along with a sampling of his responses to those reviews. The works will be treated in chronological order of publication, with the exception of the two editions of *Der grüne Heinrich*, which will be discussed first.

Keller began his literary career as a poet. Having exchanged his brush and water-colors for quill and paper, Keller began to compose verse during the early forties; his verse bore the imprint of the Swiss political fervor of his day, which reached its culmination in the Sonderbund War of 1847. The German-born

August Ludwig Follen (1794–1855), leader of political liberals in Zurich, recognized in Keller's poetry a voice for the movement, and used, or as many would contend, purloined the voice of the young poet to further the cause of the political movement. Follen edited (which he understood to mean "adapted") Keller's poetry to suit the needs of his political cause, which both irritated Keller and enraged Carl Helbling, the editor of the first critical edition of Keller's correspondence (*G.B.* IV, 23).

The political revolution in Zurich in 1848, in the aftermath of the Sonderbund War, swept Keller's closest political associates into power; they awarded their longtime friend with an unprecedented stipend as cantonal poet, thereby enabling him to study in Heidelberg and in Berlin for several years. The highly productive years in Berlin established Keller as a rising young writer and laid the foundation for his future literary endeavors.

Der grüne Heinrich
(First edition, 1855)

Keller's association with his first publisher, Eduard Vieweg, who was chiefly involved in scientific publishing and was based in Braunschweig, was strained and fraught with misunderstanding, due in part to Vieweg's lack of experience in publishing literary works and also due to Keller's procrastination. Keller was initially introduced to Vieweg through the Zurich chemistry professor Carl Löwig. The Vieweg firm had a long-standing tradition as a scientific publisher stretching back to the scientific works of Goethe and Alexander von Humboldt. Eduard Vieweg was interested in publishing belletristic literature that could be sold to the lending libraries of the day. One can conclude that Vieweg was not accustomed to dealing with lengthy works of fiction in progress and was certainly not prepared for Keller's procrastination, which was a result of his diverse interests and personal crises, as Keller alluded to in a letter to Ludmilla Assing (*G.B.* III/2, 48). Keller misled Vieweg (and himself) into believing that the work at hand, a novel of modest length, was near completion (*G.B.* III/2, 10). Keller's work ethic and Vieweg's needs as a publisher were mismatched. Over a period of many years the novel grew into *Der grüne Heinrich*, and Keller finished it only due to the pressure put on him by Vieweg. Keller's correspondence with Vieweg, Hettner, Freiligrath, and his mother reveal how difficult these years were for Keller due to constant financial difficulties and a series of unrequited loves that, together with his diverse interests, thwarted Keller's attempts to meet the deadlines set by Vieweg. And yet it must be said that the publisher gave the aspiring young author his first chance and encouraged him in every way.

Whereas Follen had edited some of Keller's poetry to the extent of rewriting it, Vieweg gave Keller complete artistic freedom. Their correspondence reveals little critical advice regarding the content of *Der grüne Heinrich*. Rather, it is filled with demands to increase the rate of production and expressed frustration over deadlines not met, while exercising enormous patience spread over years. Vieweg, in an early letter of encouragement to Keller, wrote that he would be most happy to enter into a binding contract with Keller for his impending novel (*G.B.* III/2, 19). However, this cordial beginning deteriorated rapidly into a relationship of unequals when Keller failed to deliver sections of his manuscript in a timely fashion. Almost two years later we can sense on the one hand Vieweg's frustration with Keller and on the other his paternal gesture of encouragement: "Tell me now yourself what I ought to think, what will become of this affair! I have no other alternative than to take you to court, if you force me to do so. I would like to make a suggestion. Come here and complete your work. I will give you my quarters in the city — I live in the country in the summer — and can clear out a room, etc." (*G.B.* III/2, 55). At other times Vieweg was euphoric, but he failed to understand how Keller could lose interest in the novel, indicating that Keller's exposé enclosed in an earlier letter interested the publisher greatly (*G.B.* III/2, 60). The publisher is referring to Keller's letter of August 15, 1852, in which Keller explains just how emotionally involved he is in the novel; he uses this emotional involvement as an excuse to justify delays in production (*G.B.* III/2, 58–9). Vieweg's confession in January 1853 provides us with some insight into his passionate involvement with the project: " . . . because I can assure you that I have fallen in love with your book! I have read very few novels that have given me such pleasure, very few that have such depictions of nature and the development of the soul, very few in which the burgeoning artistic endeavor shows such promise, very few that appear to be so beautiful or so true, yes I would find it difficult to set aside such a manuscript as is yours!" (*G.B.* III/2, 65)

While Vieweg rarely questioned the content of the novel, he certainly had much to say about the intolerably slow progress on the manuscript, and as a publisher he was incensed that only 150 sets of the first thousand copies of the first three volumes had been sold, due largely to the interminably slow progress made on the fourth and final volume. It was Vieweg's contention that Keller's procrastination on volume four seriously affected the sale of the novel (*G.B.* III/2, 99). For useful criticism on content during the writing process Keller had to rely on friends such as Hermann Hettner. Later, when Keller prepared the revised 1880 edition he turned to Emil Kuh, Theodor Storm, Paul Heyse, and Wilhelm Petersen for constructive criticism and advice.

The first reviews of *Der grüne Heinrich* were mixed. Keller wrote to his mother and sister that "praiseworthy reports" had appeared in German newspapers lauding his novel (*G.B.* I, 114). Keller referred here to the two reviews by Hettner and Varnhagen von Ense, both of whom were well disposed to him and knew him personally.

Hermann Hettner[1] was impressed by the first three volumes of Keller's novel. Hettner recognized as early as 1855 that the novel was born of the necessity to express and to overcome deeply perceived personal emotions; it was certainly not a single-mindedly crafted, emotionally detached work of fiction. According to Hettner, the warmth of experience could be felt throughout; it was in the most genuine sense both poetry and truth. Hettner suggests that anyone who has experienced the process of self-cultivation can find himself in this novel more clearly and more deeply depicted than he himself could express. He praises in particular the idyllic scenes in the country, the family of the pastor, the schoolmaster, the deep-souled Anna, and the sensual Judith, as well as the hero, who remains naive and at the same time clear and tactful through the many and varied situations, circumstances, and intrigues. He also praises the Goethean language and style. For Hettner the story of Heinrich's youth was a pearl.

Hettner found the third volume of the novel weaker. The fresh naturalness of the hero recedes, he says, and is replaced by a more spiritual but also more conventional character. Hettner finds the love stories between Rosalie and Erikson and between Agnes and Lys too extensive. He also finds the carnival scenes much too drawn out. Hettner hastily adds that he does not want to prejudge the novel before he has read the concluding volume (*G.B.* I, 390).

Hettner wrote in the *National-Zeitung* on May 5, 1854 on the first three volumes of *Der grüne Heinrich* that one feels the warmth of experience throughout, and emphasized that this artistic work was born of necessity and not of caprice. Perhaps no one else knew better than Hettner just how difficult and painful it was for Keller to complete the novel. For Hettner as for others, Keller's novel — even in its incomplete form — was reminiscent of Goethe's *Wilhelm Meister,* although Hettner hastens to add that it would be wrong to consider it a mere imitation, because it is far too unique and original. Hettner was the first to recognize the originality of Keller's novel; it had much in common with the Bildungsroman, but it already appeared to him, even without the ominous and highly disputed conclusion, to be unique. Hettner makes his audience aware that this is Keller's first novel, pointing out that the author had learned through the writing process the techniques of how to write, and that consequently the novel has some structural and organizational flaws. It opens in the middle of the young artist's career, turns to an extensive discussion of his youth, and returns again to the artist in Munich. But Hettner's review attempted to be objective and supportive of his friend's artistic endeavor. Keller was particularly appreciative of the

---

[1] Hermann Hettner (1821–1882) became one of Keller's closest intellectual friends and promoters. Hetter and Keller met in Heidelberg, where Hettner lectured on aesthetics and literary and art history. Their extensive exchange of letters while Keller was in Berlin, particularly on the topic of drama, enabled Hettner to write his book *Das moderne Drama,* which appeared in 1852. In 1851 Hettner was appointed to a position in Jena, and in 1855 to the Directorship of the Königliche Antikensammlung in Dresden.

review, which he felt balanced the "gemeinen Philisterquatsch" (common philistine rubbish) that Gustav Kühne had written about his novel in *Europa* (*G.B.* I,
395). In his letter to Hettner of May 6, 1854, Keller thanked him for the very
positive review.

Hettner praised the fourth volume in his letter of June 11, 1855, stating that
"The clarity of style is truly Goethean, the overall effect is purely poetic, which
one finds so seldom in contemporary literature. The idyll in the count's castle is a
masterpiece, so tender and sensitively perceived and so thoroughly fresh and
healthy that all young aspiring writers should study Keller's fiction closely" (*G.B.*
I, 412). Hettner questioned in the same letter whether the death of Heinrich is
justified. Keller conceded to Hettner in his letter of June 25, 1855 that he had
written the conclusion in haste and that one must read between the lines to follow the moral thread. His Heinrich had failed to care properly for his mother,
who had died an impoverished death, having sacrificed all she had possessed for
her son. Heinrich was therefore hardly in the position to begin again, because he
had irreparably neglected his immediate family. One who has transgressed such
a basic tenet of society cannot expect to build a new life for himself. Keller explained that he had designed a much longer conclusion consisting of three
chapters that would have constituted a formal elegy on death, in which Heinrich
would have had to grapple with his newly acquired belief that death was finite;
Keller suggested that Heinrich would have been unable to reconcile the finality
of death with his mother's passing (*G.B.* I, 414).

Karl August Varnhagen von Ense's review of the completed *Grüner Heinrich*
in the *Vossische Zeitung* on June 14, 1855 was kind and encouraging. The reviewer comments that neither self-doubt nor exhaustion has damaged the long
awaited conclusion to this excellent novel. Varnhagen von Ense finds it remarkable that Keller was able to maintain the same tone given the long period of
gestation. He remarks that Keller's novel is an uncommon one; one that entertains, but also challenges the intelligent reader's artistic sensibility: for Varnhagen
von Ense a Swiss breeze wafts over the whole, spreading freedom and personal
independence. He finds the style to be clear and dexterous. *Der grüne Heinrich*
reminds him of *Wilhelm Meister,* and has the tender charm of Novalis's *Heinrich
von Ofterdingen.* Varnhagen von Ense dislikes the conclusion; he would have
wished the hero another fate than the one he receives. Keller was pleased, if not
to say relieved by the review. Keller was encouraged by the strong praise and
strong criticism that often stood side by side in the same review, for they were
evidence that there was something worthy of discussion in his novel and that
final judgment was still to be rendered (*G.B.* III/2, 120).

Well aware of some of the flaws in the novel, Keller wrote to Vieweg in May
of 1856 that he would like to revise the novel in a few years and publish a new
edition; he would even be prepared to purchase the unsold volumes. He suggested that such flaws would never have occurred had he been able to write the

entire manuscript before it went to press. He lamented that each section was printed as soon as it was completed; this procedure made any alterations impossible and was, Keller believed, directly responsible for many of the perceived flaws (*G.B.* III/2, 133).

Julius Grosse, wrote a series of three reviews for the *Abendblatt zur neuen Münchener Zeitung* in May of 1857, entitled "Drei Deutsche Romane." He selected Gustav Freytag's *Soll und Haben*, Keller's *Der grüne Heinrich*, and G. v. Holtei's *Die Vagabunden*. Each review in the series was a full two pages long and occupied the title page and entire second page of the evening newspaper. Imagine that happening tòday! That these texts were read and deemed comparable to one another affords the modern-day reader some insight into what was commonly read in the last century. Grosse comments that out of the three novels, the subjective relationship to self-confession is most significant and deepest in *Der grüne Heinrich*, an artist-novel that has not yet been fully appreciated by the reading public, although it belongs to the most genial and poetic of creations of the age. Grosse interprets this novel as an admonishment to all those ambitious types who give themselves over to a talent they imagine they have. The reviewer is aware that Keller only became a writer after much suffering and despair as a failed landscape painter; he believes that Keller, like Goethe before him in *Werther*, had healed himself by superimposing his personal burden upon a literary character. Heinrich's fate is a tragedy of desire, because his desire to become a painter was matched neither by his talent nor his financial means, upon which his chances for attaining proper training depended. Grosse comments that Keller's book is most educational; it attains a creative fullness, a mastery of minutely illustrated details and an ideal that reminds one of Goethe and Raphael. In fact the attention devoted to description recalls Stifter's prose, who likewise wrote with a painter's eye for detail. Keller's characters, Grosse claims, are created for utopia, and that is why they appear so colorfully bizarre in their everyday context. These characters are individualists; they pursue their own instincts and ideals. Grosse finds Keller's portrayal of Heinrich as a creative, talented fellow with a full range of faults, inhibitions, and internal contradictions, to be what affords this novel its greatness. Likewise the dualism between Heinrich's idyllic love for Anna and his passionate love for Judith lend beauty to the story of Heinrich's youth. Grosse was one of the few critics who approved of Keller's conclusion; he finds Heinrich's fate appropriate and even predictable. Grosse believes that to have allowed Heinrich to live would have changed the message of the novel. However, Grosse questions whether the placing of Heinrich's fortunate encounter with the count so close to the end of the novel doesn't mislead the reader into thinking that all will end well. Grosse, in his concluding comments, reminds his readers that Keller is self-taught and a Swiss, and that the novel contains spirited reflections on God and freedom, on politics and art. He reminds his audience that the novel was warmly received by such a noted critic as

Julian Schmidt. It had not become popular because it ignored the desires of the readership of the day. Grosse agrees with Varnhagen von Ense that Keller's novel is challenging and soars over the heads of the average reader; it is a novel filled with the ideas of the times, and certainly more than just another entertaining read.

Keller often turned to Friedrich Theodor Vischer for advice, and was in general well disposed towards him, even if he was at times critical of Vischer's counsel. In 1844 Vischer was appointed Professor for Aesthetics and Literary History in Tübingen, where he wrote his three volume *Ästhetik*; he eventually accepted a position at the University of Zurich. In Zurich Vischer quickly became an important and respected member of the intellectuals who gathered at the Wesendonck home, where Keller himself was a frequent guest. Keller and Vischer established a mutually beneficial friendship over the years. In fact, Vischer even approached the publisher Georg von Cotta (1796–1863) on Keller's behalf, and persuaded the publisher to offer Keller a contract for monthly submissions that would have provided Keller with a reliable income and still allow him time to write. Keller's acceptance of the position of cantonal secretary annulled this plan.

Vischer, in his 1874 essay on *Der grüne Heinrich,* entered into historical discourse with other critiques on the novel such as *Vorlesungen über den deutschen Roman der Gegenwart* (1871) by the literary don Friedrich Kreyßig (1818–1879). Vischer accuses Kreyßig of not being able to distinguish between subjectivity and objectivity and of having precious little sensitivity for irony. Vischer questions whether *Der grüne Heinrich* is a novel or an autobiography, and tries to provide an answer with the formula: "Poesie . . . mit offenem Durchblick auf Selbstbiographie" [Poesy with an open inclination toward autobiography]. The freshness borne of genuine experience that characterizes the story of Heinrich's youth is achieved by the autobiographical element, but is lost in the last two volumes of the novel due in part to third-person narration. Greater objectivity is achieved through this distancing, but can one then speak of an autobiography? Vischer, the aesthetician, finds the conclusion to Keller's novel inorganic; he does not feel that Heinrich's death is sufficiently justified. As a professor of aesthetics Vischer was always guided in his critiques by his sensitivity for the beautiful. Disapproval of the novel's conclusion on the part of his readers and critics led Keller to undertake its revision almost a quarter of a century after its initial publication.

Der grüne Heinrich
(Second edition, 1879–1880)

The Viennese literary historian Emil Kuh wrote to Keller that he spent days, weeks, even months caught up in *Der grüne Heinrich* (*G.B.* III/1, 154). Kuh objected to Vischer's criticism of the novel; his own assessment of the book was that it was a problematic but highly significant novel, which would be read in the twentieth century and become part of the literary canon (Luck, 245). Kuh at first advised Keller against revising such a powerful work, for great authors may allow themselves poetic license (*G.B.* III/1, 158). However, in the same letter, Kuh made concrete suggestions about what ought to be changed, if Keller should decide to revise the novel. Kuh suggested striking the nude bathing scene with Judith, suggesting that a novel of such high caliber hardly needs such lewd scenes. When Keller actually struck that scene from the revised edition, Theodor Storm, among others, took umbrage at Kuh's prudishness. Kuh encouraged Keller to have the novel assume the form of an autobiography of Heinrich Lee for the sake of narrative uniformity. To resolve the unsatisfactory conclusion, Kuh suggested that Keller should begin the novel with the return of Heinrich to his native village on the eve of his mother's death. The entire novel would than be a flashback and could be left open-ended. Keller elected to follow much of Kuh's advice because it blended well with his own plans for the revision of the novel: "Ihre Gedanken über eine Renovation des Grünen Heinrich, welcher Pechvogel einmal Ihre Gunst gewonnen hat, sind mir sehr willkommen und anregend; sie treffen zum Teil mit dem zusammen, was ich selbst darüber gedacht" [Your thoughts concerning the revision of *Der grüne Heinrich*, that calamity which seems to have won your favor, are very welcome and stimulating; they correspond in part with my own thoughts on the matter: *GB* III/1, 161]. Keller advised Kuh against writing a monograph on himself and his works, indicating that it was much too early to begin such an undertaking, as he still had much more to write. Keller's personal relationship with Kuh was to remain one of cautious amicability. On the one hand, Keller shared with Kuh his own private fears regarding Vischer's desire to write an essay on his work, "Daß Vischer einen größeren Aufsatz über meine Sünden schreibt, erfüllt mich mit Grausen, besonders wenn er kritisieren wird müssen, was ich schon lange bereut und gebüßt habe" [That Vischer wants to write a lengthy essay about my transgressions (as a writer) fills me with dread, because he must criticize what I have long regretted and atoned for: *G.B.* III/1, 179]. On the other hand, Keller maintained considerable distance, and avoided several opportunities to meet Kuh personally. The correspondence between Keller and Kuh is full of attempts by Kuh to arrange a meeting and Keller's polite interest in one, followed by his deft excuses as to why he cannot keep them. Keller was incensed to learn from an article that there were those who attributed his discovery as an author to Emil Kuh. Keller's growing dislike for critics manifested itself in the healthy distance he maintained from those literary historians who pried too much and who came too close.

Keller's friendship with Josef Widmann, the literary editor of the Bernese *Bund*, was genuine. Their correspondence and Widmann's reviews in the *Bund* exhibit great respect for Keller's prose and contain encouragement from Keller for Widmann's own creative endeavors. Theirs was a friendship based upon mutual respect. Widmann provides us with some insight into literary criticism in his day when he laments how little time he has as a journalist to craft well-wrought critiques, as compared to the erudite scholarship of professors, who have the time to allow their interpretations to mature (*G.B.* III/1, 236). Widmann writes despairingly of the pressure exerted by journalism to write with expediency, a pressure that rendered impossible any well-reflected, well-wrought literary criticism.

Keller also wrote to Theodor Storm of his plans for the revision of *Der grüne Heinrich*. Storm feared, as did Kuh, that changes might harm the book, and expressed deep concern about Keller's revision plans, although he realized that such a revision was necessary if the book was ever to reach a broader reading public. Storm feared for the freshness of life and for the shine of sensual beauty captured in the original edition (*G.B.* III/1, 423). Storm believed that the artist's carnival (*Künstlerfest*) in Munich carried too much weight in the book. He was also concerned whether Judith, when she returns from America, remains still youthful enough to be an attractive woman. Storm questioned whether the death of the mother should be moved to the beginning of the novel. As already mentioned, Storm opposed Keller's plans, pursuant to Kuh's advice, to strike the scene in which Judith bathes. Keller incorporated Storm's suggestions into the revised edition, as he acknowledged in his letter to Storm of November 1, 1880: "In meinem monotonen Roman werden Sie sehen, daß ich die Judith noch etwas jünger gemacht, als Sie mir geraten haben, um die Resignation, die schließlich gepredigt wird, auch noch ein bißchen der Mühe wert erscheinen zu lassen" [In my monotone novel you will see that I have made Judith appear even younger to make the resignation at the end of the novel seem worthwhile: *G.B.* III/1, 451].

Keller discussed Otto Brahm's review of the revised edition of *Der grüne Heinrich* in a letter to Storm. The review, published in the *Deutsche Rundschau*, takes up Auerbach's discussion, in which he had questioned the right of an author to revise a work that is already in the public domain (Brahm, 1880, 466). Brahm reminds his readers of Goethe's revisions of *Werther*, and of his capricious reworking of *Götz von Berlichingen* for the Weimar theater. Brahm claims that there are two viewpoints: that of the author and that of the reader. He maintains that it is the author's right to revise his work; likewise, it is the reader's right to choose which edition he prefers.

Brahm respects Keller's desire to revise this work of his youth, to make this highly autobiographical work more closely represent the author's mature outlook on life. He sees in the new edition many parallels to Goethe's *Wilhelm Meister*, as did Hettner, Grosse, Vischer, and Kuh. Rather than choosing one edition over the other, Brahm advocates reading both, and recommends his audience to read both editions, insofar as *Der grüne Heinrich* is a perennial masterpiece, to which one returns again and again for stimulation and for sustenance.

On the one hand, Brahm's review is critical of Keller's attempt to tighten the framework of the Bildungsroman by imposing a first person narrative structure upon the novel, thereby suggesting that the narration now seems contrived. On the other hand, Brahm praises Keller's extraordinary talent: by this he means Keller's ability to combine new with old material, while maintaining the same tone and register throughout the work. He compares aspects of *Der grüne Heinrich* to *Wilhelm Meister* and to *Dichtung und Wahrheit*, and demonstrates how both Goethe and Keller were inspired by Rousseau's *Confessions*. Brahm tempers this comparison with a discussion of Heinrich's originality and modern *Weltanschauung* as opposed to what he calls Goethe's type-cast characters, such as Werther, in order to emphasize the originality of Keller's talent. He then praises the diversity among Keller's female characters, and concludes his review by lauding the diversity of color that Keller's palette affords the reader.

Brahm's review was only mildly critical of Keller's pale attempts to bring unity to the novel through revised narrative structure. But he provoked Keller's wrath by recommending his audience read both editions. With the publication of the second edition Keller had considered the original edition obliterated and underscored that fact by purchasing the remaining copies of the first edition from his publisher at his own expense; he then used them as fuel to heat his house!

Keller was also not pleased with Brahm's review because he felt that the critic had skirted the central issue of the form of the book, choosing instead to compare the old with the new, only to resurrect the problems already known to every reader of the original edition. Keller was also clearly irritated with Brahm's review because even after he had completely revised the novel, bought up and destroyed the remaining unsold copies of the original edition, Brahm had the audacity to compare the original version with the revised edition, which resulted in resurrecting all the old flaws that Keller had sought to eradicate by his revisions. Keller was particularly miffed that Brahm failed to discuss the question of what kind of novel the revised *Grüner Heinrich* was. Assessing whether it is a biography, Keller maintained, would lead to an aesthetic interpretation of the novel, which in turn might lead to new critical approaches (*G.B.* III/1, 455).

In a letter expressing similar sentiments to Julius Rodenberg, editor of the *Deutsche Rundschau*, Keller wrote that he had not yet received the newest issue of the *Rundschau*, so he did not yet know Brahm's critique first hand, but was nevertheless prepared for the philological methods with which the professors of German literature loved to attack contemporary literature. Keller speaks of a deeply rooted misunderstanding among critics of their rightful task that is only occasionally corrected when a competent critical examination of a given work is undertaken (*G.B.* III/2, 378).

Later, in a letter to Storm dated August 16, 1881, Keller again revealed his thoughts on contemporary critics, stating that the banter of the scholars becomes rubbish as soon as they intrude upon contemporary literature. He feared that a war would evolve between the grazing philologists and the authors; one that would not be dissimilar to the war that was currently raging between artists and art critics / historians, who had no feeling for art (*G.B.* III/1, 464).

The critics of Keller's day assessed the new literary works in the light of the classic tradition of German literature established in part by Gervinus, who, we will recall, upheld Weimar Classicism as its zenith. Thus many a critic compared Keller's *Grüner Heinrich* to Goethe's *Wilhelm Meister*. Others, such as Brahm, were reminded of Jean Paul Richter. Even Hettner saw in Keller's novel a direct descendant of *Wilhelm Meister*.

It is therefore not difficult to understand that Keller enjoyed his correspondence with Wilhelm Petersen precisely because he was a government counsel and not related to the literary profession in any official capacity, for he was neither a writer, a journalist, a literary critic, nor a historian. Petersen remained for Keller untainted. He was also unusual in that he had befriended and maintained contact with the literati of his day, such as Theodor Storm and Paul Heyse, among others. Keller was particularly receptive to Petersen's interest in *Der grüne Heinrich* precisely because he was a widely-read, well-meaning reader of the type Keller sought to engage. It was Petersen who in his first letter to Keller pressed for a new edition of *Der grüne Heinrich* (*G.B.* III/1,345). Petersen suggested that much of the contents could be deleted, namely all the philosophizing about art and religion, the episodes about the child who was possessed by the devil and about Römer; that furthermore Heinrich need not perish so prematurely and that he could be shown to behave more considerately toward his mother, all of which would serve to make the novel more palatable. Petersen believed that nothing prevents Heinrich from becoming a respected citizen or from marrying Dortchen, which would sweeten his mother's last days. It is too painful that the young man should perish after all that he has endured (*G.B.* III/1, 347–48). Clearly all this advice from Vischer, Kuh, Storm, Petersen, and others encouraged Keller to undertake the revision he had already conceived only months after completing the original version. Keller, in a letter to Petersen dated December 7, 1877, wrote of his ongoing mental revisions of *Der grüne Heinrich*, which represented an effort to eradicate all the earlier errors: "Jetzt gehe ich unverweilt an die Wiedergeburt des grünen Tropfes, genannt Heinrich, damit ich endlich mit den alten Velleitäten tabula rasa habe . . ." (Presently I will begin to work uninterruptedly on the rebirth of that green rougue named Heinrich, so that finally I can eradicate all the old irritations: *G.B.* III/1, 359). According to Petersen, good literature must contain an educative and ethical principles; it must be *erbäulich* (*G.B.* III/1, 373). Petersen believed that Keller's novel belonged to the canon of German literature because it would stand the test of time and be read by future generations. In a letter to Keller dated November 16, 1879 Peterson confesses that this novel is precious to him and that he will pass it on to his children; he believes that it has played a significant role in his life and has given him impressions that he could scarcely have received elsewhere (*G.B.* III/1, 374).

Keller's correspondence kept Paul Heyse abreast of the revisions. In a letter dated January 25, 1879 Keller wrote: "He is once again traveling around Munich in the process of revising the Green Henry for a new edition. Heinrich will tell his own story to the end and he [Keller] is preoccupied with the revision of the final volume, having already revised the first three volumes. All in the all the tome will only be about 18 pages shorter" (*G.B.* III/1, 37). In November of the same year Keller wrote to Heyse that he has had to revise much more than he had originally thought necessary. Keller adds that he plans to let the "Herring" live and to enable him to get together with Judith at the end of the second half of the book (*G.B.* III/1, 39). In March of 1880 Keller wrote to Heyse that his "Schicksalbuch, *Der grüne Heinrich*" was slowly approaching its second conclusion and that he was no longer enjoying the revision process. Only after the entire version was published did Heyse respond to the finished product in a letter to Keller dated October 21, 1880 and filled with exultant praise for this wondrous work whose clever transformation has succeeded beyond his greatest hopes. Full of praise for the revisions, Heyse agreed that nothing is more difficult than to re-immerse oneself into a former style and tone while augmenting the old with the new additions (*G.B.* III/1, 46).

However, not all the readers of Keller's revised novel were as pleased as Petersen and Heyse. Many of the critics reproached Keller for the new conclusion; they believed that Heinrich must remain dead; that the original version was superior. Keller, attacking a critic in the same letter to Vischer, wrote that one German scholar had actually said that he would hold onto the original edition. From that, Keller continued, he could see that the scholar had hardly read the book in the first place, since he could not recognize how much work had been put into the revision: there was hardly a page that remained untouched, and all in all over thirty pages of the original novel had been struck (*G.B.* III/1, 145). Clearly, Keller believed the new edition to be the superior one. Storm concurred, with the verdict that the last third of Keller's book had in the process of revision become something of consequence (*G.B.* III/1, 459). While there were diverse opinions and arguments surrounding the revised edition of *Der grüne Heinrich*, this was certainly not true with the publication of the Seldwyla novellas, which were recognized immediately and unanimously as some of the finest novellas in German literature.

Die Leute von Seldwyla I (1856)

During the six years that followed Keller's return from Berlin, he published two works: *Die Leute von Seldwyla* (with Vieweg in Braunschweig in 1856) and *Das Fähnlein der sieben Aufrechten* (in Auerbach's *Volkskalender* in 1860). Although the Seldwyla stories would later become the best known of Keller's works, their initial impact was less than encouraging; some of the best criticism of the period is found in the private correspondence of Keller's admirers. The discussions and critiques in the newspapers and periodicals of the day remained superficial.

Typical of the first comments on the Seldwyla stories were those of Auerbach and Gutzkow. Auerbach writes condescendingly in *Der Augsburger Allgemeinen Zeitung* of Keller's works as bright summertime reading, well suited for leisurely passing the time under an arbor on a warm July day. Karl Gutzkow writes in 1856 in his periodical *Unterhaltungen am häuslichen Herd* that the Swiss author Keller had augmented modern German literature with stories bearing a special uniqueness. Keller, according to Gutzkow, exploits his youthful memories thoroughly and draws heavily upon the provincial settings of his homeland in his exclusively narrative fiction. His Seldwyla stories reveal a creative mind that brings forth all manner of characters, adventures, and experiences from his region, which he portrays with the clarity of a painter. Awkward in Keller's fiction is his penchant for weak humor. His comfortableness and apathy do not allow his attempts at satire to flourish; this peculiar attitude, which betrays something of a hostile self-satisfaction, only deprives the reader of the impact that a great talent could bring.

The author Otto Ludwig, who coined the term poetic realism, wrote to Auerbach praising Keller's tone and sense of color and setting in the Seldwyla novellas. Ludwig admitted, not without a hint of envy, that he was also working on a novel set in a provincial setting, but that it would not have the range of Keller's Seldwyla stories. Ludwig lauded Keller's healthy, rugged Swiss torpor that is characteristic of a peculiarly Swiss vein of romanticism and affords Keller's works the firm flesh and blood physicality that makes poetic truth possible.

The private comments of the diplomat Alexander von Villers in his letter to A. von Warsberg reveal some of the most perceptive early comments on *Romeo und Julia auf dem Dorfe* (Zäch, 1952, 43). Villers praises the detailed observation of Sali and Vrenchen as they play with and eventually destroy the doll; however, he finds the language of the dialogue between the two children completely unsuited. The portrayal of this scene is sufficient to convey the message; the conversation between the children takes away from the scene rather than augmenting it. He also cites other instances in which the characters speak in a manner that is not suited to their origin or lifestyle. Villers writes that for a while he ate mock turtle soup and grew so accustomed to the taste that when he was served real turtle soup he did not like it. Applying this example to the realists, he suggests that those who depict their reality well enable it to become our own. An example of such a successful author is Homer. Keller, Villers admits, cannot match Homer despite many a successful brush stroke. Villers finds Keller's introduction to *Romeo und Julia* superficial, grammatically incorrect and unnecessary; one could hardly twist language and thoughts more curiously in order to say something completely unnecessary. He also criticizes Keller's title, suggesting that Sali and Vrenchen's situation is hardly comparable to the two lovers of Verona, who die as a result of a misunderstanding. Villers finds nothing tragic about the death of Sali and Vrenchen. In his judgment the story is without motive; even fear of shame after the deflowering is unacceptable, because the two young people have been robbed of honor and honesty from the very beginning. Villers fails to recognize the critique of middle-class society in Keller's story, but he raises questions concerning the motivation for suicide that are still puzzling to many even today.

Paul Heyse, in the introduction to his *Deutschen Novellenschatz,* praises Keller's talent as a first-rank writer of novellas. Keller's tone is related to Goethe's through its moderate objectivity, but transcends the latter through its much more brilliant subjective palette of color and through the fullness of its humor. These stylistic attributes augment Keller's inclination for contrast: the endearing character stands next to the peculiar, the merry next to the tasteless, the sensually seductive next to the frightfully terrible. Heyse believes that a humorous perspective on life is the basis of Keller's writing. This humor enables Keller to portray all the cracks and fissures in the social order; it prevents him from having to make things seem better than they are. According to Heyse, Keller has the realistic courage to call things by name rather than cloaking them in sentimental idealism. Keller knows how to manipulate light exaggeration in order to achieve an effect attained by the baroque artists, who transformed the trivial and the ridiculous into the sublime. Heyse believes that in this regard, Keller only has one predecessor — namely Cervantes in his *Don Quixote.*

Sieben Legenden (1872)

Keller's *Sieben Legenden* were published at Easter of 1872 by Göschen (of Stuttgart) to a surprised and joyful readership. Surprised, first and foremost, because the legends represent the first substantial publication by Keller since the first volume of the Seldwyla stories in 1856, and perhaps secondly, because the word *Legenden* in the German title refers to stories of religious content. Those readers who knew Keller's works well were astonished by the notion of Keller writing religious tales. Of course, upon reading the work, Keller fans were enraptured by his deft handling of the religious material, while other less broad-minded readers were offended. Friedrich Theodor Vischer wrote to Keller on April 1, 1872 to thank him for sending him a copy of the legends; he promised that he would write a critique of them, certainly not without a few criticisms, but in the spirit of a warm friendship.

Writing in the *Wiener Neuen Freien Press* on May 17, 1872, Julius Stiefel (1847–1908) reacted negatively to Keller's legends. Stiefel writes that of the seven legends, four (*Der heilige Eugenia, Vitalis, Dorothea,* and *Musa*) make a travesty of the holy stories. Three of the stories are about the life of the Virgin Mary; laced with humor, they are the least offensive of the transposed legends in Stiefel's view. However, Stiefel contends that there is much in the other four legends that is offensive: while the religious plots of the original stories, adapted from a two-volume collection entitled *Legenden* by Ludwig Theobul Kosegarten (1758–1818), remain untouched, the atmosphere is so fundamentally changed that the saints lose their sainthood and become secular citizens in a world republic. The morals of these stories, which arise from the Scriptures, give the appearance that Keller did not merely pilfer the legends for malleable material, but transformed sacred material in order to show his contempt for it. Stiefel takes the overwhelmingly positive reception of these legends as a sign of morally impoverished times.

The Viennese literary historian Emil Kuh was enamored with Keller's fiction. In a letter to Keller dated February 20, 1871, Kuh wrote that he could formerly have named only two individuals besides Goethe who had guided him throughout his life: the dramatist and writer Friedrich Hebbel and the philosopher Arthur Schopenhauer. After the publication of *Der grüne Heinrich* and the Seldwyla stories Kuh was forced to acknowledge a third individual — namely Keller himself. It is perhaps of no surprise that Kuh was enchanted by the appearance of the *Sieben Legenden*. Kuh, in a letter to Keller dated January 8, 1874, referred to the *Sieben Legenden* as the purest of Keller's fiction because of their rigid form, adding that Keller was the greatest poetic talent of the time. Kuh believed that, while Storm was an admirable poet, he was restricted by his material; Keller, on the other hand, transcended all provinciality, as the discerning reader would recognize. No German poet besides Keller possessed the humor that only a handful of Englishmen, such as Sterne, could claim as their own. Likewise, in a letter dated June 7, 1872, Keller's friend Weibert communicated a highly complimentary reception of the legends by the author Eduard Mörike (1804–1875). Mörike had allegedly said that he had never had greater reading pleasure than with Keller's legends; that furthermore he knew of no other recent book that was so complete in its art of portrayal.

Die Leute von Seldwyla II (1874)

The reception of the second volume of the Seldwyla novellas, published with Göschen in Stuttgart in 1874, was conceptually influenced by the first volume, although in the preface to the second volume Keller clearly conveys his awareness of the social and economic changes that had occurred since the completion of the first volume. The stories in the second volume were compared with and judged against the growing acclaim of the original stories. While few critics gave the first volume of stories the attention they deserved, most reviewed them in a positive light and recognized them as destined for a permanent place in nineteenth-century German letters. Robert Prutz (1816–1872), the poet and literary historian who was professor in Halle, writes in his *Die deutsche Literatur der Gegenwart 1848–1858* that he held Gottfried Keller to be an author of limited talent. He refers to Keller's novel as a portrait of the soul (*Seelengemälde*). He praises its fine sense of perception and observation, but finds the conclusion unsatisfactory. Prutz refers to the novel as his romantic dream world, reminiscent of Rousseau's famous confessions. However, Prutz was known for discussing texts he hadn't read; instead of reading Keller's original text, Prutz had read Julian Schmidt's literary history and had mistakenly understood that Heinrich had gone insane at the end of the novel, confusing Heinrich's fate with that of the mentally disturbed painter Römer! In the Seldwyla stories Prutz finds Keller's fiction more anchored in reality. He still believes that Keller prefers to suffuse the events in the Seldwyla stories with a romantic aura. He concedes that *Frau Regel Amrain und ihr Jüngster* and *Romeo und Julia auf dem Dorfe* are the pearls among the Seldwyla novellas.

Berthold Auerbach, in his review of the five new novellas in the second volume of *Die Leute von Seldwyla*, was well disposed toward Keller and his talent. Auerbach writes that a new work by Gottfried Keller is really a celebration, a feast, where the reader will sample new gastronomic creations and not merely warmed-up leftovers (Auerbach, 1875, 34). Auerbach takes pride in the fact that he had been one of the first to recognize Keller's significance almost two decades earlier. In his review he reminds his readers that Keller is special because he writes when the muse speaks; he does not attempt to support himself with his writing and can afford to wait until the creative spirit moves him. By comparing Keller's literary legacy to Mörike's, Auerbach suggests that Mörike, like Keller, writes for enjoyment, and that they both derive personal satisfaction from the creative process. Neither Keller nor Mörike are particularly concerned with the wishes of their readers. In this regard Auerbach agrees with Varnhagen von Ense's earlier comment in his review of *Der grüne Heinrich*; namely, that Keller wrote challenging works for an experienced readership.

According to Auerbach, Keller is further set apart from his contemporaries because of his Swissness, which he defines as an acute political and religious awareness that permeates Keller's thought and being. This political and religious consciousness, Auerbach asserts, separates Keller from German authors, whose traditional aversion to such themes is exemplified by Schiller's journal *Die Horen*, in which religion and politics were taboo. The Germans, says Auerbach, are accustomed to evaluating the education of an individual primarily according to his aesthetic insights, but the average Swiss achieves through his participation in the democratic process a political consciousness and a Helvetian patriotism that are both the source and the reaffirmation of individual honor.

After this introduction Auerbach draws our attention to Keller's characters, who are fashioned from everyday life and embellished with a uniqueness that only Keller's fantasy can provide. Keller is intimately involved with each of his characters and each of his stories, over which he reigns as master (Auerbach, 41). He avoids clichés and stock phrases; his language is fresh and original. Keller draws the reader into his stories; he unabashedly ignores the fashionable desires of the reading public.

In the last third of his review Auerbach discusses each novella. He draws parallels between *Kleider Machen Leute* and works of the Romantics. Auerbach categorizes *Der Schmied seines Glückes* as a farce, and is impressed by Keller's ability to portray both the unsightly and evil with humor. In *Die mißbrauchten Liebesbriefe*, Auerbach recognizes Keller's attempt to treat the less admirable aspects of the publishing industry of his day with humor. He finds the structure of *Der Schmied seines Glückes* and of *Die mißbrauchten Liebesbriefe* contrived, which he believes is not true of the last two stories of the collection, *Dietegen* and *Das verlorene Lachen*, on both of which he lavishes praise. He lauds *Dietegen* as a well-rounded composition, admires Keller's portrayal of Dietegen's youth, and is impressed with Keller's ability to lend the story a believably authentic fifteenth-century historical context. Auerbach's discussion of *Das verlorene Lachen* ties into his long introduction on Keller's Swissness, which he says is responsible for his unabashed penchant for discussion of political and religious matters. Auerbach suggests that the novella has captured the essence of the time (45). He claims that Keller offers poetic solutions to many of the questions and problems raised in *Das verlorene Lachen*; he notes in particular the educative influence and praises the remarkable strength of Justine and Jukundus. Justine comes to terms with her faith and Jukundus acquires a manly sense of civic duty (46). Characters such as these exemplify a measure of humanity through strength of character that will transcend their own time. In concluding his laudatory review, Auerbach emphasizes just how rare it is to encounter an author whose stories one can read again and again, and yet always with the expectation of feeling the same joy of the first reading, of encountering the same unforgettable moments and the same genuine emotions.

The concluding novella in the collection, namely *Das verlorene Lachen*, which Auerbach had praised, received mixed reviews. Keller had sought to conclude the "schnurrpfeiferliche" (quaint) collection with an earnest depiction of contemporary society (*G.B.* III/1, 183). Keller conceded in a letter to Vischer in 1875 that he had perhaps "forced" the material for a short novel into the form of a novella, for which it was not well suited (*G.B.* III/1, 139). The second half of the novella, Kuh suggests in his letter to Keller of December 12, 1874, does not carry the same weight as the first part, because the relationship between Jukundus and Justine is not isolated, not intimate enough (*G.B.* III/1, 187). Kuh believes that their relationship is motivated too much by the events and conditions around them. He is of the opinion that this last novella may not be received well by posterity. He finds fault not with the abbreviated strictures of the novella into which the material has been condensed, but rather feels that the material inherent in each character has not been fully exploited. Keller, thanking Kuh for the copy of his review of the Leute von Seldwyla, chastised him for his comments on Das verlorene Lachen: "With the last novella you perfidiously refused to defend me, just like Vischer, who, I have heard, found the last novella too tendentious and provincial. I had sought to create a true depiction of modern society in an effort to round out the unique peculiarities in the second volume by delivering something well crafted" (G.B. III/1, 190).

On the other hand, Widmann, in a letter to Keller of January 8, 1875, seemed to understand what Keller was attempting to achieve in this last novella. He was surprised that Keller had decided not to leave Zurich given the reaction to Das verlorene Lachen. Widmann comments that Keller's closing novella makes him aware of Keller's message, which suggests that noble, gracious, and humane attributes can be upheld independent of any religious conceptions that one might have. This is exemplified by the two pious women, Agathchen and her mother, who are humble and good, not because of their religious beliefs, but almost in spite of them (G.B. III/1, 215). Keller may have been inspired to write this final novella by a letter he received from one Frau Josefine Stadlin-Zehnder, a teacher who had worked closely with Pestalozzi. Stadlin-Zehnder had asked Keller in 1873 to consider revising and updating Pestalozzi's Lienhard und Gertrud so that it would correspond to contemporary tastes and the needs of the times; Keller had declined the invitation, suggesting that one could not revise Pestalozzi's book; rather, something new would have to be written and that would require another Pestalozzi (G.B. IV, 151). Stadlin-Zehnder's request was timely, and one can speculate that it may have influenced Das verlorene Lachen. From the diverse critiques on this novella one could further hypothesize, as Keller has led us to do, that the materials and ideas that were seen by some as overflowing the restrictive form of the novella eventually found their way into Keller's last novel, Martin Salander.

Züricher Novellen (1878)

Wilhelm Scherer (1841–1886) in his review of Keller's Züricher Novellen in the Deutsche Rundschau concentrated on an analysis of the architectonic structure of the novella cycle. Scherer shows how the story of Herr Jacques creates the frame for the cycle by establishing the theme of the search for originality through talentless efforts and mere charlatanism ("talentlose Treiben und Scheinenwollen") which is then substantiated by the central characters in Der Narr auf Manegg and by the positive example of Salomon Landolt in Der Landvogt von Greifensee (Scherer, 324). This theme of originality is pursued in Hadlaub and Ursula, and would also be applicable to the much earlier story included in this collection, Das Fähnlein der Sieben Aufrechten (The Banner of the Upright Seven). Scherer also draws the reader's attention to the different phases of Zurich's history represented in these stories: *Der Narr auf Manegg* takes place there during the Middle Ages, and the setting of *Ursula* portrays the city during the Reformation, while *Der Landvogt von Greifensee* depicts eighteenth-century Zurich.

After discussing the architectonics of the cycle Scherer turns to each individual novella, but seems most fascinated by *Ursula*. Scherer is impressed with Keller's ability to transport his audience into another historical era; in *Hadlaub* for example, Keller brought to life the era of the *Minnesänger* for the modern reader. Scherer acknowledges the extraordinary talent required to recreate the aura of a historical period which the author could not have experienced; he appreciates how difficult it must be to make that setting believable to a modern reader. Scherer is also particularly enamored with *Der Landvogt von Greifensee*, and is quite taken by the host of characters Keller presents in this novella. Scherer wonders how it possible for anyone to come of up with such an array of personalities, which leads into a discussion of Keller's characters that he divides into two categories: symbolic characters, such as Viggi Störteler in *Die mißbrauchten Liebesbriefe*, and individualists, such as Salomon Landolt in *Landvogt von Greifensee* (326).

Scherer characterizes *Ursula* as a melancholy story that concludes peacefully enough. The literary historian hints at but does not elaborate on the deeper religious significance of this novella. Scherer avoids any in-depth discussion of Keller's reflections, other than to suggest that such religious sects as the Anabaptists cast their spell over many innocent individuals such as Ursula, who were too meek to challenge their rhetoric. Even strong individuals, Scherer comments, such as Hansli Gyr are susceptible to the power of religious rhetoric, for which Gyr becomes something of an apostle. Ultimately, Ursula's innate innocence and Gyr's strength of character enable them to overcome their respective ordeals and to establish a life together.

Scherer concludes his review with a discussion of Keller's original style, a style that rests with the unique quality of his creative images as well with his unusual choice of vocabulary. Scherer praises Keller, claiming that he cannot name another author who can manipulate the language so that something new always emerges from the banal; Keller achieves this uniqueness through his clever choice of expressions and by creating unique contexts. Scherer readily admits that Keller's prose is not for everyone; nevertheless, he reports that Keller's readership is increasing and that he interprets this as a positive sign of the growing aesthetic education among the public.

Keller corresponded extensively with Storm and Petersen about the *Züricher Novellen*. One advantage of publishing works in serialized journals — perhaps one of the few — is that it afforded authors the opportunity to test the waters, to air their progeny publicly, thereby allowing time for reflection and revision before the final publication as a book. The publication of the *Züricher Novellen* was the catalyst that encouraged Storm to strike up a correspondence with Keller. Storm's first letter to Keller on March 27, 1877 expressed both praise and gratitude for the new novellas, and touched off a long and fruitful literary correspondence. Storm suggested rewriting or rather amending a section of *Hadlaub*. He encouraged Keller to include a love scene following the extensive *Minne*-courtship that brings Hadlaub and Fides together (*G.B.* III/1, 412). Keller was receptive to Storm's suggestion; he conceded that the conclusion was hasty and did not have the proper time to mature. On the other hand, Keller did not feel that he, at his age, should try to write such a scene; he would rather let things be, assuming that readers can read between the lines, adding that he would ponder Storm's suggestions, saying that they must be of significance if a Lutheran judge in Husum, who has sons of his own, sent them by way of the imperial mail to an old chancellor of Helvetian persuasion to encourage his diligence in the art of erotic portrayal! (*G.B.* III/1,413)

In his correspondence with Storm about the novella *Ursula* Keller expressed his own dissatisfaction, complaining that it is incomplete, for which he blamed the Christmas book market that forced him to commit the manuscript to the press before it had properly matured. On this topic Storm concurred with Keller completely, suggesting that *Ursula* ought to be expanded, asserting that what is there is far too good to leave in its fragmentary form (*G.B.* III/1, 426).

Keller exercised patience in his correspondence with his friend Wilhelm Petersen, who embodied his ideal reader. Petersen questioned whether the Governor of Greifensee, in respect to his light-hearted party, shouldn't have fallen prey to his former love, Figura, but added that he understood Keller's melancholic outlook on life and love, and that such merry conclusions fail to suit his disposition. Keller responded in a slightly testy manner, indicating that this novella could not end in marriage because the central tenor is that of the elegiac waft of resignation that hovers over the afternoon gathering of the bachelor and his five former loves. (*G.B.* III/1, 356–57).

It is significant that Keller learned more from and was more receptive to the criticism from his friends, whether avid readers such as Petersen or fellow writers, than he did from the literary historians of his day such as J. Schmidt, Brahm, Prutz, Kuh, and Scherer, among others, for whom he harbored increasing distrust and even disdain.

Das Sinngedicht (1882)

As the correspondence between Keller and Julius Rodenberg, editor of *Die Rundschau*, reveals, *Das Sinngedicht* underwent a long period of gestation before it was finally serialized in the *Rundschau* and later published by Hertz in Berlin in 1882. Although Keller began discussing *Das Sinngedicht* with Rodenberg in late 1879, the first installment did not appear until January 1881, and then only after several postponements. Rodenberg wrote to Keller that he found the frame unusually ornate, well suited and aesthetically pleasing (*G.B.* III/2, 377). In response Keller discussed the proper genre designation and suggested that the term "Novella" is the most suitable. Keller feared that the entire piece might appear too empty and droll; Keller was paraphrasing Storm, who referred to the *Sinngedicht* as his "Spezialerfindungen Lalenburger Geschichten." However, Storm was of the opinion that one has to take advantage of poetic license to preserve or achieve the hybrid, less stringently structured novella that will allow the embellishment of reality to the furthest extent of creative possibility (*G.B.* III/2, 378).[2]

Rodenberg praised the cycle for its richness and diversity. He believed it would remain Keller's crowning achievement because of the colorful array of characters, the sheer breadth of creativity, the aura of originality that pervades the whole and finally because of the classical style, which he found to be reminiscent of Boccaccio (*G.B.* III/2, 189). Reporting on his lecture tour to Vienna in March of 1881, Rodenberg wrote of the phenomenal approval with which the *Sinngedicht* had been received by the Viennese. Rodenberg related that he was approached by professors, students, and readers alike, who all claimed that this was Keller's most aesthetically pleasing work (*G.B.* III/2, 385). Keller's Austrian friend, Adolf Exner, was a bit more reserved in his commentary than Rodenberg in a letter dating from December 28, 1881. While he praised the *Sinngedicht*, he found the overall French influence distasteful.

Heyse feared that Keller's novella cycle suffered from the serialization, but was delighted to discover on a second reading how well it all fit together (*G.B.* III/1, 55). Agreeing with a suggestion from Petersen, Heyse encouraged Keller to expand the conclusion to give it greater impact before publishing the cycle as a book. Keller was receptive to Heyse's suggestion and went on to discuss the *Sinngedicht* at length (*G.B.* III/1, 56).

The popular novelist Friedrich Spielhagen discussed Keller's *Sinngedicht* in *Westermanns Monatsheften*, where he attributed many an accolade to the work and praised Keller as an author who fully controlled all the aspects of his art. He refers to some incongruities that he fears may damage the popularity of the work, referring specifically to minor aberrations in the actions of some characters that remain unmotivated and may detract from the work as a whole. Spielhagen was more concerned with the interests of his readers, and with not offending them; precisely that sensitivity may help to explain why his own works were as popular as they were. Keller was never concerned with popularity. He sought to craft fine art that would communicate his message to the discerning reader.

Paul Schlenther (1854–1916), a leading critic in the last decades of the nineteenth century, praised Keller's *Sinngedicht* in *Die Tribüne* of December 11,

---

[2] Storm is writing about the novella or a kind of hybrid novella, and taps into Keller's concept of the *Reichsunmittelbarkeit der Poesie,* which is explained in chapter 4 as part of the discussion of realism.

1881 for its original creativity as manifested in the wealth of unusual situations that are rendered believable because they are tied into everyday life. Schlenther asks which of the modern naturalists was capable of carefully constructing and motivating all these happenings. He asserts that Keller stands upright in the realm of monumental reality; he knows the place where the golden poetry lies buried and has the craft to resurrect and use it as no other author of the time. Schlenther asks how it is that Keller is less known, is less lauded and is less often read than his contemporaries. He attributes this to a largely female reading public, which he claims has not yet developed a true understanding for Keller. Schlenther believes that women should appreciate the multiplicity of female characters in Keller's works and suggests that this is a strength of the *Sinngedicht.*

Eduard Engel praised Keller's language in the *Sinngedicht.* Engel later became a professor of literature who was known for purging the German language of foreign words. Writing in *Das Magazin für die Literatur des In- and Auslandes* he lauded Keller's well-wrought prose, particularly his sense of feeling for language, his clarity, his originality, and especially his grammatical correctness. He asserts that this cycle of novellas could only have been written by one who has great respect for his material and artistic talent for the language. He suggests that superficial readers who claim the book is boring should take a few lessons in classical German rhetoric. Engels awards the *Sinngedicht* a place of honor among the classics.

Gesammelte Gedichte (1883)

Keller, writing to Emil Kuh as early as 1871, was already thinking of revising his poetry (*G.B.* III/I, 161–62). He would prefer that the existing volumes go unnoticed, because he would like to make a fresh start by editing and expanding the collection, suggesting that one is always guilty in youth of foolishness and of yielding to bad advice. Responding to Kuh shortly thereafter, Keller wrote: "It's all right if you do not love my poetry; I don't either. Nevertheless I must spruce up and harmoniously cloak these unsuccessful youthful rhymes, simply because they exist already. With a thoughtful reworking and a substantially augmented volume I hope to make the unfinished and immature volume vanish" (*G.B.* III/1, 164).

In a letter to Heyse, Keller mentioned that he was sweltering in his poetic purgatory while roaming about consuming many cigars (*G.B.* III/1, 75). On good days he completed five or six poems; sometimes he needed two days to revise, rewrite, or eliminate just one poem. Keller claimed that he was occasionally composing new poetry. Indeed, Storm showered Keller with praise for his now famous "Augen, meine lieben Fensterlein": "The purest gold . . . . such pearls are seldom" (*G.B.* III/1, 441). Keller, writing to Vischer in 1881, spoke of another "task" that stood in his way, namely his poetry: he must collect and edit his po-

etry (*G.B.* III/1 147). Keller's volume of revised poetry was published by
Wilhelm Hertz in 1883. Otto Brahm lauded Keller's volume of collected poems
that brought together the poetic achievements of some forty years (*Deutsche
Rundschau* XXXVII, [Dec. 1883]). Many of the poems of the first two books of
poetry, published in 1846 and 1851, as well as those published in newspapers,
journals, and diaries have since that time become available in one volume, allowing the reader to appreciate fully the wealth of Keller's poetry.

Brahm ascribes Keller's exceptional poetic hues to three sources: they are the
poems of an epic poet, a humorist, and a Swiss. For Brahm the most important
measure of quality in poetry is the ability to convey sensitivity. The most significant measure of quality in the epic is fantasy. Brahm maintains that fantasy is the
driving force in Keller's writing. The liveliness of Keller's fantasy enables him to
portray uniquely: sensations, moods, and feelings in magnificent images. His
images range from the wondrous to the wonderful; his fantasy gives birth to the
fantastic. The fantastically horrible, however, can be transformed into the delightful through Keller's seemingly inexhaustible creative imagination. Keller's
Weltanschauung is optimistic; although never skirting the serious, he often views
the world with gentle humor that ranges from benevolence to biting satire.

Quite often, Brahm contends, what begins as a nature poem evolves into
critical reflections with social, political, or ethical purport. He reminds us that
Keller's first published lyrics consisted of passionate political verse, and believes
that it was the patriot in Keller that brought forth the first poetry. The fervent
passion of the forties has given way to the more benevolent graciousness that
comes with maturity. The astute ethical observations are ever present; the radical
tone in the political poems of the 1840s has taken on the milder, gentler tone
expressed in the form of folk festivals (*Cadettenfest, Sängerfest,* and *Schützenfest*).
Keller has written poems for special occasions (*Gelegenheitsgedichte*) in the best
tradition of Goethe's poetry. On the one hand, the political, philosophical, and
ethical are expressed with such finesse and sensitivity revealing the true poet in
Keller; on the other hand, this sensitivity reveals convictions, for which Brahm
holds the true Swiss in Keller accountable.

Brahm concludes his review with a brief discussion of *Der Apotheker von
Chamounix,* which he interprets as Keller's satire of Heinrich Heine. He speaks
of Keller's appreciation of Heine as a poet, but suggests that Keller refused to
accept the capriciousness of Heine's epics, which he satirizes in this little Romanzero. Brahm insists that had Keller published this work in the early fifties,
his reputation as a poet of talent and promise would have been recognized immediately.

Rodenberg was equally enamored by Keller's volume of collected poems. In a
letter to Keller dated November 16, 1883, Rodenberg expounded expansively on
Keller's poetry. He concurs with the sentiments in Brahm's review, but aug-
ments the critic's reflections as follows: what the critic Brahm did not express,

nor could he have expressed it, is the simultaneous sensitivity for both melancholy and joy that Rodenberg recalls from having read Keller's poems at an earlier time and has recognized again in reading the revised edition of his poems today (*G.B.* III/2, 405). For Rodenberg the volume contains infinite wealth, to which he will return again and again, as one would to a good friend; it will remain close to him and he will often turn to it as a refuge according to the changing moods of the day (*G.B.* III/2, 406).

Widmann, editor of the Bernese *Bund*, wrote of how powerful an impression Keller's poems had made upon him, particularly such a poem as the "Schillerfest"; he asks who else in the nineteenth century could have written such poetry besides Keller? He finds that Keller has transcended Goethe's poetry in the promotion of and progress toward a greater humanity. Widmann believes that Keller's poetry exhibits boldness in pure artistic conception (*G.B.* III/1, 244).

Keller, reflecting over the diverse responses to his volume of poetry in a letter to Storm, wrote that its publication had stirred up considerable discussion; that discussion brought forth more contradictions than the poetry itself contained, which in turn had quieted his guilty conscience (*G.B.* III/1, 494).

Martin Salander (1886)

Keller mentioned in a letter to Storm dated August 16, 1881 that he had thought out a new novel of one volume that would be very logical and contemporary; to which Keller added with a flourish that it would be a novel in which rather strong tobacco would be smoked (*G.B.* III/1, 465). This single volume became *Martin Salander*. In a letter to Heyse dated January 1882, Keller wrote that his novel would draw upon the political, social, and moral issues discussed in the closing novella of the Seldwyla collection, *Das verlorene Lachen*. Keller envisioned a modern novel, and hoped before his days were over to transcend the eternal reporting and to produce lively portrayals without dissipating into endless dialogue He writes that he has made an impressive beginning, has created several scenes and has drawn up the major characters as well as the other rogues. The only thing missing is a racy woman who will assume a life of her own, beyond that of her creator (*G.B.* III/1, 70). Keller, in a later letter, wrote to Heyse that his little novel was coming along, and requested Heyse's advice as to whether the title "Excelsior," which Keller wanted to borrow from a Longfellow poem, was suitable or not (*G.B.* III/1, 86). Heyse advised Keller in January 1883 against the title because it was not typical of Keller and reminded one of the titles of inferior stories in literary journals such as the *Gartenlaube* (*G.B.* III/1, 86).

In a letter to Heyse dated June 4, 1884 Keller described the long process of gestation that *Salander* had undergone, reaffirming his desire to allow a literary creation to run the full course of maturation before committing it to paper. Keller was laboring on his single-volume piece, which was slowly transforming itself and becoming more ponderous and hopefully more aesthetically pleasing (*G.B.* III/1, 102). Keller, in his effort to write a "modern" novel, knew that the book was going to be more realistic, more austere than his earlier works. Keller lamented to Heyse that he found himself caught up yet again in the dreadful treadmill of having to crank out a novel for regularly scheduled installments of the *Rundschau*. Producing manuscripts in this manner did not allow his prose to mature (*G.B.* III/1, 116; see also *G.B.* III/1, 110). Keller complained to Heyse of what had become the bane of his literary career: that meeting deadlines was at loggerheads with his unbridled muse (*G.B.* III/1, 116).

The initial reaction to the first installment of *Martin Salander* in the *Rundschau* came from Wilhelm Petersen, who found the piece splendid and who was enamored by the beauty, the warmth, the color and health, and the didactic power of the novel. Petersen fell in love with Frau Salander because of her integrity, her diligence. Petersen found in the novel a certain freshness with which he had come to associate all of Keller's works. Petersen placed great value on Keller's outstanding ability to portray characters who were not only full of passion, but were also portrayed in their civic and social roles. This art of portrayal is simple and healthy, like a draught of fresh spring water; this side of Keller's craft has been sadly neglected by the critics (*G.B.* III/1, 405).

Heyse began his letter to Keller of December 12, 1886 with the words of his wife, "that this is not a novel, but a book designed for one's edification," thereby underscoring the educative tone already noted by Petersen above; an assessment with which Heyse agreed. Heyse intended to stand up for Keller against the critics, who would surely misread this book and accuse Keller of mislabeling it a novel (*G.B.* III/1, 120). In his correspondence, Keller had provided his readers with the source for his last novel by referring them to the concluding novella in *Die Leute von Seldwyla, Das verlorene Lachen*. The village of Seldwyla has been transformed and urbanized — it has become Münsterberg, the setting for *Martin Salander*. Widmann referred to Keller's novel as having much in common with a national epic, and even made a reference to Schiller's *Wilhelm Tell* in his review which was not well received by his readers. Widmann defended his choice of the term epic on the grounds that *Martin Salander* had the material and contents of an epic designed for late nineteenth-century Swiss life. The reference to Schiller's *Tell*, Widmann assured Keller, was not an attempt to place to works side by side as equals, but rather an attempt to draw attention to the edifying nature of Keller's novel (*G.B.* III/1, 259). As Helbling has indicated in his introduction of the Keller-Widmann correspondence in the critical edition of Keller's *Gesammelte Briefe*, Widmann was the first to recognize the significance of Keller's last novel, claiming that it was dedicated to the development of the soul of a people and as such ought to be characterized as a modern Swiss national folk epic (*G.B.* III/1, 211).

By December 1886 Keller had recognized — and was perhaps himself persuaded by — the overwhelming frustration and disappointment expressed by critics and friends alike over the novel. In a letter to Storm dated December 29, 1886, Keller wrote that Storm need not write to him about *Martin Salander*, he already knew what was wrong with the book and what he must change, "in order to help it [the novel] to the light" (*G.B.* III/1, 500). Nevertheless, Storm wrote to Keller on January 12, 1887 expressing his disappointment with *Martin Salander*:

> Ihren "Salander" habe ich in drei Fortsetzungen vor Mai in der Familie gelesen, und ich leugne nicht, etwas verschnupft worden zu sein, und nicht nur die bei mir saßen, auch von meinen Korrespondenzfreunden kamen verwunderte Fragen. . . . aber ich wußte mit dem Dinge nicht recht was anzufangen . . . .
>
> (*G.B.* III/1 502).

> [I read your "Salander" prior to May in three sittings with my family and friends and I cannot deny being somewhat peeved; from my family and friends as well as from correspondents came incredulous questions. I really did not know what to make of the novel.]

Keller was despondent over what many perceived to be his miscast novel; in any case he never responded to Storm's perceptions of the novel and never answered Storm's letter, even after the latter wrote again, suggesting that he would like once again to wander through Seldwyla or old Zurich or in the youthful paradise of *Der Grüne Heinrich*, where it was less frighteningly realistic than in *Martin Salander*.

Rodenberg, on the other hand, viewed the novel as important as a *Zeitroman* (novel of the times) (*G.B.* III/2, 423). The manifold and at times disappointing reception of this novel did not prevent Keller from planning a sequel, in which Martin's son, Arnold Salander, was to become the central character, as we are told by C. F. Meyer (XV, 184) and Adolf Frey (33). Perhaps Paul Schlenther's review of *Martin Salander* for the *Rundschau* in 1887 strives more than most for a balanced review of Keller's last novel.

Schlenther concentrated on Keller's depiction of the world in the novel. The review praises Keller's successful attempt to present a mirror image of his time, whose poignancy and accuracy was received with astonishment in Switzerland. Schlenther suggests that Keller fashioned Salander's *Weltanschauung* according to his own and that Salander therefore represents Keller's generation. Through the actions and ethics (or lack thereof) of the Weidelich twins, Keller afforded his readers keen insight into political and social life in Zurich during the 1880s. In his gentle ridicule of Salander, Keller mocks himself and all Swiss of his generation. Keller suggests, in Schlenther's interpretation, that while everything is tolerable at the present time in Switzerland, it could be better; thus Schlenther detects some optimism in the novel. Strong figures such as Marie Salander, continued the Stauffacher tradition of strong female characters so prevalent in

Keller's earlier works. Schlenther suggests that Arnold Salander is introduced too late in the novel to convincingly fulfill the expectations placed upon him as a well-educated member of the next generation (149). Surprisingly, Schlenther never mentions the style of the novel, which had disappointed individuals such as Storm and Petersen, who had expected the poetic magic of the Seldwyla novellas.

The new style of *Martin Salander* also disappointed many of Keller's readers. They too sorely missed the poetic beauty of the Seldwyla novellas, which had become Keller's trademark. Interpretations ranged from those that misunderstood Keller's purpose and therefore attributed what they perceived as stylistic weakness to old age, to others, such as Widmann, who saw in this last work the beginning of something new, defined by later literary historians as naturalism. The publication of *Martin Salander,* while not it did not increase the sales of Keller's other books during the 1880s, cannot be said to have depressed them. Keller's correspondence with his last publisher, Wilhelm Hertz of Berlin, reveals that both enjoyed the growing renown and increased sales of Keller's books. Keller was clearly pleased that Hertz had already announced in December of 1882 a third edition of the *Sinngedicht,* which had been first published in 1881 (*G.B.* III/2, 434); the third edition would have a run of 1250 copies. In October of 1885 Hertz suggested publishing a fourth edition of the *Züricher Novellen.* In 1886 Keller signed a publishing contract for *Martin Salander* that stipulated the publication of four editions, of one thousand books each, to be printed at the outset (*G.B.* III/2, 455). The large printing attests to Keller's growing popularity and to Hertz's confidence in his talent. In the same year Hertz published a further edition of the Seldwyla novellas (*G.B.* III/2, 458). In 1887 Hertz announced a fifth edition of the *Sinngedicht* (*G.B.* III/2, 461), in 1888 a fourth edition of the *Sieben Legenden* and a third edition of the *Gedichte* (*G.B.* III/2, 462). In 1889 Hertz undertook the publication of the first edition of Keller's *Gesammelte Werke,* in which the author was directly involved. Its publication was completed by the fall of 1889, less than a year before Keller's death. Hertz's high regard for Keller, evident from their correspondence, and the ever-increasing sales of Keller's works indicates the respect, high regard, and popularity that Keller's prose and poetry had achieved during the last decade of his life.

Keller's significance was recognized first by Friedrich Theodor Vischer, who wrote an influential early essay on Keller in 1874 and expanded it in 1881, and then by Otto Brahm, who made the first attempt at a comprehensive monograph on Keller during the early 1880s. Both Vischer's essay and Brahm's monograph represent some of the best and most extensive criticism on Keller in the nineteenth century.

Friedrich Theodor Vischer was a faithful advocate of Keller's craft, although not an uncritical one. Vischer's 1874 essay on Keller did more to introduce Keller to a broader audience than any essay before that of Otto Brahm in 1883.

Vischer's study of Keller, which he had begun in 1874, went through several revisions in 1880 and again in 1881, after the revised edition of *Der grüne Heinrich* (1879–80) had been completed. Vischer's essay sought to promote Keller's works while defending them against what he perceived to be an unjust appraisal by Friedrich Kreyßig. Kreyßig, in his lectures on the modern German novel, *Vorlesungen über den deutschen Roman der Gegenwart*, delivered in Berlin in 1871, was primarily interested in whatever modern content could be extracted from Keller's *Grüner Heinrich*; he overlooked any aesthetic value that the work might contain. Kreyßig, according to Vischer, had absolutely no understanding for Keller's irony; he failed to differentiate between what was subjective and what was objective. Vischer compares Kreyßig to a bird of prey (*Stoßvogel*) that hastily extracts from an aesthetic work that which he wants to see or needs to further his own line of interpretation (351). According to Vischer, Kreyßig rushes through the text to determine whether or not the basic tenor in *Der grüne Heinrich* is modern, while discarding all that is strange, rather than explaining it (Luck, 242). Vischer devotes an extensive portion of his essay to the debunking of Kreyßig's criticism of *Der grüne Heinrich*; Vischer finds it unscrupulous that Kreyßig only considered Keller's first novel, his first work of prose, and never examined *Die Leute von Seldwyla*. Vischer asserts that Kreyßig allowed the conclusion of the novel to influence his overall interpretation, suggesting that Kreyßig read the entire novel in reverse and then based his overall assessment upon the novel's less-than-fortunate conclusion. Vischer argues correctly that Keller's novel, despite its classification as a novel, is really a blend between a novel and an autobiography. Kreyßig had taken Keller at his word that the book was a novel, and as a result compared the work to other novels: he was misled from the very beginning. Vischer believed that no one who was reasonable could fail to recognize the epic breadth, the organic spirit and depth inherent in Heinrich's development (345). He compared Keller's work to Goethe's *Dichtung und Wahrheit*, recognizing that Goethe's work was an autobiography interwoven with fiction and poetry, whereas Keller's work is a novel with many fictional interludes, punctuated by autobiographical impulses.

Vischer, unlike Kreyßig, attempted to explain the conclusion of the first edition of *Grüner Heinrich*. He does so by positing questions about the conclusion: Did Keller condemn himself to death? Did he have some other reason for this ending, stemming perhaps from guilt toward his mother? Vischer asks if the author wants to willfully condemn the old Heinrich, so that a new one could arise in his place. Heinrich is dead — but Gottfried Keller, his creator, lives. This twist is evidence enough for Vischer that this book walks a fine line between an autobiography and a novel.

Vischer moves on to discuss the *Sieben Legenden*, *Die Leute von Seldwyla*, and *Der grüne Heinrich*. The poet, he exclaims, is really arisen from the grave, filling his readers with merriment and *Lebensgefühl* (352). Vischer concedes that before it attained poetic maturity, Keller's prose reminded him in places of the prose of the German Romantic writer Jean Paul Richter (1763–1825), and that an example was the capricious conclusion to *Der grüne Heinrich*. The Seldwyla collection reveals that Keller was striving for a "Lebenstüchtiger" realism (a realism able to cope with life), which understood the genuine ideal (*Idealität*) within itself (359). Keller's spirit, according to Vischer, is genuinely civic-minded. The characters in Seldwyla are not educated to become world leaders or humanists, but to become solid citizens (360). They strive to attain what any individual with a rational worldview can achieve. Earnest thinking goes hand in hand with conscientious morals. Keller's attempts to discuss the ethical in his fiction are suffused with piety.

Vischer asserts that there are two types of readers: those who admire the portraits the writer paints and those who are only concerned with the purport of the book. Some readers are sensitive and some are not (367). Vischer believes that Keller will never be popular, because he is a poet. He heralds Keller's talent as an ability to illustrate with an artist's eye, which reminds Vischer of Goethe. Keller draws both young and old, women and men with an assured hand. His seemingly bottomless treasure chest of character types are drawn from everyday life. As a painter Keller shows rather than tells; he does not confuse the occupation of the poet with that of the historian.

Vischer concludes that to condemn Keller on the basis of his first novel, frankly an unripe youthful publication, while simultaneously ignoring the Seldwyla novellas, is to do him an injustice. He refuses to discuss the many flaws of *Der grüne Heinrich* again, but would rather turn his attention to a well-rounded composition such as *Romeo und Julia auf dem Dorfe* (397). Vischer maintains that Keller has learned much from the style of old novellas, chronicles, and from Luther's German. He writes that Keller coined his own golden language (400). He achieves this style through syntax, rhythm, and acoustic movement within the language. One has the sense that one is listening to a storyteller from a bygone age. Keller has also benefited from the Old High German that is still present in the Swiss dialects. Vischer lauds Keller's linguistic creativity; he creates new words, original expressions like every born poet. He writes for an audience who will appreciate such artistic flourishes. Vischer believes that Keller has remained little known because of his ambitious prose and because he was cantonal secretary for fifteen years, interrupting his career as a writer. The majority of readers want to encounter the usual prosaic portrayals in their reading and have no sense of beauty or ear for style and rhythm.

Included in the 1881 edition of the original essay was Vischer's discussion of the final volume of the revised *Grüne Heinrich*. Vischer still finds the original conclusion to be of interest, even if it had been supplanted by the revised edition. He recommends a comparison of the two editions. Vischer approves of the new Heinrich, who in the revised edition becomes a successful member of society; he claims that the persuasiveness of this conclusion depends on how this hero is inwardly motivated to become liberated from his troubles and guilt. Vischer is uneasy about Keller's decision to reintroduce Judith, whose love for Heinrich — and his for her — has attained a platonic plateau that is powerful enough in terms of its resignation to motivate Heinrich to forsake fulfillment of his sensual desires in order to embrace a socially respectable position as a civil servant. The Heinrich of the revised version, taking Judith's lead, places community needs before personal desires. Vischer questions whether there is enough substance in the text to enable Heinrich to make the transition from independent artist to civil servant believable. A letter from Frau Lee, in which she admits that she has perhaps been too lenient in educating her son, alleviates some of Heinrich's guilt; she shoulders some of the responsibility for her son's misguided ways. A further letter from the count indicates that Dorothea has not remained true to Heinrich, but has become engaged to another; this development helps Heinrich to liberate himself from his guilt and those languishing elements of his past. This preoccupation with the self leads Vischer to categorize the book as a blend of an autobiography and a novel. Vischer suggests that Keller is again drawing upon his experience as a cantonal secretary. While this experience was not yet his own when the original version of the novel was written in 1855, it enabled him to portray Heinrich as a civil servant in the revised edition of 1880. Overall he finds the new conclusion filled with beautiful, emotional, and picturesque situations, wrought through and through with deep reflection and expressed in stunning language achieved by Keller at the height of his poetical prowess.

Otto Brahm's 150-page critical essay on Keller, published in Leipzig in 1883, was the first and to my knowledge only volume to have been published on Keller's works during his lifetime. Brahm is well disposed toward Keller's fiction and poetry from the outset. He seeks to assess Keller's fiction by comparing it to that of his contemporaries, and attempts to show how it grew organically out of the German literary tradition and is therefore a natural continuation of that tradition. Although Keller received praise in the 1870s and 1880s from such notable literary historians as Friedrich Theodor Vischer and Wilhelm Scherer, and from such authors Auerbach, Heyse, and Storm, Brahm believed that Keller had not yet received the wider recognition he deserved from the German reading public, and aspired to introduce others to Keller's fiction. Brahm's essay, which addressed a general readership, remains the most comprehensive study of Keller's prose written during the author's lifetime.

Unlike later scholarship by such literary historians as Jacob Baechtold, whose biography of Keller we shall discuss in the next chapter, Brahm concentrates on interpreting Keller's literary work; he devotes one paragraph to Keller's biography. Brahm immediately begins with the theme of Swissness in Keller's writing which he believes to be most often misunderstood and has, as a consequence, unfairly relegated Keller to the position of a provincial author. Brahm attempts to identify what is peculiarly Swiss in Keller's works, listing his characters, the setting of his stories and what Brahm defines as an honorable sense of civic duty (14). He maintains that the Swiss element in Keller's works is realistic (15). Brahm also places Keller in the tradition of Jean Paul Richter and the Swabian school of poets; he hints at the influence of Goethe, thereby attempting to discredit the notion that Keller is a provincial writer. Quoting Keller, Brahm allows the author to declare himself a German as well as Swiss (15). Keller was rather vocal in his rejection of the idea of a Swiss national literature (*G.B.* III/I, 244). Brahm defines the German (as opposed to Swiss) in Keller's writing as the romantic element (16). This blend of the realistic and the romantic, according to Brahm, is the essence of Keller's art. Brahm sees in this blend the direction that literature will take. Keller uses the romantic to paint aesthetic arabesques, but he remains committed to the principles of realism: he is always in control of the romantic element which he infuses into his realism. Brahm recognized Keller's ability to embellish realistically, making the improbable seem possible.

Brahm divides Keller's literary career into three phases. The first is characterized by the youthful struggle with subjectivity. The second phase is distinguished by the transition from subjectivity to objectivity, and the third phase is characterized by the author's creativity and originality. Keller's first literary efforts were political poems which reflect the author's views during the 1840s. In *Der grüne Heinrich* Keller addresses various topics such as immortality, an indestructible respect for nature, as well as many personal issues that preoccupied Keller in the early 1850s. Brahm refrains from criticizing the first poems, for reiterating flaws already discussed would serve no purpose. Rather, Brahm focuses on the central issues of Keller's first novel, including the question of subjectivity. Brahm asserts that the novel moves from autobiographical mode in the beginning to fictional mode toward the conclusion. Brahm discusses at length the death of the hero, and his sympathy for the psychological necessity that influenced the author's conclusion. Brahm believes that Heinrich must meet his own demise, because he is incapable of bringing his inner world into harmony with his outer world (32). Comparing Keller's novel with Goethe's *Werther*, Brahm suggests that both authors created literary figures on whom they imposed death, so that they, the authors, might live. Both Goethe and Keller distanced themselves from their first novels; Keller completely rewrote his novel, replacing tragedy with resignation. Brahm agrees in part with Vischer, who described Heinrich's death as incomprehensible, but who was equally disenchanted with Keller's new conclusion in the revised edition of 1880. Brahm likewise questions whether Keller improved the conclusion in the revised edition. Could Werther's or Tasso's tragedy have been averted and replaced with resignation he asks and would that have been desirable? (35) Brahm, unlike Vischer, is clearly in favor of the tragic conclusion; he believes it to be suggested in the text from the first chapters of the original edition (35). Brahm suggests that revisions should have been made in the episode at the count's residence, for it is there and not in the conclusion that life becomes more pleasant for Heinrich. As a result the reader is confused by Heinrich's departure from the count, and by his tragic end. Brahm refers to the conclusion as "skizzenhaft" (sketchy) when compared with other highly detailed sections, such as the artist's festival in Munich, but concedes that this is the sign of great artists such as Shakespeare who reign sovereign over their art. Brahm also questions Keller's decision to switch to a first-person narration; he considers such alterations to be merely cosmetic, suggesting that the laborious task was in vain. Comparing the conclusions of the two editions of *Der grüne Heinrich* leads Brahm to pose the question, already raised by Auerbach, concerning the right of an author to revise a novel already in the public domain. Brahm contends that the author has the right to revise his own work, but readers also have the right to decide which edition they prefer. Although Brahm favors the original tragic conclusion, he concedes that the new conclusion is a reflection of Keller's mature outlook on life; whereas the original conclusion was reminiscent of Goethe's *Werther*, the revised conclusion was more in the spirit of the mature Goethe's *Wilhelm Meister's Apprenticeship*.

In addition to that of Goethe, Brahm acknowledges the influence of Jean Paul Richter on *Der grüne Heinrich*, and believes that Richter's *Titan* served as the model for Keller's work. Echoing Vischer's comments on Richter, Brahm suggests that Keller's naivete is founded upon his indestructible respect for nature; this respect, when joined together with his sense of humor, make Keller a literary heir of Richter. Brahm quotes at length from Keller's novel, proving Richter's strong influence. For instance, the two female characters, Anna and Judith, opposites with whom Heinrich falls in love, have their precursors in the figures of Liane and Linda from Richter's *Titan*. In particular, Anna, "das zarte ätherische Wesen" (that gentle ethereal being) is the image of Liane, the youthful love of Richter's hero. Likewise the fascination with death in *Der grüne Heinrich* — a motif which is not in Keller's later works — is a romantic element that Brahm traces to Richter's influence. Keller's portrayal of landscape in *Der grüne Heinrich* also reminds Brahm of Richter's idyllic landscapes and villages. Brahm's comments conclude with a seven page excerpt from the story of Heinrich's youth which again shows the influence of Richter on the two female characters Anna and Judith and their relationship to Heinrich. Lest Keller be accused of being an epigone, Brahm is swift to demonstrate that there are significant differences between Goethe and Keller. Goethe's heroes in *Werther* and *Wilhelm Meister* are cast character-types (*Typen*), with which readers can easily identify. The characters in Keller's novel are rugged individualists. Heinrich, for example, is much too much an individualist; his character is too subjectively portrayed to be a cast character and is therefore not able to carry the symbolic weight of a Werther or Wilhelm Meister. Many a youth of Werther's time could identify with his philosophy of life. Although many may share Heinrich's views on aesthetics, politics and religion, they have more trouble identifying with his person, and this is detrimental to the novel's popularity. Heinrich remains unreachable and incommensurable (Brahm 44).

Brahm closes this section with a discussion of education and pedagogy in the two novellas that have parallel themes to *Der grüne Heinrich*, namely *Frau Regel Amrain* and *Pankraz der Schmoller*. Both of these novellas and the theme of education provide Brahm with the bridge to the second phase of Keller's career.

This second phase concerns the shift from the subjectivity prevalent in *Der grüne Heinrich* to objectivity in such works as *Romeo und Julia auf dem Dorfe*. These works show that Keller is less preoccupied with himself and therefore more inclined to consider the social issues of his day. Brahm concentrates on *Romeo und Julia auf dem Dorfe*, the story that has become the most widely read and highly praised of Keller's stories. Brahm claims that the realistic depiction of village life is still tainted by the black fiddler, a romantic figure more reminiscent of creations by Tieck or Eichendorff. The motif of death is also transformed, and no longer glorified (69). This emerging objectivity contains a growing didacticism, as Keller distances himself from the romantic influence. Brahm notes that *Romeo und Julia* is the only novella of Keller's that ends tragically. In all the others, the protagonists are cured and become honorable citizens, which Brahm likes to refer to as "das Schweizerische Realistische" (the Swiss realist element: 70). Brahm lauds Keller's imagination and originality which bring forth a seemingly endless line of new and unique characters (71). Keller's inexhaustible fountain of creativity is undisputed testimony of his creative genius. Brahm contends that Keller's fiction represents a continuation of the German literary tradition in the spirit of Goethe and Richter.

Brahm's discussion of this second phase concludes with an analysis of the *Sieben Legenden*, which demonstrate Keller's vivid imagination as well as his ability to write no longer as a romantic, but with the moral sensitivity and earnest artistic achievement of a modern realist (82). Keller thoroughly transforms highly religious material into stories for the secular world; his characters clearly prefer life on earth to life in heaven. Though Feuerbach's philosophical influence on Keller is clear to the modern reader, Brahm curiously enough never even mentions Feuerbach's name. Perhaps he was afraid of offending prospective readers who were believers, because Brahm explains that Keller is not maliciously mocking religious ritual (83). Indeed, Brahm praises what he refers to as the ethical in the *Sieben Legenden*, stories which he believes represent the pinnacle of Keller's creative powers (87).

The third phase of Keller's career is exemplified by the realism of the *Züricher Novellen*, the 1880 edition of *Der grüne Heinrich*, and *Das Sinngedicht*. Brahm detects a further withdrawal from the romantic influence, and senses that Keller is mocking the romantic ideal. With the move to realism, the historical element also takes on a more important role, most notably in *Dietegen* and in *Der Narr auf Manegg*. Zurich replaces the imaginary Seldwyla as a backdrop.

The delivery becomes broader, more folksy and popular. The sparse exchanges in the Seldwyla novellas and in the *Sieben Legenden* are replaced by extensive speeches and dialogues, and by word games in *Das Sinngedicht*. The didactic and practical thread, and the ethical themes present in the Seldwyla novellas continue in the *Züricher Novellen*, where they are further developed and their resonance deepened: the poet has become a teacher (96). Brahm interprets this didactic trend in Keller as a peculiarly "Swiss" phenomenon, recalling the great Swiss educator Heinrich Pestalozzi and reminding the reader that Keller had written a textbook for elementary schools.

After further discussing the pedagogical context, Brahm turns his attention to the unique literary form of the then recently published *Das Sinngedicht*, a cycle of novellas that had focused new attention on Keller. Brahm begins by comparing Reinhart, one of the two main protagonists in the cycle, to Faust, the learned but estranged scholar, thus anchoring *Das Sinngedicht* in the Goethean tradition. Brahm quotes eight pages from *Das Sinngedicht* before taking up his interpretation of the text, which begins on an enthusiastically congratulatory note (120). Brahm finds that Keller's blend of the romantic and the modern has led to a new genre, which he labels a realistic fairy-tale of the modern age. Comparing the *Decameron* of Giovannni Boccaccio (1313–1375) with *Das Sinngedicht*, Brahm demonstrates that *Das Sinngedicht* is composed of six interconnected, yet independent novellas that while imperfectly joined, do achieve a greater degree of integration than those in the *Decameron*. He discusses what he believes to be the central topic of the novella-cycle, namely Keller's examination of the women's emancipation movement. Brahm highlights Keller's skill in discussing this topic, not through empty theory and parliamentary speeches, but by allowing his characters to represent different sides of the movement. Keller swiftly narrows the topic to the relationship between women and men. In *Das Sinngedicht*, marriage, equal partnership in marriage, and the role of both parties in marriage are aired as well as the socially divisive question of marriage between different classes Here again is evidence of Keller as the modern writer not afraid to discuss current social topics. Brahm concludes his interpretation of *Das Sinngedicht* by comparing it to *Nora* by Henrik Ibsen (1838–1906). He finds Ibsen's satire much more earnest, whereas Keller's is more playful and humorous. Brahm contends that *Das Sinngedicht* is a poetic realization of certain social problems, he lauds it as Keller's most balanced creation (124).

The remainder of Brahm's essay discusses Keller's male and female characters. Brahm sees Heinrich Lee as representative of many of Keller's male characters, all of whom share inhibitions regarding their ability to express feelings and who usually resort to sulking. Keller's female characters who, though predominantly mischievous, are much more open and often try to liberate their male counterparts from these inhibitions.

In the final section of his essay Brahm pays tribute to Keller the landscape artist turned poet, who paints with words what the artist would compose on canvas. The painstaking attention to detail, the precision of the images, the symbolism as well as the propensity to complete all stories, to answer questions and to solve problems raised, all these emanate from Keller's training as a landscape artist. Keller also conveys abstract concepts such as immortality in concrete visual images that are accessible to every reader (148). Brahm disagrees with several of his contemporaries, in particular Vischer, who reads into Heinrich's death the symbolic death of the author which will lead to his resurrection. Similarly, Brahm refuses to accept the interpretation of the Swiss literary historian Robert Weber (1824–1896), who interprets Anna's death as the fading of Idealism and sees in Judith the brilliant natural embodiment of Realism; for Weber, both are examples of bad German aesthetics (141). Brahm concedes that Keller has not written as voluminously as some of his contemporaries, but emphasizes that what Keller may lack in volume is outweighed by his diversity of form, color, characters, imaginative plots, atmosphere, moods and motifs that spill forth from his creative genius (148).

Brahm's essay is the most comprehensive critique of Keller's fiction written during the author's lifetime. It does not discuss the collection of *Neue Gedichte* (1883) or the novel *Martin Salander* (1886) which were published later. In fact, Brahm makes no attempt in this essay to discuss Keller's poetry. The overriding positive tone of this essay reveals a deep respect for Keller's literary work; Brahm is constructively critical and does not hesitate to state his views or to dispute the opinions of his contemporaries. His purpose is to anchor Keller firmly in the canon of nineteenth-century German literature, first by establishing clear ties to the lineage of German authors, specifically Goethe and Jean Paul Richter, and finally by demonstrating Keller's originality while emphasizing his ability to blend the German romantic tradition with realism to produce what Brahm envisioned to be the modern. The overall tone of the essay in its breadth and depth was aimed at a broad audience, ranging from literary scholars to the general reading public, who were offered Brahm's interpretation along with tantalizing samples of Keller's prose.

The reviews of Brahm's book were mostly positive. Erich Schmidt writes in *Die Deutsche Literatur-Zeitung* that this task fell to the right man. The essay, he continues, is not filled with empty praise; one can feel Brahm's understanding for Keller and his fiction. J. W. Widmann enthusiastically endorses Brahm's monograph in the Sunday edition of the *Bund*. He points out how rare it is to have a book of this nature written on a living author by a literary historian who has sufficient time to be thorough in his examination. By comparison, the journalist does not have sufficient time to carry out extensive research on a book or author, because he always has deadlines to meet. Furthermore, Brahm's study will greatly enhance our understanding of Keller's fiction: "Seldom has a book appeared that captures the intellectual presence of a living author. What the journalistic critics hastily put to paper is worked out here in the quiet study of the a literary scholar. Brahm's book embodies this careful scholarship and presents a complete picture of Keller's fiction."

Brahm's essay was unusual in that it was a daring attempt to write a comprehensive study of the fiction of a living author who had not yet ceased to write. There can be little question that Brahm's book helped to further Keller's reputation. It also transformed Keller's prose into a standard against which his contemporaries would be measured.

Of course, there were those who disagreed with Brahm. While Theodor Fontane (1819–1898) did not challenge Brahm's assessment of Keller as a great writer who has earned his place in the canon of nineteenth-century German literature, he did question Brahm's vision regarding the direction of future literary development. Brahm had distanced Keller from the Romantics by emphasizing his blend of "controlled" romanticism with dominating realism which Brahm saw as the wave of the future (Brahm, 17). Fontane places Keller one notch above Arnim, Tieck, and Eichendorff, but questions just how large the difference actually is between the Romantics and Keller. Fontane respects Keller's talent, humor and art, but diagnoses the disturbing aspect in Keller's writing as his "style" (*Stil*), a word Fontane uses not in the antiquated sense of writing style, but in the sense of objectivity. Fontane defines style as follows: "A work is more stylish when it is more objective; in other words, the more objective, the more the characters speak for themselves — the more liberated the work is from the contradictory peculiarities of the author." (Fontane, 264). Fontane strives for objectivity by allowing his characters to speak their minds without noticeable auctorial influence. Keller, he asserts, imposes on his characters a distinct tone, which is at times appropriate and at other times leads to complete dissonance (265). Fontane cites the *Sieben Legenden*, asserting that the tone of these seven legends is more like that of a fairy-tale than a religious work. Fontane is put off by this overriding tone (266). As much as he appreciates Keller's humor, and understands Keller's intent to illustrate Feuerbach's triumph of earthly life over the promise of the hereafter Fontane nevertheless finds the title misleading and inappropriate. Fontane finds this fairy-tale tone prevalent in all of Keller's writing and claims that it is responsible for the inconsistency in his works Though left unstated, it is Keller's subjective style that forces Fontane to view him as a romantic rather than a realist author.

Fontane also challenges Brahm's critical methodology. He accuses Brahm of studying the minutest details as if he were researching Goethe. Though Fontane does not question the need for a minute study of such consistently great writers as Goethe, Shakespeare, or Dante, he does question Brahm's propensity to research Keller as if he were another Goethe. He maintains that not everything Keller wrote was uniformly good. One is tempted here to accuse Fontane of jealousy: why criticize a literary historian for his thoroughness? Quoting August

Wilhelm von Schlegel, Fontane claims that Keller "never drew back the curtain on uncharted terrain" (268–69). Keller produced an excellent wine, raised some spectacular vintages, but the mountain and the vine-stocks were long present. Keller was a good writer, but he was not a genius and does not deserve to be examined as though he were. Moreover, Brahm's essay tends to talk about the stories, their contents, rather than interpret them. We understand little more after reading Brahm than we did before (268).

Nevertheless, Fontane concedes that Brahm's twenty-page interpretation of *Der grüne Heinrich* is right on course. Fontane agrees with the parallels Brahm drew between Keller's novel and Goethe's *Werther, Wilhelm Meister* and *Dichtung und Wahrheit*. But, after demonstrating the parallels between Goethe and Keller, Brahm confuses the reader by emphasizing the differences: Werther and Wilhelm Meister are shown to be mere cast characters, whereas Heinrich Lee is an individualist. Of course, it is precisely here that Brahm is attempting to pull back Schlegel's curtain, to demonstrate that Keller has gone beyond Goethe, that he has broken new ground.

It seems appropriate to conclude this chapter devoted to criticism written during Keller's lifetime with the tribute to Gottfried Keller published shortly after his death by Julius Rodenberg, the editor of the *Deutsche Rundschau*. Rodenberg emphasizes the unbridgeable artistic void left behind by Keller's death. While claiming Germany to be Keller's spiritual homeland, Rodenberg acknowledges that he remained a Swiss patriot. Zurich and the Swiss landscape formed the backdrop, indeed the essence of all his fiction and poetry. But Keller's allegiance was not blind patriotism. Rodenberg cites such critical works as *Martin Salander* as a sign of Keller's integrity and of his honesty toward his own people. Rodenberg relates his own long affiliation with Keller, recalls the celebration that overwhelmed the author on his seventieth birthday, and concludes his tribute appropriately enough with Keller's poem "Feueridylle."

Works Cited

Auerbach, Berthold. "Gottfried Keller's Neue Schweizergestalten." *Deutsche Rundschau* 4 (July–September, 1875): 34.

Brahm, Otto. *Gottfried Keller. Ein literarisches Essay.* Berlin: Auerbach, 1883.

———. "Gottfried Kellers Gedichte." *Deutsche Rundschau* 32 (Oct.–Dec., 1883).

———. "Gottfried Keller's 'Grüner Heinrich'" *Deutsche Rundschau* 25 (Oct.–Dec., 1880): 466.

Eduard Engel. "Gottfried Keller: Das Sinngedicht," *Das Magazin für die Literatur des In- und Auslandes,* February 4, 1882.

Fontane, Theodor. *Sämtliche Werke.* Vol. 21/1: 262. Munich: Nymphenburger, 1963.

Frey, Adolf. *Erinnerungen an Gottfried Keller*. 1891; rpt. Zurich: Rotapfel-Verlag, 1979, 33.

Grosse, Julius. Review of *Der Grüne Heinrich*. 3 parts. *Abendblatt zur Neuen Münchener Zeitung*. May 2, 9, 19, 1857.

Hettner, Hermann. Review of *Der Grüne Heinrich*, vols. 1–3. *National-Zeitung* (Berlin) May 5, 1854.

Keller, Gottfried. *Gesammelte Briefe*. Ed. Carl Helbling. 4 vols. Bern: Benteli, 1950–54.

Kuh, Emil. "Die Leute von Seldwyla." *Wiener Abendpost*, Dec. 28, 1874.

Luck, Rätus. *Gottfried Keller als Literaturkritiker*. Bern: Francke, 1970.

Meyer, Conrad Ferdinand. *Sämtliche Werke*. Vol. 15. Bern: Benteli, 1985. 184.

Rodenberg, Julius. "Gottfried Keller." *Deutsche Rundschau* 64 (July–September) 1890.

Spielhagen, Friedrich. *Westermanns Monatsheften* 52 (June) 1882, 309.

Scherer, Wilhelm. "Gottfried Keller's Züricher Novellen." *Deutsche Rundschau* 17 (Oct.–Dec., 1878), 324.

Schlenther, Paul. Review of *Martin Salander*. *Deutsche Rundschau* 51, April–June, 1887, 148.

Varnhagen von Ense, Karl August. Review of *Der Grüne Heinrich*. *Vossische Zeitung*, June 14, 1855, 6.

Zäch, Alfred. *Gottfried Keller im Spiegel seiner Zeit. Urteile und Berichte über den Menschen und Dichter*. Zurich: Sientia, 1952.

3: The Circle of Friends: Keller Scholarship 1890–1919

THE LITERARY HISTORIAN OTTO BRAHM wrote the only book length interpretation of Keller's fiction during his lifetime. Immediately following Keller's death in July 1890, works about him consisted largely of tributes composed by fellow authors such as C. F. Meyer and Paul Heyse and by such friends and admirers as the *Rundschau* editor Julius Rodenberg or the Schleswig government councilor Wilhelm Petersen (1835–1900). The critical scholarship of this period began with such literary historians as Adolf Frey (1855–1920) and Jacob Baechtold (1848–1897): scholars who had known Keller personally. It gradually progressed to a circle of critical admirers such as Baechtold's successor Emil Ermatinger, who had not known Keller personally and who was therefore able to judge his fiction with greater objectivity. However, the efforts of Frey and Baechtold were also significant. They documented conversations with Keller about his fiction and preserved such material as his verbal plans for the continuation of *Martin Salander*, which might otherwise have been lost to successive generations, because it was not extensively documented in his literary estate. In fact, Baechtold's biography and Frey's monograph became the main sources of documentation for many Keller scholars during the first two decades of the twentieth century.

Rodenberg's tribute to Keller in the summer edition of the *Deutsche Rundschau* was followed by Adolf Frey's description of the author's last year, which in tone and style was to epitomize much of Keller scholarship during the last decade of the nineteenth century (Frey, 1890, *Rundschau*). Frey begins his account with the celebration of Keller's seventieth birthday, which Keller attempted to avoid by leaving Zurich to take the waters on the Seelisberg in central Switzerland. Frey emphasizes what he calls Keller's republican humbleness. The article provides a month by month account of Keller's final year, closely documenting the author's physical deterioration, while emphasizing his composed acceptance of impending death. Frey recalls moments of alertness which revealed a sharp mind still sensitive to the world around him and capable of spinning new yarns. He also verifies Keller's famous confession to C. F. Meyer, "Ich schulde, ich dulde" (I owe, I suffer), a little phrase that continues to influence scholarship.[1] The account of Keller's last year concludes with a description of his death and of

---

[1] Such statements have contributed to new psychoanalytical approaches to Keller in our own time. See: Muschg, A. (1977) *Gottfried Keller*. Munich: Kindler. and Kaiser, Gerhard (1981) *Gottfried Keller — Das Gedichtete Leben*. Frankfurt/M: Insel.

the funeral procession which Keller would probably have found too elaborate. The tone is friendly and uncritical and tries to capture the final moments of a great mind for posterity.

Frey's initial essay evolved into an ever popular little volume, *Erinnerungen an Gottfried Keller*, which is still in print today. In his book, Frey expounds upon his friendship with Keller, recording his earliest encounters and first impressions of the by then celebrated Swiss author during the 1870s, while Frey himself was still a student. Of particular interest are the descriptions of Keller's reflections regarding both his craft and the chore of "authoring," as well as his attitude toward critics, together with the author's frustration over the questionable ability of literature to influence society. Frey describes Keller's position as cantonal clerk, his political views, and his plans for works that never materialized. He also offers a glance into Keller's personal life and shares some keen firsthand insights into Keller the human being. As the title implies, this is a personal biography and is aimed at a general readership.

Frey devotes one section to Keller's relationship to his craft. Keller did not have a regimented schedule, except perhaps when literary journals such as the *Rundschau* serialized his work. Even then he was known for delaying sequels and conclusions. If he was dissatisfied with the end result, he would simply set the work aside. To quote Frey, "Die Stunde mußte es bringen" (The muse must be present: 44). Keller also had an ambivalent attitude toward literary critics. While there were those, such as Hettner and Vischer, whom he respected, there were others, such as Auerbach, whom he tolerated, and, there were those, such as Gervinus and Prutz, whom he despised. Frey discusses at length Keller's reflections on Goethe, Schiller, Lessing, Shakespeare, Gotthelf, and Mörike. Keller was also a bibliophile and an avid reader whose impressive library revealed as one for whom books were nourishment borne of necessity (30).

Of particular interest for the modern reader not familiar with domestic Swiss politics is Frey's description of Keller's position as cantonal secretary, which Frey uses as a forum to discuss the author's political views. Keller's position hampered his writing for some fifteen years, but it did provide him with financial stability. In retrospect, his position inspired *Martin Salander*, while also supplying him with considerable raw material that later found its way into that novel. Frey relates Keller's frustration over the failure of his literary endeavors to improve the ethical bearing of his reading public. Although he was not surprised that his political poems and his last novel had had little effect upon the problems in his homeland, it saddened him to be so powerless, and this frustration contributed greatly to his bitterness in his final years (Frey 71). Those of his countrymen who celebrated his fame, knew him mostly for the poems that had been set to music and for the more famous of the Seldwyla novellas. Frey also reports a conversation with Keller, in which Keller speaks extensively about his planned continuation of *Martin Salander*, explaining how Arnold would liberate his threatened family, how the Salander daughters would remarry the right men this time. Frey has captured much that has come to form our impressions of Keller's character, his many moods, his relationship to family and friends, and his humble, forthright spirit.

Upon Keller's death, a fellow author from Zurich, Conrad Ferdinand Meyer, expressed his sympathy and respect for Meister Gottfried by emphasizing Keller's love of country, his proper ethical personality, and his sense of duty, all of which were wed to a powerful imagination tainted by many moods. This unique combination of characteristics would not repeat itself in the near future (Meyer, 15, 178). Meyer and Keller maintained a distant friendship; both harbored mutual respect for one another's talent, but were not well suited for each other's company, a fact well documented in Keller's correspondence. In August 1890 Meyer also wrote an essay titled, "Erinnerungen an Gottfried Keller," in which Meyer speaks of the genuine reverence he felt not only for Keller's talent, but also for the moral strength of Keller's character. In their conversations Keller avoided discussing aesthetic observations and shunned such empty terms as realism and pessimism; he preferred discussing individual cases and motifs, and always spoke to the heart of the matter. Often he would speak of the source of his various literary motifs. Meyer reports that Keller was uncomfortable with historical material, because he could not verify the historical information or for that matter any situation beyond his realm of experience. Meyer praises the *Sieben Legenden* as psychological masterpieces, and believes the *Züricher Novellen* to be Keller's greatest achievement because of the way the themes of frugality and of being oneself are handled. Meyer recalls his unsuccessful attempt to convince Keller to discuss religious themes. Similarly to Frey, Meyer closes his essay with two memorable encounters with Keller. In the first, Keller spontaneously and eloquently elaborated upon the dramatic elements in a photograph of a tapestry by Raphael of Ananias and Saphira. This surprised Meyer, because he had no idea that Keller had such profound knowledge of drama. Keller's knowledge and understanding of drama was discovered only later with the publication of the dramatic fragments in Keller's unpublished writing.[2] In the second, Meyer recalls his last visit with Keller, shortly before the author's death. Keller filled the room with a "Spinnen und Weben der Phantasie" (spinning and weaving of fantasy), revealing transposed biblical scenes as literary material (*Stoffe*), and confirms Frey's record of Keller's plans for the second part of *Martin Salander* which would have concluded with a great flood (Meyer, vol. 15, 184). The episode closes with Keller's and Meyer's intuition that this would be their last meeting,

---

[2] Meyer, as a distant friend of Keller, could not have known at that time how extensive Hettner's and Keller's discourse over drama had been during Keller's years in Berlin. The question remains unanswered and perhaps unanswerable as to why Keller, beyond his dramatic fragments such as "Therese," never completed a drama despite his intensive study of the genre and his early professed intention to become a dramatist.

one framed by Keller's now famous words "Ich schulde, Ich dulde!" which Meyer interpreted to mean death (136).

The Austrian poet and playwright Hugo von Hofmannsthal wrote an unusual tribute, composed as a discussion between a *Legationssekretär* (legal counselor), an estate owner, a painter, a musician and Hofmannsthal himself (II, 266). The conversation opens with a discussion of the many festivals that appear in Keller's works. The counselor recalls the long-winded artist festival in Munich described in *Der Grüne Heinrich*, a festival that he felt was unnecessary, commenting that the book would be better served had the second half simply been lost. The story of Heinrich's youth is so rich in life's experiences, that one forgets one is reading fiction. The estate owner values above all else Keller's ability to lend form to the most ridiculous and most diverse events, and to cast light at the proper moment, thereby illuminating the whole. The counselor agrees with the estate owner. He refers to the diversity of situations, the multiple layers of personality ranging from pompousness, boasting, vanity to cowardliness and helplessness: no other author has painted embarrassment in so many rich hues and tones. The painter suggests that Keller the landscape artist expresses these emotions in colors, shadows, and hues that are not given to every author, citing the "Scharlachroten" (scarlet red) nightshirt of the Gutsbesitzer in *Der Schmied seines Glückes*, or the interplay of light and shadow in the house of the Ölweib (a malicious old woman) in *Das verlorene Lachen*. When the painter recalls Keller's works, he thinks only of the mystifying rhythm of light and shadows (Hofmannsthal, 271). This rhythm in Keller's works is also perceived by the musician. The musician hears a harmonious melody through the diverse destinies of Keller's characters in an ordered world, a harmony which does not exist for example in the works of Dostoyevsky. The estate owner concurs, stating that the author must have an unbelievably fine and proper conception of the distribution of volume and weight, otherwise it would be impossible to have created any one of these stories which reflect a well balanced, fully rounded life. The painter concludes the discussion, suggesting that the deeply felt boredom and joy in Keller's works flow directly into our veins, and that this merriment helps us through life, something he believes cannot be said of Goethe. Hofmannsthal's little tribute to Keller remains as timeless as it does eloquent.

The literary historian Jakob Baechtold became Keller's first biographer. Baechtold was commissioned by his colleague and friend, Professor U. Schneider, the executor of Keller's last testament, to oversee, organize and thereby to preserve Keller's literary estate. In the preface to his three volume work, Baechtold informs the reader that a shadow had fallen on his friendship with Keller in the last years of the author's life, as Keller grew increasingly suspicious of literary historians. A letter from Keller to Baechtold dated January 28, 1877, in which Keller entrusted his future literary estate to Baechtold, persuaded the biographer to accept Schneider's commission (*G.B.* III/1, 283).

Baechtold began his work in 1893, just three years after Keller's death. Since Keller held truth and honesty to be the greatest virtues, Baechtold pledges to apply these virtues as his guiding principle in his portrayal. The biography of Ludwig Uhland (1787–1862) was to be Baechtold's model, thereby setting up a structure, that would allow Keller to speak for himself. The biographer's voice is only heard during the poet's childhood or when letters or sufficient documentation are either unavailable or unsuitable. Baechtold takes Barthold Georg Niebuhr at his word that it is not appropriate for the world to know the innermost thoughts and feelings of an individual; there are clothes for the soul, which one should no more remove in public than one's clothes for the body. Following Niebuhr's principle, Baechtold selected six hundred letters out of the thousands in the archive which he believed could be published without offending the living. However, Baechtold did not omit the Munich correspondence between Keller and his mother, exposing Keller's pitiful financial hardship at that time. Perhaps Baechtold intended a tribute to the difficult early years in Keller's life and sought to provide tangible evidence that he was not hiding the unpleasant episodes in the author's life.

Baechtold's biography fills three volumes, and was published by Keller's last publisher, Wilhelm Hertz (1822–1901); the volumes appeared sequentially in 1895, 1896, and in 1897. The first volume relates Keller's youth and concludes with Keller's Heidelberg years. The second is devoted to Keller's productive years in Berlin, and the third spans his years as cantonal secretary, as well as the intense literary production of the seventies and early eighties. Baechtold relates Keller's life by allowing Keller to speak as much as possible. He provides background information and documentation to Keller's artistic works, but generally does not offer literary interpretation or analysis. Each volume concludes with an appendix that contains some unusual materials, a few unpublished poems, some early prose, fables, dramatic fragments, and newspaper clippings about Keller. Baechtold had known Keller, and this carried with it both advantages and disadvantages. He could report on conversations as Frey and C. F. Meyer had done. Nevertheless, his friendship with Keller and his own sense of propriety made him reluctant to pass judgment on Keller, a reluctance that Emil Ermatinger, Baechtold's successor, did not possess. Even so, Baechtold's work served even after Ermatinger's revisions and expansions of 1915 as *the* source for all Keller scholars until the first critical edition of Keller's works was completed in 1948.[3]

---

[3] The first critical edition of Keller's works, which culminated in an extensive twenty-two volume collection, was published beginning in 1926 under the direction of Professor Jonas Fränkel of Bern. Volumes 9, 10, 12, 15/2, 20, 21 and 22 were edited by Dr. Carl Helbling of Zurich and were completed in 1948. The five volume critical edition of Keller's correspondence, also edited by Carl Helbling, was begun in 1950 and completed in 1954, over a half a century after Baechtold first published his selection of six hundred letters.

Albert Köster's seven lectures on Keller were delivered in Hamburg at the end of the century and published with B. G. Teubner Verlag in Leipzig in 1900. Köster's goal was both to strengthen the acquaintance some readers had already made with Keller's fiction and to introduce new readers to Keller. Indeed, it was Keller's lack of renown, Köster laments, that inspired him to deliver these lectures. Köster approaches Keller's works chronologically, using his biography as backdrop.

The first lecture explores the Keller family history, Keller's education, the various stages of his artistic development as a landscape painter, and his failure to succeed in that medium. The second lecture discusses Keller's years in Zurich during the 1840s, the transition from visual arts to poetry, and Keller's development from highly subjective political poetry toward greater objectivity in epic forms. Köster also provides a representative sampling of Keller's poetry. He tries to differentiate between poems that reflect Keller's experience as a landscape painter and those that point toward his development as an author of prose. On the one hand, Keller's portrayal of nature reminds Köster of the Romantic author Joseph von Eichendorff (1788–1857), while also reflecting the melancholy of Nikolaus Lenau (1802–50). On the other hand, Keller's patriotic poems reveal his liberal political views, and also recall the wit and humor of Heinrich Heine (26).

The third lecture treats Keller's year in Heidelberg and discusses the influence of Jakob Henle (1809–1885), Christian Kapp (1790–1874), Hermann Hettner, and in particular the pronounced influence of Ludwig Feuerbach's philosophy. Feuerbach's philosophy claimed that man was not created in God's image, rather that man created God in his own image and for his own needs. Köster believes that, at the time, these teachings addressed Keller's own thoughts on God and on eternal life as manifested in the *Neue Gedichte* and in the first edition of *Der grüne Heinrich*, but that Keller later tempered and even overcame Feuerbach's teachings (47). Comparing Keller to Goethe, Köster claims that Goethe had decided that rather than to research the unknowable, it would be better simply to revere it. Köster discusses Keller's interest in drama, believing that he had a refined sense of judgment about drama, including a fine sense for situations that would make for good dramatic conflicts. But Keller's chief talent, according to Köster, lay in the epic and not in drama.

The fourth lecture focuses on the *Der grüne Heinrich*. Jean Jacques Rousseau (1712–1778), Goethe and Jean Paul Richter are cited as those predecessors, who had the greatest influence on this first novel. Although Köster concedes that some of Keller's initial humor in the *Der grüne Heinrich* resembles the sentimental humor of Jean Paul, he shares Brahm's opinion that Keller swiftly overcame this sentimentality. Köster criticizes the shapelessness of the novel the first person and the third person narratives, and the misplaced long-winded, but admittedly very beautiful story of Heinrich's youth contribute to this problem.

Köster insists that the tragic end, criticized by so many readers, is already inherent in the story of Heinrich's youth (65). The dramatic framework misleads the reader into believing that Heinrich has the chance to redeem himself at the count's residence. However, these readers have failed to see this as a dramatic moment of retardation before the inevitable fall. Heinrich knows that he has failed as an artist and that neither good fortune nor Dorothea's love can transform that failure. Moreover, he has a moral and social obligation to return home to his mother; his failure to arrive in time to help her destroys his last hope of self-restitution. Köster believes that from its start, the narrative prepares the sensitive reader for its tragic end (71). He agrees with those who praise the story of Heinrich's youth, and attacks the literary historians Friedrich Kreyßig (1818–1879) and Robert Prutz (1816–1872) for their criticism of this magnificent section.

Köster still detects shades of the impending tragic in the revised edition of *Der grüne Heinrich* (1880). He commends the unifying first-person narrative, the introduction of the Zwiehahn-skull, and the episode of the seamstress Hulda. He insists that the hue of the tragic hangs over the entire work, suggesting thereby that the new conclusion is not entirely justifiable (Köster, 77). Judith's return makes it possible for Heinrich to trust life again, to resign himself to a lifelong commitment in service of society.

The fifth lecture is devoted to the first volume of *Die Leute von Seldwyla*, which according to Köster transcends subjectivity. An artwork must not be capriciously produced, but must allow the warmth of experience to shine through; it must be a blend of the artist's experiences and creative genius. Köster feels that *Spiegel das Kätzchen* is misplaced in this collection and sees in it a remnant, a last tribute to the Romantic age. Both *Pankraz* and *Frau Regel Amrain und ihr Jüngster* were inspired by the relationship between Keller and his mother during Keller's years in Berlin, where these novellas were conceived. Köster finds the didactic tone in these first two novellas too strong, too much in the tradition of Pestalozzi and Gotthelf. One already observes a more mature, less obviously didactic tone in *Die drei gerechten Kammacher*. Keller pushed back the frontier of Swiss literature with this work, because he transformed a traditional romantic motif suffusing it with his humor, thereby severing the connection to the romantic (90).

Köster praises *Romeo und Julia auf dem Dorfe* as a masterpiece because of its vivid portrayal, masterful characterization, and its fine architectonic structure. Keller has taken two real events, and has combined and embellished them to convey the ethical message that evil deeds breed evil. Therefore, the deaths of Sali and Vrenchen are justified, despite much criticism to the contrary, because they planned only to spend one last day together and did not originally plan a joint suicide. During that one day, they realize that they could not live without one another, but also that they cannot build their happiness upon the ruin of their respective parents. Köster explains how Keller despised the feigned tension with which many modern storytellers focus the readers' attention on the end result. Keller sought to dispel the tension through premonitions, so that his readers could think about the process (97). Köster commends Keller for his linguistic style that, unlike that of Jeremias Gotthelf (1843–1918), Peter Rosegger (1843–1918) or Fritz Reuter (1810–1874), does not succumb to dialect, but which instead insists that folksy material can be communicated in high German.

The sixth lecture focuses on the author's return to Zurich in 1855 and his life thereafter. Köster shows how Keller incorporated the changes in Zurich into the second volume of *Die Leute von Seldwyla* while maintaining the humorous critique of the original volume. Seldwyla transcends itself; Keller is drawn toward earnest ethical problems. Köster interprets both *Kleider machen Leute* and *Dietegen* as part of a transitional phase for Keller that prepares the way for more serious material and for the historical fiction of the *Züricher Novellen*. He believes these new directions become manifest in *Das verlorene Lachen*, where Keller reveals the impact of the general social and economic upheaval of the day on the family. Köster concentrates on Keller's attempts to develop a sense for the historical in *Die Züricher Novellen*. Much like Walter Scott (1771–1832), Keller did not choose exotic backdrops to his novellas, but rather familiar situations from Swiss history. Despite their success, however, Köster decides that historical fiction was not Keller's element, and is therefore not surprised when Keller returns in his last work to issues from contemporary life and focuses on the problems brought on by social and economic change.

The final lecture is devoted to those works completed during the last period of Keller's life, in particular *Das Sinngedicht* which Köster heralds as Keller's magnum opus. It is testimony to the originality of Keller's genius and is evidence that Keller's imagination and wit, far from having been diminished by his bureaucratic past, were as vivid as ever. Although in Köster's time, Keller was best known for his Seldwyla stories, Köster believes that *Das Sinngedicht* represents Keller at the height of his artistic ability, because it demonstrates the author's ability to bind together in a persuasive and believable fashion all of these novellas into a single framed tale.

If *Das Sinngedicht* was Keller's artistic masterpiece, then *Martin Salander* was his political legacy. Köster defends what many have interpreted as the novel's pessimism. Keller was seeking the appropriate form and style to express concern for the problems inherent in the modern age. The author turned again to the novel form, knowing full well that his material had already proven too extensive for the novella *Das verlorene Lachen*. Keller felt it necessary to incorporate contemporary language, catchwords, and journalistic phrases. After five years of thinking about the novel Julius Rodenberg finally persuaded Keller to send him the first installment for the *Rundschau*. Keller once again wrote to meet deadlines possibly resulting, according to Köster, in the weak conclusion. Köster reminds us that *Martin Salander* is only half of the novel. Keller did not write the proposed second volume on Arnold Salander, so that we are rendering judgment upon a fragmentary work. Köster encourages us not to read the work pessimistically, asserting rather that there is much evidence to suggest that Keller meant the work to be critical, but also optimistic.

Köster's interpretations take the form of lectures addressed to an audience that in all probability knew only the Seldwyla stories. Thus the lectures devote considerable time to plot summary, while also offering some of the first substantive interpretation of Keller's work. They form a bridge between Baechtold's biography and Emil Ermatinger's critical revision and expansion of that original biography.

A milestone in Keller scholarship appeared in 1904: the slender but wonderfully perceptive volume on Gottfried Keller by Ricarda Huch (1864–1947). The first volume on Keller authored by a woman — the first woman admitted to the University of Zurich — it offers a different perspective on the Swiss author and his fiction. The study is organized chronologically. Huch sees "dies göttliche Umfassen und lächelnde Durchschauen" (this heavenly embrace and benevolent ability to see through) as that which constitutes the subtle tone permeating his works (Huch, 29). Keller is particularly kind in his depiction of women and Huch writes that women should revere Keller, because they will not find a better friend among authors (31). Despite Keller's disenchantment with women's liberation, he created in some of his female characters images of the ideal woman who aspired to freedom while maintaining a balance between the feminine and the masculine. All Keller's female characters reveal purity of spirit — and pluck (31). She discovers in his work a well balanced set of female characters, who are not imaginary ideals, but realistic role models. Nor was Keller fearful of presenting a woman with negative characteristics such as Züs Bünzlin. Huch believes that Keller admired health, honesty, openness, candor, and strength. His female characters embody this whole range of emotions. Huch finds it refreshing that Keller's characters do not succumb to unrequited love and failed relationships. They tend, rather to collect themselves and to go on living. Likewise, Huch reports that Keller's letters reveal respectful and honest interaction with women of all ages and in all walks of life.

Huch next discusses *Das Sinngedicht*, which she considers the most artistically complete of Keller's novella cycles, although one can well understand why many prefer the Seldwyla novellas because they radiate Keller's unique personality and warmth (44). She describes the *Sieben Legenden* as the golden fruit, the apex of Keller's career, and refers to *Martin Salander* as the work of an aging author, transparent, closed, well rounded, not emanating from the chaotic workshop of the poet's internal fantasy (45).

Huch admires Keller's linguistic style for its freshness, attributing his unique style and diction to the richness of his Swiss dialect (47). The veracity of Keller's mind, according to Huch, enabled him to hone his language so that it is neither stilted nor coquettish, but carefully wrought. Keller's raw material also came either from his own experience (*Grüner Heinrich, Pankraz, Frau Regel Amrain*) or from newspaper articles (*Romeo and Julia*). The study closes with an analysis of Keller's philosophy of life, discusses his melancholy (*stille Grundtrauer*) and points to his unique blend of Swiss and German elements that make his fiction so special. She hopes that Meister Gottfried will live on and continue to show us through his own pure sight "den goldnen Überfluß der Welt" (the golden abundance of the world: 55).

Literary histories published after Keller's death were more inclined to include an interpretation of his works than those that appeared during his lifetime. Richard M. Meyer, a professor at the University of Berlin, in the second volume of *Die Geschichte der deutschen Literatur* concentrates on nineteenth and twentieth century authors; he hails Keller and Fontane as the two outstanding literary craftsman of nineteenth-century German prose. Not only does Meyer rank Keller as one of the two greatest nineteenth century German authors, but he also compares Keller's prose and experience to other great European authors past and present. Feuerbach's influence on Keller and consequently on his artistic endeavors is comparable to the influence of Goethe on the philosopher Benedict Spinoza (368). He compares Keller's years in Berlin and their ramifications for his future artistic endeavors with Ibsen's sojourn in Munich (369). Meyer sees in Keller the greatest epic poet since Goethe, which he justifies based on three criteria. First, the epic poet must have the talent to make his material vivid and of timeless interest. The descriptions of the French naturalist Emile Zola (1840–1902) leave Meyer cold; likewise, the emotional depictions of Clemens Brentano (1778–1842) blur our vision. Keller illustrates most successfully those events that he has personally experienced. Second, a great epic poet must possess an unlimited creative imagination. Meyer suggests that the wealth of creativity that Keller lavished on the *Sieben Legenden* is Homeric and contains enough material to keep a dozen folklorists and writers of novellas busy for a lifetime. Third, is the ability of the writer to lend his artistic endeavor, regardless of how varied and diverse, an inner unity; this structural and thematic unity is Keller's forte (1921, 375). Meyer attributes Keller's unique style to a fundamentally folksy tone colored by the many hues of Keller's Swiss dialect, with which he infuses his impeccable high German. Keller's rich vocabulary and his unlimited creative play with language produce such original expressions as "schwarzäugige Höllenbrätchen" [dark-eyed daredevil]. This folksy aspect of Keller's language, Meyer contends, also reveals itself through the frequent diminutives (*Sümmchen, Weinchen*) and in the Swiss penchant for nicknames, such as "der kinderfrohe Schweizermann." Meyer demonstrates how Keller's sentence structure has been schooled by his reading of Goethe; Keller's sentences are almost always composed of two equal halves, which maintain an acoustic balance. But the hallmark of Keller's style, according to Meyer, lies in his inexhaustibly rich visual images. Keller has the ability to take well worn images, such as the tree tops of a forest, and recreate them so that we become cognizant of them for the first time: "Wie ein leichtes grünes Seidenzelt schwebte die zarte Belaubung in der Höhe, von den schlanken Silberstangen emporgehalten" (Like a weightless green tent of silk swayed the gentle foliage upon high, supported by the slender silver trunks: 377). Keller's goal is to inspire his readers with a new *Lebensfreude*, to provide them with hope and optimism while also humoring them. His philosophy of life is grounded in reality. Keller's epic greatness lies in his ability to portray things and events vividly and concretely, in the inexhaustibility of his imagination, in his creative language and uniform style, and finally in the unity of his philosophical outlook on life.

A perennial study from these burgeoning years of Keller scholarship is Hans Dünnebier's monograph, *Gottfried Keller und Ludwig Feuerbach*. Published in 1913, this volume explores both eruditely and thoroughly the enduring influence of Feuerbach's philosophy on Keller. While numerous studies published in more recent decades have taken issue with the extent and degree of Feuerbach's influence on Keller,[4] no other single study published since has been able to match Dünnebier's thoroughness. Dünnebier is convinced that Keller's study of Feuerbach's philosophy, which was motivated by his encounter with Feuerbach in Heidelberg, was the single most influential educative and philosophical force in Keller's life. Dünnebier believes that Feuerbach was for Keller what Spinoza was for Goethe. Dünnebier examines Keller's attitudes and thoughts regarding religion, based on Keller's reading of the German Romantics and his early pantheistic conception of God. The particularly informative third chapter examines those religious and philosophical forces that influenced Keller's thinking during the 1840s. Keller maintained his belief in God and immortality until his encounter with Feuerbach in Heidelberg in 1848. Dünnebier relates Keller's ac-

---

[4] While the following Keller scholars would not deny Feuerbach's influence on Keller, they do dispute the extent of that influence and certainly the longevity of that influence. Fränkel, the chief editor of the first critical Keller edition takes issue with Dünnebier's thesis. Lukács, in his 1938 essay on Keller, suggests that Feuerbach merely provided Keller with an organized framework in which he could sort out his ideas (Lukács, 1938, 167). H. Reichert in his 1949 study, *Basic Concepts in the Philosophy of Gottfried Keller* essentially agrees with Lukács; he analyzes in great detail Keller's concept of freedom and how it relates to ethics, aesthetics, politics and social relations. Locher's (1969) painstakingly thorough study reconstructs Keller's Weltanschauung based upon his earlier poetry and shows that Keller arrived at ideas similar to Feuerbach, before his contact with Feuerbach. In 1954 Zollinger-Wells in his *Gottfried Kellers Religiosität* is bent on depicting Keller as God-fearing and suggests that Feuerbach's influence was limited. Karl Fehr in his 1972 study *Gottfried Keller* acknowledges Feuerbach's influence, but questions the longevity of that influence, particularly in his interpretation of Keller's late poem, "Golgatha." Locher in his 1985 study of Keller's ethical posturing also discusses the limits of Feuerbach's influence.

quaintance with Feuerbach and examines the poet's correspondence from the period, demonstrating how Keller gradually came to reverse his original negative inclinations toward Feuerbach's teachings and indeed became an adherent of his philosophy. More recent studies reveal how close Keller's original thinking was to Feuerbach's philosophy, suggesting thereby, that it was only natural for Keller to adopt Feuerbach's philosophical framework. Dünnebier clearly and precisely summarizes the major tenets of Feuerbach's philosophy as follows: Man created God because man needed an image, an ideal, in which he could believe and toward which he could strive. God, created in the image of man, by man, could also be dismantled by man (Dünnebier, 139). Immortality offered hope and a means of transcending death for the believer who led a righteous and pious life. But nature according to Feuerbach is a republic unto itself; it has no need of a God. Thus Feuerbach advocates that man, not God, become the focus of our attention. Belief in God becomes belief in oneself. Man, in Feuerbach's teachings, becomes God. If we eliminate God, we also eliminate immortality. Without immortality man is forced to concentrate on earthly life and to acknowledge the inevitability of death; thus man must fashion his life according to the dictates of his inner life. In Keller's words, life in the light of Feuerbach's teachings looms more beautifully before us. Dünnebier believes that Feuerbach's philosophy was as important to religious development as Luther's teachings. Feuerbach completed what Luther had begun. Feuerbach's philosophy exposed Christian dogma and prepared the transition from Christianity to humanism. True Christianity, according to Feuerbach, is founded on the innate goodness in man and not on threats, guilt of sin, and fear of mortality. Feuerbach considered such institutions as marriage, friendship, and the right of material possession to be the cornerstones of his new humanism. As we know from Keller's correspondence, this philosophy spoke directly to the young poet. Dünnebier shows in his discussion of *Der grüne Heinrich* just how well Keller understood and was influenced by Feuerbach. Dünnebier insists that Keller's drama *Therese* and the *Sieben Legenden* are manifestations of Feuerbach's influence and could not have been conceived without his teachings.

Religion was, according to Feuerbach, the most primitive form of education (Dünnebier, 108). Education toward humanity will replace former religious instruction. Feuerbach and Keller believe in the goodness of man and in the triumph of good over evil. Each individual must establish his own goals in life according to internal drives and in accordance with fundamental virtues that lie within us. The state can only partially educate the individual; the burden of education rests with the family and the individual. Dünnebier cites many examples of Keller's characters who err in their attempt to establish and achieve suitable goals. For example, Heinrich Lee suffers from his inability to fulfill Feuerbach's axiom "Erkenne Dich selbst" (Become cognizant of thy inner self). Dünnebier compares Heinrich to a modern Parzival (137). Feuerbach agrees with Goethe that each individual possesses a character that is steadfast and educable (138). Heinrich's embattled personal position lies between his misinterpreted inner drive to develop himself as a landscape artist and his obligation to serve society. Marriage and family remain the core social unit of the community. Dünnebier maintains that Heinrich's death is justifiable in the light of Feuerbach's philosophy because he has neglected and even exploited his family and particularly his mother in order to achieve goals that were unattainable because he had failed to acknowledge his inner self and therefore his limitations.

Dünnebier takes issue with Ricarda Huch's assessment that Keller represents the completion of German Romanticism. Heinrich Lee might be a romantic, but his creator, Keller, is a realist, and his philosophical outlook, like Feuerbach's, is orientated toward the future (156–57). Dünnebier cites *Der Apotheker von Chamounix* as Keller's manifesto against the Romantic school, contending that Keller had fashioned the realistic Seldwyla novellas in his head already while writing *Der grüne Heinrich*.

Dünnebier sheds light on the theologians who influenced Keller, such as David Friedrich Strauß, a disciple of Jakob Böhme and Friedrich Schelling, who viewed religion as an incomplete form of philosophy. Keller, on the other hand, disapproved of such theological movements as the Reform Theology Movement led by Heinrich Lang, and takes them to task in *Das verlorene Lachen*. Lang sought to reinvent Zwingli's church. Keller wanted no part in these reforms. Indeed, the teachings of the fictional pastor of Schwanau in *Das verlorene Lachen* have something of the cabalistic, the alchemy of a bygone era, through which Keller caricatured Lang's reforms. Justine is drawn into the pastor's theological reforms until she realizes too late that they lack substance and offer little comfort. Following the example of her husband Jukundus, she must turn inward to examine her innermost drives, beliefs, and virtues. Sustenance and inspiration must come from within. Keller demonstrates in *Das verlorene Lachen*, the failure of theology in general and certain theological reforms in particular to offer answers to modern problems or comfort in the modern age. Dünnebier places Keller's Feuerbachian philosophy of life in the context of the reform theology of the day.

In removing the theological hierarchy, Feuerbach does not want to destroy the moral parameters of European culture. Each individual, must follow the example of Jukundus, must set goals for himself. Keller believed that one's external actions should correspond to one's internal beliefs and thoughts, that one's conscience represents the individual. Keller disliked mere appearance (*Schein*); he strove for truth, genuineness, honesty, the essence (*sein*). Dünnebier believes that no other author has created such an array of characters (schoolmaster Wilhelm, Pankraz, Viggi Störteler, John Kabys, Heinrich Lee, Strapinski,) who struggle to find themselves and who come to self-cognition (*Selbst-Erkenntnis*). Keller differentiates the incorrigible characters (Wohlwend) from the educable (Jukundus) by their ability to recognize in themselves an ideal toward which they can aspire. Cognizance of the self, trust in the self (*Selbstvertrauen*) and self-confidence (*Selbstbewußtsein*) are the foundations of character development for both Keller and Feuerbach.

The shaping and fashioning of the character (*Persönlichkeit*) become a life-long process for Keller. Keller's ethic, according to Dünnebier, can be summed up by the following questions: What are my moral values as an individual? What are the values held by the family for whom I am spokesperson? Have I and my family conducted ourselves in such a fashion that we serve the community, and can stand as a community? More recent studies, which question the degree to which Feuerbach may have influenced Keller, do not diminish the depth of Dünnebier's scholarship, nor do they compromise this grand overview of those issues, historical, political, theological, and philosophical, that directly or indirectly influenced Keller's philosophy of life and his view of the world.

The publishing house of J. G. Cotta, the successor to Keller's last publisher, Wilhelm Hertz, assumed the rights to the Baechtold biography in 1901. Hertz approached Emil Ermatinger, Baechtold's successor, to edit a new edition of the biography. Ermatinger accepted the commission to prepare a new edition that would ultimately become a new biography. In the preface Ermatinger acknowledges Baechtold's extraordinary achievement as Keller's first biographer and as the first archivist who safeguarded and organized Keller's literary estate. He admires the thoughtfulness and deference that hallmarks Baechtold's biography, a sensitive reserve that was necessary for one who had been both Keller's contemporary and friend. He compares Baechtold's achievement to that of building a house: Baechtold sought to erect a strong foundation and ground floor, but intentionally left the upper floors and the interior design for future generations of Keller scholars. Baechtold's effort has served some twenty years of scholarship, but it is now time to expand the original structure. The passage of time allows Ermatinger to cast aside earlier precautions and to expand Keller-scholarship with emotional detachment.

Ermatinger reorganized and rewrote Baechtold's biography, but retained all the documentation as well as the reported conversations between Keller und Baechtold. He abandoned the interlacing of biographical text, letters and other documentation, which he found too unwieldy. He removed all the material in Baechtold's appendices, arguing that it belonged in a critical edition of Keller's works and not in a biography.[5] He relegated all the letters, now including two hundred more than Baechtold had published, and supplementary supporting documentation, to volumes two and three, leaving the first volume for the biog-

---

[5] Ermatinger, 1915, viii; Ermatinger was justified in omitting the material in the appendices, because he knew that the administrators of Keller's unpublished works and the Cotta Publishing House were laying plans for a critical edition of Keller's works.

rapher's text. Ermatinger provides deep psychological insights into Keller's character and expands in detail the literary and historical inter-connections which influenced Keller and his works. Ermatinger attempts to present a more balanced view of Keller's philosophy of life and his view of the world than Dünnebier had. It was Ermatinger's goal to write a biography that would be accessible to the lay reader and of interest to the literary scholar.

Ermatinger reveals the craft of Keller's art and does not hesitate to offer literary interpretations of specific works to the extent that a biography primarily concerned with the author's life will allow. Looking at his analysis of one of Keller's texts, *Martin Salander*, the artistic merits of which are disputed even today, will reveal how distance and personal detachment enabled Ermatinger to assess Keller's work with greater objectivity than earlier literary historians had. The biographer shows how Keller used actual historical occurrences of public corruption during the 1880s as material for his fiction. Keller refashioned those historical events into the masterful mosaic that became *Martin Salander*. Ermatinger seeks to dispel the earlier claims that this last work was essentially pessimistic, the last novel of a crotchety, aging author, whose talent was in decline. Ermatinger contends that it is Keller's right as a citizen and his responsibility as a respected Swiss author to expose public corruption. Ermatinger includes Baechtold's conversation with Keller regarding a planned sequel to the novel, in which all the characters were to meet on a mountaintop and fall prey to a natural catastrophe (I, 647).

Ermatinger concludes his biography with an analytical depiction of Keller's philosophy of life. Taking issue with Baechtold's suggestion that Keller had too little good will, Ermatinger contends that one cannot reduce a complex life to a simple formula. He believes that Baechtold's evidence is partial and should be balanced by other evidence from friends such as Marie von Frisch and Paul Heyse, who knew Keller better. Citing a letter in which Baechtold refers to Keller as a maniacal egoist, Ermatinger demonstrates how seldom one has the ability, even when one is closely befriended, to penetrate the mind of a great individual (I, 660). Baechtold had thought that Keller's humane side would be seen less favorably once all his correspondence had been published. Ermatinger disagrees; during the preceding two decades, many new letters and much supplementary documentation have been published, but these have not cast a shadow. By taking issue with Baechtold, Ermatinger began a discussion of Keller that his own contemporaries and future Keller scholars would continue.[6] With Ermatinger's biography, Keller scholarship entered a new phase, one that transcended the circle of friends and opened untraversed avenues toward greater

---

[6] For contemporaries of Ermatinger analyzing Kellers Weltanschauung see Max Hochdorf (1919, 1921). For more recent studies see: H. Reichert (1949), R. Wildbolz (1964), K. Locher (1985), and E. Swales (1994)..

objectivity and diversity in interpretation. It remains as respected today as it was in 1915.

In his Keller essay "Beim Lesen des Grünen Heinrich," originally written in 1907 and revised in 1917, Hermann Hesse tries to determine why Keller's novel is a classic and therefore worthy of belonging to the canon. According to Hesse, *Der grüne Heinrich* as an autobiography need not appear to be objective. Keller tells us everything, holding nothing back and does so without any affected self-importance. The artistic material reflects an average life filled with average events. There is hardly any original thought in the novel. Hesse claims that the secret that Keller's novel shares with works by Homer, Dante, Boccaccio, Shakespeare and Goethe can be reduced to two fundamentals: the timelessness of his material and the power of his language (II, 298–99). First, suggests Hesse, what makes Don Quixote, Hamlet, or Wilhelm Meister and Heinrich Lee interesting to us today is not just that they were representatives of their age, but rather that they are human beings to whom we can relate today. We can empathize with Heinrich Lee and still find his story touching, because his experiences are as relevant today as they will be tomorrow and in a hundred years. Hesse concedes that his generation was perhaps still too close to Keller to make such a pronouncement, but he willingly projects that Heinrich Lee will assume his place together with Don Quixote and Wilhelm Meister among those timeless enduring characters for all posterity (299).[7] Second, Hesse maintains that Keller's is the only creative and genuinely artistic German since Goethe's. Keller incorporates the linguistic color and elasticity of his native Swiss into artistic prose, yielding a language and style that had an originality no other German writer besides Luther and Goethe had ever achieved. Keller had a natural feeling for rhythm and for rhetoric that was given shape and rigor by his study of earlier writers. Hesse believes that one only has to read Keller aloud to recognize the well rounded sentences and hear the polished harmony of the cadences, because they emulate natural rhythmic and breathing patterns. Hesse admits that one will not become a great author by reading Goethe or Keller, but one will become cognizant that Keller did not simply write whatever came into his head.

Though Keller's works and his fifteen years as cantonal clerk invite closer scrutiny of his political views, the first monograph on this topic did not appear until 1916. Surprisingly, perhaps, it was written in English by Edward Hauch, a Canadian graduate student of German.[8] The first extensive analysis of Keller's

---

[7] Hermann Hesse wrote a tribute to Keller in 1930, that he later revised in 1951. This tribute is discussed in chapter four and can be found in: Hermann Hesse. *Eine Literaturgeschichte in Rezensionen und Aufsätzen* edited by Volker Michels. Frankfurt: Suhrkamp, 1972. vol. II. 293–298.

[8] Edward Hauch. *Gottfried Keller as a Democratic Idealist*. New York: Columbia UP, 1916. This text will be discussed in chapter five which is devoted to the Anglo-American tradition of Keller scholarship.

political views in German was Hans Max Kriesi's *Gottfried Keller als Politiker* published in 1918, though it actually refers to Hauch's book published two years earlier. Kriesi's study is the first substantial work on Keller as a political thinker and author who plies his craft to further a given political cause.[9]

Kriesi succinctly presents the political scene in Switzerland during the Napoleonic wars, and sketches the events which led to the emergence of the modern Helvetian state. He then discusses the political sentiments of Keller's father, who extolled a strongly unified Switzerland, and believed firmly in a political education. Keller received such an education from his earliest years. Later, in the 1840s, a period of political ferment in Zurich, while Keller made the transition from painting to writing, he found himself entangled in diverse political debates which engaged and stimulated him. Keller was born at a time during which the sharp contrasts between aristocrats and democrats, between conservatives and liberals, between orthodox and free thinkers, federalists and unitarians had become increasingly marked (Kriesi, 47). This political turmoil stimulated Keller; his acquaintance with the poetry of Georg Herwegh (1817–75), Anastäsius Grün (1806–76) and others inspired him to try his own hand at that medium.

Kriesi divides the political poetry of Keller into three categories: the general poems espousing freedom, those on German politics, and those devoted to Swiss politics. He then interprets the poems in light of historical events and Keller's political views. According to Kriesi many of the poems devoted to regional Swiss politics lay unpublished in the archive. (Of course these have since been published in the critical edition of Fränkel and Helbling).

Keller's period of intense political activity during the 1840s resulted in the first volume of poetry and it brought Keller into contact with those political agitators who became his friends, and also became part of the new Zurich cantonal government in 1848. They awarded him a cantonal scholarship that enabled him to study in Heidelberg and Berlin. Keller's political fervor gave way to political reflection. Keller even wrote in his "Book of Dreams" that it was no longer permissible to have a private life; every individual must fulfill his civic obligations. Fulfilling one's obligations in the public sphere would help one to lead a conscientious life in private. Kriesi suggests that the opposite is also true, and refers to the first edition of *Der grüne Heinrich*, in which the protagonist, who has failed to care for his family affairs, cannot expect to find his place in society.

When he returned from Berlin in 1855, Keller had become a successful novelist, much more mature and self-assured than the failed landscape artist who had returned from Munich over a decade earlier. Zurich had also changed. Keller viewed industrialization, the mass migration from country to city, as well as the increasing individual greed that permeated the air with distaste. Thus his frequent depictions of folk festivals provide an escape from the contemporary

[9] See also Fränkel (1939), M. Kaiser, (1965), H. Richartz (1975) and E. Swales (1994).

individualistic, self-centeredness while promoting a political education toward a sense of community of shared freedoms under the umbrella of the Swiss national superstructure. Also discussed in this context is Keller's essay "Am Mythenstein," in which Keller envisions dramatic singing companies involving hundreds who would put on political plays written for the common people with the aim of politically educating them toward the establishment of a national identity.

Kriesi provides fine analysis of Keller's years as first cantonal clerk, and discusses his attitude toward the Democratic Movement of the 1860s, as well as his thoughts on the constitutional revisions and political turmoil of that era. Kriesi also analyzes Keller's *Bettagsmandate*,[10] which summarized the current political situation and simultaneously sought to stimulate the people to lead morally better lives and to strive for a stronger sense of community. The corruption in the public sphere that Keller had witnessed as cantonal clerk and which he observed in the late seventies and eighties provided the historical material for *Martin Salander*. Kriesi draws on Ermatinger's examples of scandals from public life in Zurich during the 1880s and uses these historic events to interpret the political element in *Martin Salander*, which Kriesi reads as the author's political legacy to his countrymen. The study closes with a quotation from C. F. Meyer's *Erinnerungen*, in which Meyer compares Keller's attitude toward his homeland to that of a protecting spirit (240). The appendix contains a wealth of Keller's political essays, editorials, reports from the cantonal government, *Bettagsmandate* and a host of useful political documents.

Max Hochdorf's study *Zum Geistigen Bilde Gottfried Kellers*, published in 1919, explores those aspects of Keller's life that helped to shape his mind and fashion his view of life and the world. Hochdorf suggests that Keller's disappointments in love subjected him to melancholic moments that profoundly influenced his writing. Examining Keller's style, Hochdorf is the first literary historian to show convincingly that Keller's prose anticipates naturalism. While he concedes that certain romantic stylistic elements crop up even in Keller's later work, he insists that the overall artistic direction, beginning with the Seldwyla novellas, is firmly based in realism and in fact already anticipates naturalism He emphasizes throughout that Keller writes with the landscape artist's critical eye; he portrays images and scenes which reveal rather than tell. His visual images are ablaze with color, shadows, and light. The painter in Keller has a predilection for genre painting (*Sittengemälde*) which instructs by showing rather than by explaining. Hochdorf explores these aspects of Keller's style in the two editions of *Der grüne Heinrich*. He concedes that the revised edition (1879–80) is more unified in its structure and offers greater overall clarity and moderation. However, primarily for stylistic reasons, Hochdorf seems to prefer the original 1855 ver-

---

[10] The *Bettagsmandat* is the public address delivered by an official of the cantonal government on the Swiss National Day of Prayer which always falls on the second Sunday in September.

sion. He attributes Heinrich's death in the original version to one of Keller's melancholic moods and recalls the author's struggle to complete the novel. He substantiates this view with an unknown citation from Keller's autobiography in 1876, overlooked by both Brahm and Köster, in which Keller claims to have willed Heinrich's death because of his own melancholic disposition at the time of writing.[11] Hochdorf refuses to accept that Heinrich's guilt is the primary reason for his death, arguing that he is not any less guilty of neglecting his mother in the second version than in the first. Hochdorf suggests that other characters, including Heinrich's own mother, were responsible to his failures and consequently for the guilt he feels, and argues that the older, more resigned Keller sought moderation and reconciliation; he wanted to temper Heinrich's burden of guilt The young Keller had acted as an angry God who had condemned Heinrich; the mature Keller, who had himself learned to accept resignation, sought reconciliation.

Hochdorf asserts, that if *Der Grüne Heinrich*, even in the original edition, anticipates naturalistic issues despite the remnants of a romantic style, one would have to concede that *Martin Salander* was a naturalist novel. First conceived in 1881, when Zola published his collected theories in *Le roman expérimental*, Keller, in the best of naturalist tradition, sought to reveal the animal instinct and the lack of righteousness in man. . The best of intentions were marred by Rodenberg's deadlines for the *Rundschau*, and by the author's advancing years. Nevertheless, the power of the landscape painter prevails in Keller's verbal images that illustrate far more than any dialogue could reveal.

It seems fitting to conclude this phase of Keller's criticism with a sampling of two commemorative lectures delivered on the one hundredth anniversary of Keller's birth. The first was delivered by the Swiss poet and Nobel prize laureate Carl Spitteler (1845–1924). While the entire Swiss nation is celebrating Keller's birthday, Spitteler reminds his listeners that the author was not always so well known. He recalls his own student days in Zurich during the mid-1860s when his professor repeatedly felt obligated to say that he was discussing Gottfried Keller and not one Augustine Keller. Spitteler asks how it was possible that Keller, years after the publication of his first novel, was still so little known. He suggests that the newspapers of the day only printed articles on recently published books by authors who were in vogue and who published regularly. By comparison, Keller's publications were much more erratic. His novel did not get off to a good start, nor was it promoted as well as it should have been by the publisher. Keller became known because certain professors (Brahm, Kuh, Vischer) taught some of his works regularly and because powerful publishers such as Rodenberg promoted Keller's works in widely read journals such as the *Deutsche Rundschau*.

[11] Hochdorf refers to page 35 in Brahm's 1883 essay on Keller and to pages 71 & 72 in Köster's book on Keller.

Keller's works, according to Spitteler, had become widely read and familiar because of certain traits. Keller conveys a truthfulness and directness; there are no superfluous sentences or words. Keller wants to learn and is not afraid to err or fail. Spitteler admires Keller's language, which comes from deep within. Keller always finds the right word or the exact image necessary to convey his thoughts. For Spitteler, Keller's humor is the poetry of his prose, stimulated by the sharp contrast between poetic endeavor and realistic reproaches. Spitteler also praises Keller's keen and independent sense of judgment for its gracious quality and for its accuracy Spitteler is inclined to agree with Fritz Mauthner that Keller's narrative prose is better than Goethe's (474).

Spitteler is also careful to temper his praise, and admonishes his listeners not to deify Keller as the Germans have nearly deified Goethe, for this would mean the end of Swiss literature. It is harmful to raise any writer or poet to unassailable heights, for it makes that poet's work unsurpassable. It would be wrong to make Keller the measure against which all future Swiss writers would be judged.[12] Glorification produces despair and a sense of hopelessness among the young poetic talents; it leads to a fossilization of our understanding of the great writer who has risen above criticism. Spitteler is not afraid to rank C. F. Meyer's poetry as at least equal to Keller's, but he also maintains that many young writers have been driven by their respect for Keller to become better at their craft.

The other commemorative lecture was delivered in the great hall of the University of Bern on July 19, 1919 by Professor Harry Maync. Maync focuses his lecture on Keller's place in the canon of German and world literature. He places Keller predominately in the nineteenth-century realist tradition. He sees romantic elements in some of Keller's works, but is careful to define what he understands by "romantic." Maync suggests that romanticism in the modern age is the poetic license to fashion and embellish realistic material to the limits of one's fantasy, and he asserts that for Keller, the terms German and romantic were one. His romanticism was not that of the preceding literary period, but rather an empirical romanticism. Keller synthesized romanticism with realism. Maync also places Keller's early writing in the tradition of Jean Paul Richter, and in the first edition of *Der grüne Heinrich*, he senses the distant echo of Eichendorff's *Taugenichts*. However, *Der grüne Heinrich* does not dissipate into romantic feeling and aesthetic moods, rather, it depicts lively human beings in a secure and familiar world (17). Maync believes that Keller the painter exhibited a much greater romantic bent than Keller the poet. Keller never accepted the l'art pour l'art of the early German Romantics. Moreover, the modern German audience demands not only well rounded artistic forms but substantive, realistic content as well. He concludes that Keller's childhood and education, his environment, and

---

[12] Spitteler refers to a trend in German letters in the nineteenth century touched off by the historian Gervinus to deify Goethe. See chapter one.

not least of all his Swissness required that he counterbalance the romantic elements with realism (14).[13]

Of course, a festive lecture on a native son and poet would not be complete without comparing Keller's art to Goethe's. Maync suggests that Keller's Bildungsroman resembles *Wilhelm Meister* much more than it resembles *Heinrich von Ofterdingen* or *Sternbald*. Heinrich Lee, like Wilhelm Meister, recognizes the error of his dilettantish, artistic endeavors and, like Wilhelm Meister, secures a worthy position in society without relinquishing his idealism. Maync takes great pains to show that Keller is a German realist writer, whose encounter with Feuerbach enabled him to make the transition from spirituality to sensuality and, on the artistic level, from romanticism to realism. Romanticism ignores the world. The realist observes the world. Keller, trained in landscape painting, had learned to observe the world around him; his eyes become his windows on the world, his prose and poetry are visual art (20). Keller's realism is stylized reality, eliminating all that is not crucial and elevating what remains, affording it a higher symbolic truth. Through this stylization of events, Maync contends that Keller fulfills Schiller's twofold expectation of the artist, namely that he rise above the realistic events, while also remaining within the bounds of the material and sensual world.

Keller's philosophy of life, like Goethe's before him, emphasizes the purely humane (*das Reinmenschliche*). Keller believed in the basic goodness of man and in the power of good in the world. Keller had both feet planted firmly in this world, as indicated by the Seldwyla novellas and by the *Sieben Legenden*. His life and works reveal his belief in the desire of every human being to become a useful member of society.

Although Maync hesitates to call Keller a total realist, much less a naturalist, he concedes that Keller maintains a consistently high level of reality in his fiction. He places Keller between Gotthelf, who often remains mired in banal reality, and Auerbach, who cloaks reality all too idealistically. Maync claims that of all the German realists — Hebbel, Ludwig, Freytag, Reuter, Raabe, Fontane, Storm and Heyse — Keller crafts the finest art. Keller's linguistic talent enables him to suffuse his impeccable and imaginative German with a Swiss resonance uniquely his own; language was artistic material for Keller, and his humor is a hallmark of his prose; ranging from roguishness to the grotesque, it appeals to readers of diverse social and educational background.

In his conclusion Maync states that we will undoubtedly be commemorating Gottfried Keller's two hundredth and three-hundredth birthdays in celebration of his artistic achievement and of the timeless wisdom they collectively espouse (48). Maync's prophesies have been fulfilled. Keller scholarship has continued to grow and deepen in quality and diversity during the twentieth century. The next

[13] Maync equates Keller's Swissness with a genuine love of reality anchored in a deeply rooted earthy love of all things Swiss expressed in concrete terms.

chapter will focus on the fifty years of Keller scholarship following the centennial celebrations in 1919.

Works Cited

Baechtold, Jakob. *Gottfried Keller Bibliographie (1844–1897)*. Berlin: Wilhelm Hertz, 1897.

Baechtold, Jakob. *Gottfried Kellers Leben. Seine Briefe und Tagebücher*. 3 vols. Berlin: Besser, 1894–97.

Dünnebier, Hans. *Gottfried Keller und Ludwig Feuerbach*. Zurich: Ketner, 1913.

Ermatinger, Emil. *Gottfried Kellers Leben, Briefe und Tagebücher*. 3 vols. Stuttgart & Berlin: J. G. Cotta, 1915–1918.

Frey, Adolf. *Erinnerungen an Gottfried Keller*. Leipzig: Haessel, 1892; rpt. Zurich: Rotapfel Verlag, 1979

Frey, Adolf. "Gottfried Keller — Das Letzte Jahr" *Deutsche Rundschau* 65 (October–December 1890).

Hesse, Hermann. *Eine Literaturgeschichte in Rezensionen und Aufsätzen*. Vol. 2, ed. Volker Michels. 298–302. Frankfurt am Main: Suhrkamp, 1972.

Hesse, Hermann. "Seldwyla im Abendrot: Zu G. K. s 100. Geburtstag am 19. Juli." *Vossische Zeitung*, July 19, 1919.

Hochdorf, Max. *Gottfried Keller im europäischen Gedanken*. Zurich: Rascher, 1919.

Hofmannsthal, Hugo von. *Gesammelte Werke*. Vol. 2, 266–275. Berlin: S. Fischer, 1924.

Huch, Ricarda. *Gottfried Keller*. Berlin: Schuster & Löffler, 1904. (Subsequent editions appeared with Insel Verlag.)

Köster, Albert. *Gottfried Keller. Sieben Vorlesungen*. Leipzig: B. G. Teubner, 1900. (Reprinted 1907, 1917, and 1923.)

Kriesi, Hans Max. *Gottfried Keller als Politiker*. Frauenfeld & Leipzig: Huber, 1918.

Maync, H. "Gottfried Keller, 1819–1890" Bern: K. J. Wysse, 1919. (Commemorative lecture at the University of Bern on July 19, 1919 as part of the Keller Centennial celebration. Reprinted in 1928 by Huber.)

Meyer, C. F. *Sämtliche Werke*. Vol. 15, 179–85. Bern: Benteli, 1985.

Meyer, Richard M. *Die Deutsche Literatur des 19. und 20. Jahrhunderts*. 364–87. Berlin: Georg Bondi, 1921. (Earlier editions appeared in 1906 and 1912.)

Spitteler, Carl. "Gottfried Keller-Rede in Luzern." Luzern: Otto Wicke, 1919.

4: Keller Scholarship 1920–1969

THE HALF CENTURY THAT FOLLOWED the centennial of Keller's birth in 1919 saw a veritable explosion in Keller scholarship, including the establishment of the Gottfried Keller Society which in turn promoted the publication of the first critical edition of his works. New critical approaches provided a wealth of original interpretations that have also served to deepen and broaden discourse. Keller's role in the tradition of German and European realism has been investigated by such pre-eminent scholars as Lukács, Martini, and Preisendanz. Keller's philosophy of life and view of the world have been re-interpreted by Roffler, Reichert, Wildbolz, and Locher. Sociological approaches by Benjamin, Lukács, Pascal, M. Kaiser and Richartz opened up new avenues of investigation. Keller's relationship to the Divine has been explored by Zollinger-Wells, Wenger, and Fehr with very different interpretations. Demeter, Staiger, von Wiese, Lemke, Preisendanz, and Adey have thoroughly examined Keller's humor. Keller biographers such as Ackerknecht, Boeschenstein, and Breitenbruch augmented the solid work begun by Baechtold and Ermatinger. The continuing scholarship in the mid-twentieth century is evidence of Keller's enduring power to inspire modern readers, to address contemporary problems, and to offer sustenance in a changing world.

The most important event of the 1920s was the decision to commence publication of a definitive and comprehensive critical edition of Keller's oeuvre. Jonas Fränkel, a professor of German at the University of Bern, received the commission to begin work on this extensive undertaking which enjoyed considerable financial support from the governing authorities in the canton of Zurich. This critical edition would be completed some two decades later by Carl Helbling.

In addition to the comprehensive critical edition, the early decades of the twentieth century saw several scholars publish Keller editions. Max Nußberger published one in eight volumes that was not based on the original manuscripts, but rather on the first published edition of Keller's works by Hertz. This meant that many of the errors made by previous editors and typesetters were duplicated. Keller's collected works were published by Hertz in 1889 during the final year of Keller's life, when he seventy and ill, and thus was no longer physically able to perform the rigorous duties of an editor. Much of the burden fell on the publisher's shoulders. The errors in this first edition also resulted in misinterpretations of those texts. Nußberger's commentary focuses on biographical relationship between the author and his works; it relies heavily on Keller's biography to determine the source of and inspiration for the various texts, and is less concerned with the interpretation of the works.

Harry Maync edited an annotated six-volume edition of Keller's collected works published by Propyläen in Berlin. He also neglected to use the handwritten manuscripts as the basis for his text so, unfortunately, this edition is also based upon Hertz's flawed original edition and it too has merely reproduced its errors.

Max Zollinger's five volume edition opens with a clear and well rounded introduction and concludes with an excellent contribution from Paul Schaffner about Keller's virtuosity as an art critic. This edition also contains insightful commentary by Karl Polheim of *Sieben Legenden* and the *Sinngedicht*.

Jonas Fränkel's approach to the comprehensive critical edition would be a departure from the existing publications. He believed an editor should delve into the heart of the fiction; one must know how to read literature in order to edit an author's works. Too many literary histories on Keller seem to move on the periphery of the artistic works, a regrettable situation, and one which he sought to rectify. Fränkel established three principles that guided him through the seventeen volumes he completed. His first goal was to achieve an accurate text based primarily but not solely on the handwritten manuscripts, which he in turn compared with Keller's galleys. This would eliminate the errors that mar the earlier publications of Keller's works. Second, he sought to present those texts in an accurate and tasteful manner. Third, he wanted to apply strict scholarly standards in order to elucidate these texts in terms of their originality and artistic craftsmanship. Fränkel did not see it as his task to present every last word Keller had ever put on paper, nor did he want to register every punctuation error that clutter the appendices of so many scholarly editions (Fränkel, 1954, 162). With these strict guiding principles in place, Fränkel set out to accomplish his task. The first volumes began to appear in 1926. By 1934, fourteen volumes had been published and by 1939 seventeen volumes. In 1942 Carl Helbling was commissioned to complete the critical edition. Helbling published an additional seven volumes completing the critical edition in 1948. Volumes three to eight were published by Eugen Rentsch in Erlenbach-Zurich and the others by the Benteli publishing house in Bern.

While Fränkel was working on the critical edition, Bundesrat Robert Haab and government councillor Oscar Wettstein joined Hermann Escher, Hans Bodmer, and Karl Naef on July 9, 1931 to establish the Gottfried Keller Society, which would be based in the canton of Zurich, and whose purpose it would be to remember and to promote Keller and his works. This would be accomplished through the restoration of Keller memorials, through exhibitions in Zurich, and through the support of critical editions. The society also seeks to renew and increase Keller's renown through lectures and presentations. It also supports publication on and by other significant authors from Zurich such as C. F. Meyer. The society, in its original constitution of 1931, also undertook to promote the critical edition. As its first task, the society restored Keller's last study in the house *Zum Thaleck* in Zurich's Zeltweg. On Sunday, October 30, 1932, the initial meeting of the Gottfried Keller Society took place in the great chamber of the Zurich town hall for the first annual Jahresbott or Herbstbott as it has come to be called. Professor Fritz Hunziker presented a lecture on "Gottfried Keller and Zurich," which formed the centerpiece of a celebration that included a festive program of Keller's poetry set to music and sung by the Zurich Men's Choir and the University Choir. By the end of the first year membership had grown to include 186. Keller's restored study in the house at Thaleck on the Zeltweg was first opened to the public on July 19, 1933. By 1943 the society had grown to include almost 400 members. In more recent years the society has been instrumental in establishing the Gottfried Keller Center in Glattfelden, the author's birthplace. This center was completed in 1985 (*Jb. GKG*, 25, 25). The Gottfried Keller Society has also promoted the historical-critical edition of C. F. Meyer's works, and over the years, seven of the annual Herbstbote presentations have been devoted to the life and works of Meyer, Keller's contemporary and compatriot. Today the society ranges from some 250 to 300 members. It continues to hold the annual Herbstbott in the Zurich town hall each October, to publish the annual public lecture and an annual report of the society's proceedings.

While the society sought to promote the critical edition, several members of the society's board wanted someone other than Fränkel to perform the task. While Fränkel's work was exemplary, various intrigues forced Fränkel to relinquish the editorship (*Jb. GKG*, 1940, 6). In the society's tenth report Fränkel is chastised for the slow progress of the edition. The eleventh annual report announced the appointment of Carl Helbling to succeed Fränkel.[1]

Carl Helbling assumed the editorship of the critical edition and is responsible for volumes IX, X, XII, XV/2, and volumes XX–XXII, which brought the critical edition to a close in 1948. Fränkel in an acerbic and justifiably bitter tone, well substantiated with examples, reveals how Helbling abandoned the critical objectives that had served as Fränkel's unswerving principles. Fränkel accuses Helbling of possessing too little scholarly rigor, questions his academic integrity and finds him lacking in systematic principles (1954, 188). Helbling was not at home in Keller's language and consequently, failed to understand Keller's style and rhythm, leading to innumerable errors in punctuation and spelling (154). Fränkel reproaches Helbling for not using the original handwritten manuscripts as his primary source and accuses him of reproducing the mistakes found in all the previous collected editions. The sheer number of errors Fränkel cites to prove his point leave the reader little reason to doubt his assertions. Fränkel referred to his critical edition of Keller as a torso, destined to remain a torso, to which the seven volumes by Helbling were appended (194). Nevertheless, while

---

[1] Those interested in the historical details of this critical edition should turn to Jonas Fränkel's publication: "Die Gottfried Keller-Ausgabe und die Zürcher Regierung. Eine Abwehr." (Kommerzdruck und Verlags AG.) 21–40. Also: Jonas Fränkel, *Dichtung und Wissenschaft*, Heidelberg: (Verlag Lambert Schneider, 1954), 96–194.

this chapter on the first historical-critical edition was not a happy one, it remains the most accurate and the only complete critical edition of Keller available.[2]

Whatever one might think of Helbling's contributions to the critical edition, most scholars agree that his five volume critical edition of Keller's correspondence has been an essential contribution to Keller scholarship. Over the years, countless readers have exclaimed that reading Keller's correspondence is as invigorating as reading his fiction and poetry. Helbling was well prepared to edit Keller's correspondence, having worked on Keller's letters for over a decade prior to the publication of this five volume edition. In 1940, he published the selected letters of Keller, a slim volume containing some eighty-eight letters with annotations and an index. Already in 1938 he had been asked to give the Herbstbott, a public lecture, on Keller's correspondence. It is not surprising, given his experience, that Helbling was asked to edit the five volume critical edition of Keller's correspondence which appeared between 1951 and 1954.

Helbling's editions of Keller's letters are carefully wrought and well organized. All letters with a given correspondent are grouped chronologically. The editor begins each section of correspondence with a brief introduction to the correspondent with pertinent background information and an explanation of the relationship to or friendship with Keller. Occasionally, the correspondent's response to Keller was also included, depending upon its significance and availability. Some facsimiles have also been included. The first volume contains the correspondence between Keller and his mother and sister, as well as with friends from his youth such as Johann Müller, Johann Salomon Hegi, Ferdinand Freiligrath, Wilhelm Baumgartner and Hermann Hettner. The second volume includes the correspondence with lifelong friends such as Ludmilla Assing, the Exners, Maria Melos, and Ida Freiligrath, among others. Volume three consists of two separate volumes. The first contains Keller's extensive correspondence with fellow authors, such as Paul Heyse, C. F. Meyer and Theodor Storm as well as with noted literary historians and critics such as Friedrich Theodor Vischer, Emil Kuh, Jakob Baechtold and Josef Viktor Widmann. The second consists of correspondence with Keller's publishers such as Vieweg, Duncker and Hertz along with editors of literary journals such as Auerbach and Rodenberg. The fourth volume contains miscellaneous letters and includes an index of the letters, a chronological table which moves from year to year showing when the letters were written and to whom, and concludes with an index of all the correspondents, including.those names mentioned in the correspondence or in Helbling's introductions to the correspondent.

---

[2] Those working on Keller today still use the Fränkel and Helbling critical edition. A new historical critical edition has just been published by Deutscher Klassiker-Verlag under the editorship of Thomas Böning, Gerhard Kaiser, Kai Kauffmann, Dominik Müller and Peter Villwock. This new edition will undoubtedly become the definitive critical edition in the years ahead.

The critical edition by Fränkel and Helbling became the standard work, on which Keller scholarship was based. The fifty years of Keller scholarship from the centennial of his birth in 1919 until 1969 saw an explosion of new ideas and the proliferation of Keller scholarship, due in part to the availability of the Fränkel-Helbling critical edition, and to Helbling's critical edition of Keller's correspondence.

In 1927 Walter Benjamin wrote an insightful tribute to Keller, in which he also welcomed the critical edition, which would set the stage for a necessary re-evaluation of Keller's work and indeed of the nineteenth century as a whole. Benjamin reminds his readers that Keller's fiction and poetry reflect a society in transition as a result of industrialization, increased materialism, Darwinism, and atheism, and that his works therefore serve well the impending reassessment of the nineteenth century. Benjamin suggests that the upper echelons of Swiss society maintained the characteristics of the pre-industrial middle-class much longer and were relatively unaffected by the ideological changes wrought by the German Reich. Benjamin believed that even the Switzerland of his own time lacked the air of speculation that such states as the Soviet Union had come to harness and exploit (285). The Swiss possessed more love of their cantons (*Heimatliebe*) and less national spirit. "Heimat" in Switzerland connotes the place where one's regional dialect is spoken. It is a country where political ideology places cantonal autonomy above centralization of power. There was a strong movement in Keller's time to strengthen the Federalist structure, and to this end, the ruling patricians in Zurich sought to influence Keller to become a Swiss national poet by granting him the first renewable cantonal scholarship in Zurich. Keller did favor a stronger central government in Bern, but a federalist one. He eventually did "repay" the investment made on his behalf by becoming a significant author and by serving as cantonal clerk (286).

What Benjamin refers to as Keller's radicalism, his ability to stay the course, to portray the problems inherent in the social transitions of his day, his ability to work in his capacity as cantonal clerk with individuals whose political views were antithetical to his own, are manifestations of his stalwart, single-minded views. Such stories as *Romeo und Julia auf dem Dorfe* prevented him from becoming party to the stultified generation to which Auerbach and Heyse belonged (287). Benjamin finds many similarities between Goethe's *Elective Affinities* and Keller's novella *Romeo und Julia auf dem Dorfe*. In Goethe's novel all the actions proceed from adultery. In Keller's novella the future of two lovers, naturally attracted to one another, is destroyed by the illegal and uncontrolled actions of their greedy parents.

Benjamin compares Keller's humor to that of Homer. It is not superficial, but arises from the depths of his melancholic being. A sweet, but stalwart skepticism is also part of Keller's prose; this skepticism is inseparable from the vision of happiness, which this prose transforms into reality (289). In this vision lies the secret of the epic poet, who alone can communicate this happiness by weighing each small cell of the world as though it were all of reality. Keller's works are built on unromantic foundations. Keller's hedonistic atheism did not permit him to portray nature with Christian attributes as Gotthelf had done before him. Benjamin observes something of the ancients in Keller's portrayal of the landscape. The early Renaissance painters and poets sought to portray antiquity and only succeeded in portraying their own time. This is not true of Keller. Rather, he sought to portray his own time and in doing so portrays antiquity (290). Keller's fiction is full of the genuine wisdom of classicism. Benjamin also praises Keller's thorough command of German from the most original dialect to the latest foreign expression, which no other German author had possessed since Grimmelshausen (291). The saturation of the narrative and the poetic in the post-romantic period is brought to full fruition in Keller's descriptive prose (292).[3] Of course, mimesis or portrayal of reality should not be confused with the content of art. Keller's world is a mirror of reality, the world of the epic poet, who has captured in both image and rhetoric a great epoch of social and economic upheaval. He used a classical form, that he imbued with his great sense of humor, which was born of the *Grundtrauer* (melancholy) that was peculiarly his own. Benjamin's essay is brief, but it contains highly insightful truths that have made a lasting impression on Keller scholars in this century.

In 1931 Thomas Roffler published his volume on Gottfried Keller, which has become one of several standard interpretations of Keller's philosophical outlook on life, forming a foundation for later studies (Wildbolz, Locher). Roffler sees in Keller the eternally optimistic humanist, who sought to bring all classes together for the commonweal, to strengthen the democracy by encouraging civic duty. He was able to accomplish this with far greater success than Goethe, because Goethe allowed himself to be drawn into aristocratic circles. Keller was born into a petite bourgeois family. Roffler believes that Keller's revised *Grüner Heinrich* is the Bildungsroman of the century; none other can match the depth and profundity of Keller's novel (65). Heinrich's sense of ethical correctness, of civic duty, is an inherent trait in many of Keller's characters (168). Roffler cites three sources of Keller's inspiration: Jean Paul's and Goethe's prose, and his own deeply felt humanity. Keller's fiction belongs to Germanic culture because he created an image of the bourgeoisie (*Bürgertum*) that is Germanic. Keller's sensitivity for the fairy-tale, the legend, for folk literature, combined with his awareness of the changing social and economic climates, enables Keller to capture the hearts and minds of a wide variety of readers. In a changing world, Keller was able to reach out through his fiction to all levels of society; his fiction aspires to engender humanity in an age not given to humanity. Keller belongs to those

---

[3] "Durchdringung des Erzählerischen und des Dichterischen — der wesentliche Zuwachs, den dem Deutschen die nachromantische Epoche gebracht hat — ist in Kellers beschreibender Prosa am vollsten verwirklicht." (292)

treasured figures of Swiss history who have, as educators of the people, fulfilled their civic duty in an exemplary fashion (161). Keller's *Sinngedicht* and his revised *Grüner Heinrich* have granted him a place in the canon of Western Literature.

One central issue in both in literary criticism in general and in Keller scholarship in particular during the 1930s, 1940s, and 1950s was the lingering discussion over what constituted realism. How does one reconcile the transition in Keller's fiction from the romanticism in *Der grüne Heinrich* to the stark realism of *Martin Salander*? In an illuminating lecture for the Gottfried Keller Society in 1937, Emil Staiger revealed those elements in Keller's works that came from the German Romantic tradition. The term European realism has been applied to much of the post-romantic art in the latter two-thirds of the nineteenth century. The discussion of what constitutes realism can be traced back to antiquity, most notably to Plato and Aristotle. The debate was revived during the nineteenth-century and reached its pinnacle in the theoretical works of Georg Lukács, Erich Auerbach, Richard Brinkmann, Fritz Martini, Wolfgang Preisendanz, and Peter Demetz.

Mimesis in Aristotelian terms is "the continuous dynamic relation between a work of art and whatever stands over against it in the actual moral universe, or could conceivably stand over against it" (Whalley, *Studies*, 73). The expression "mimesis" is often translated as "imitation," which may be misleading because it suggests something static, a copy as a final product, missing its connotation of a dynamic process: an active relationship to a living reality. Aristotle held that the fundamental task of mimesis is to reveal universals, a task which, when achieved, makes poetry more philosophical than history. Aristotle found these universals inextricably bound up with concrete characters and events. His concept of mimesis also implies the notion of enactment: poetry and prose do not merely describe or narrate; rather, they dramatize. Modern scholars continue to debate whether Aristotle's understanding of mimesis constituted a simple replication of reality (of nature, events, and individuals) which would make it akin to historical writing, or whether Aristotle meant a realistic yet artistic replication of nature and reality which would then be evaluated as an artistic endeavor. Indeed in his *Politeia* (Book X), Plato looks condescendingly upon exact replication of a given situation or reality. In his *Poetica*, Aristotle assigns mimesis a central role, but amends the mere replication of reality to allow for creativity. In this sense, mimesis does not precisely reflect empirical reality in every detail; rather, the reality becomes the point of departure for artistic endeavor.

German realism, as a literary epoch, evolved as a reaction to historic, social and economic events and in reaction to classical idealism and romanticism. The political suppression of the Austrian Restoration under the guiding hand of Prince Metternich ushered in the cultural era of Biedermeier, exemplified by its apolitical focus on family, nature, and functional art, an era whose tenets were seriously questioned by the political revolutions of 1848. Moreover, the revolutions of 1848, together with increasing industrialization, continued to fracture the feudal social structures, while enabling the middle-class to gain greater power and establishing what became known as the proletariat. Ironically, the bourgeois aspired to the cultural traditions of their political opponents in the aristocracy. Much of the representative fiction written after 1848 portrays this tendency to gravitate toward the external trappings and customs of pre-revolutionary social traditions, as occurs for instance in the Rosenhaus in Stifter's *Nachsommer* and in the Grafenschloß in Keller's *Der grüne Heinrich*.

The author Otto Ludwig (1813–1865) is generally credited for having coined the term poetic realism (*poetischer Realismus*), which he understood to include the pursuit of social reality.[4] The goal of the realist author is not to establish a cold objective tone, but rather to transfigure reality. Authors such as Keller, whose works fall under poetic realism, sought to poeticize or stylize their replications of reality. Bourgeois or "bürgerlicher" realism implies a broader social consciousness or awareness. The literary historian Fritz Martini sees in *bürgerlicher Realismus* the individualization of classical idealism. The bourgeois conscience, guided by its liberal ideas, feels justified in trying to preserve a personal humanity in the face of a changing society that it finds increasingly difficult to comprehend.

Keller's conception of realism has much in common with Aristotelian mimesis and with Ludwig's definition of poetic realism. Keller, both in theory and practice, embellishes his depiction of reality with his creative imagination. In a letter to Paul Heyse, Keller defines the poetic freedom of the realistic writer as the *Reichsunmittelbarkeit der Poesie* (*G.B.* III/1, 57). With this term Keller expresses the right of the realistic poet to immerse himself in a world of dreams that may or may not have been generated by real events. The author as artist possesses the license to embellish actuality with his own fantasy. The only restrictions which hold the poet's imagination in reign are the obligation to make his characters and their actions credible. The banal event, the character, or the landscape is to be embellished by the author's own fantasy until the resulting patchwork of fiction and reality constitutes something far deeper than the original event could convey. As we have already noted, Otto Brahm associated the Swissness of Keller's prose with realism (1883, 16). Brahm's essay demonstrates how Keller's work moves from subjectivity in the early works to greater objectivity in the later works, a transformation best exemplified by the two versions of *Der grüne Heinrich*. Aristotle, Ludwig, and Keller all believe that the author must proceed at least one step beyond the historian. It is the task of the author not merely to record historical events as objectively as possible, but rather to make

---

[4] It should be noted here, that Schelling, in an entirely different context, applied the term "poetischer Realismus" in a lecture titled "Die Methode des academischen Studiums" in 1802. This must be seen as pure coincidence which has little bearing on the meaning of the term for our context.

the reader more aware of this event. The author must transport the reader to a higher form of consciousness. The critics of Keller's day were obsessed with what Sammons calls an "idealistic transcendental dimension in realism" that expressed itself through ethical purpose, toward which all good realist writing should strive (12). Keller came to view his fiction as an influential force that embellished real events in an effort to capture and enliven the reader's conscience. In a letter to Auerbach, Keller writes that it is the task of the writer to show the reader a slightly better image of himself and of the world around him, to flatter him, so as to be able to criticize or reprimand him all the more harshly (*G.B.* III/2, 195). Keller believed that he must offer the reader an optimistic depiction of reality, he must humor the reader, in order to capture and hold his attention long enough for the reader to reflect upon his reading. Keller's objective was to strive for ever greater humanity, which Martini views as representative of the German realist authors. Literary scholars such as Lukács, Auerbach, and Martini continued to discuss the tradition of realism in its nineteenth-century German context; their interpretation will be taken up later in this chapter.

Modern scholarship also focused on the nature of Keller's humor. The German term "Humor," particularly as used in the nineteenth century, is imbued with a different meaning from the corresponding English term. It is idealistic and tends to describe an harmonious condition, an harmonious whole that soars above the fray and the tribulations of everyday life. It is perhaps best exemplified by Jean Paul Richter, who referred to it as "sich selber belächelnde Hausväter-lichkeit" (Richter, 11, 120). Richter's humor is very down-to-earth, and Keller's humor shares this empirical trait, which contrasts with the more speculative humor of German idealism. The metaphysically laden humor of German Idealism had given way to a new epoch in which a worldly humor would embrace life. Hildegard Demeter claims that humor is the new force with which the great realist authors bridged the eternal chasm between the spiritual and the material, between freedom and necessity (Demeter, 48). In contrast to romantic irony that supposedly lifts the real being up, the realist humorist reaffirms that which he poeticizes, not falling prey to poetic fantasy, but rather attempting to reconcile fantasy and reality with humor. Humor rescues him from the extremes of romantic extravagance on the one hand and from bourgeois provinciality on the other.

Hildegard Demeter's book on Gottfried Keller's humor was published in Berlin in 1938. Though published under the Nazi regime, it constitutes an extensive and rewarding study. In her introduction Demeter defines German humor by tracing its development from Idealism to Realism. She then explores the models she sees as influential for the development of Keller's own special brand of humor. In her discussion of humor in Keller's lyric, Demeter disagrees with Ermatinger, who views Keller's humor as a further development of Heine's romantic irony. For her, Keller's work that best reveals his attitude toward life and art is *Der Apotheker von Chamounix*.

Turning next to the epic, Demeter suggests that in *Der grüne Heinrich* the tragic overshadows the refined humor. She then concentrates on selections from *Die Leute von Seldwyla*, in which she stresses the ethical and pedagogical nature particularly in *Pankraz* which, she contends, is neither didactic nor moralizing, but life-affirming. In *Romeo und Julia auf dem Dorfe*, she discusses the masterful blend of the tragic and the comic, in the *Kammacher* the hilarious caricature, in *Kleider Machen Leute* the blend of humorous situations and characters, and in *Das verlorene Lachen*, Keller's point that the inability to laugh is the worst fate that can befall anyone. Demeter believes that the broad spectrum of Keller's humor is contained in *Die Leute von Seldwyla* (28).

The final section of the text is devoted to an analysis of Keller's humorous style, its sources, forms and techniques. Demeter reminds us of Keller's fondness for the plays of Aristophanes, of his Berlin encounter with the works of Rabelais and Shakespeare, and of his admiration for Laurence Sterne, Theodor Gottlieb von Hippel, and Jean Paul Richter. Keller also admired Charles Dickens, Fritz Reuter and Karl Immermann and praised Eduard Mörike's convincing roguishness. Her analysis of Keller's technique runs the gamut, including comical attire, domestic life, mindless palaver, use of peculiar names, word play, metaphor, foreign phrases, original phrases, hyperbole, anachronisms, and diminutives.

Demeter's study of Keller's humor is evidence that solid objective scholarship could be carried out under a repressive regime. Unfortunately, Demeter's study is more the exception than the rule. Although Keller's works were not harmfully misinterpreted and exploited by the cultural demagogues of the Third Reich, as were Raabe's and Nietzsche's, his years in Munich and Berlin, his belief in a Germanic literature, reinforced by his opposition to a Swiss national literature, made his artistic work fertile ground for a government bent on establishing a pan-German state. It is therefore not surprising that in 1939 Jonas Fränkel, editor of the first critical edition of Keller's works, published a collection of lectures on Keller, and it was hardly coincidental that these lectures, delivered at the University of Bern in 1936, should have been published just one year after the National Socialists in Germany annexed Austria, and that they were entitled *Gottfried Kellers Politische Sendung*. Fränkel's title communicates a very different message than does the title of Kriesi's book, *Gottfried Keller als Politiker*. As general editor of the critical edition in progress, Fränkel had access to archival materials that had been unavailable to Kriesi in 1918. Kriesi's work is a fine piece of investigative scholarship, while Fränkel's exhibits a highly polished rhetorical flourish substantiated by well chosen citations from Keller's fiction and poetry that are carefully organized to depict Keller as a staunch patriot of Swiss sovereignty. The Swiss concept of sovereignty, a real issue in the nineteenth and early twentieth centuries, had been resolved. Keller attributes the Swiss national character not to ancestry, Swiss sagas, realia, or to material wealth, but asserts that it is founded upon a love for freedom and independence (Fränkel, 19). Keller saw strength in Swiss cultural and linguistic diversity. Beyond language the bond of a common political faith grants freedom and independence to diverse cultural entities in Switzerland. Fränkel clarifies Keller's poetic line "Ich Schweizer darf und Deutsch sein" "I am allowed to be Swiss and I belong to Germanic culture" suggesting that it is wrong to assume, as many have, that Keller felt both Swiss and German. Other citations that follow show that Keller could only conceive of Switzerland as a political entity alongside a free and independent democratic Germany. Fränkel makes a careful distinction between Keller's patriotic fervor for a free and independent Switzerland and his sense of belonging to a larger Germanic culture. Fränkel claims that Switzerland is the only place in 1938 in Europe where the tradition of German culture reflected in the German (philosophy, music, literature, the arts) can be preserved for posterity (48, 122). Culturally, Keller felt himself part of the larger German community. Politically, Keller was Swiss. He did not believe in a Swiss national literature, which he thought would lead to provinciality. Fränkel suggests that great German literature, preserved and cared for on neutral and free Swiss soil, could serve as a bridge to the grand tradition of German culture (49).

Fränkel reminds us of Keller's active participation in the promotion of a modern democratic Swiss state through his direct involvement in the constitutional revisions of 1874. In the annual *Bettagsmandat*, Keller encouraged his countrymen to take an active part in the democratic process. He spoke out for labor laws protecting children long before they were introduced in the legislature and was instrumental in advocating equal rights for Jews in the canton of Zurich (86). In 1863 Keller also appealed to his countrymen to accept over 2,000 Polish refugees, who had attempted to revolt in occupied Poland and were forced to flee. The parallel between Keller's support of the Poles, and the then-current situation of the Jews in the Third Reich is all too transparent. While Fränkel does not state openly that Switzerland should open its doors to refugees from Hitler's Germany, he lets Keller address the issue and allows his readers to draw their own conclusions: " Let us doff our hats, brothers, in face of this great misfortune and thank God that we are granted the privilege of providing those poor outcasts with a refuge" (91). Keller's greatest political legacy lies in the sentiment that our destiny is not determined by outside forces, but rather by powers that we each preserve in our soul and allow either to flourish or to perish (109). In the final chapter, Fränkel plainly identifies the German menace to the north (119) and appeals to the Swiss to preserve their freedom and independence which will in turn enable Switzerland to preserve the tradition of German scholarship, academic freedom, and belles lettres. Although Fränkel uses Keller's fiction as a voice of authority to promote the sovereignty of Switzerland, he does not misinterpret Keller to accommodate a particular political agenda as August Follen had done a century earlier. Instead, Fränkel represents Keller's political thoughts objectively and fairly

In 1939, a single-volume biography of Keller written by Erwin Ackerknecht was published in Berlin. It affords both the Keller scholar and the lay reader with an eminently readable volume. Ackerknecht's study does not attempt broad scholarly interpretations of Keller's works already available in Ermatinger's biography, but rather seeks to provide a better understanding of Keller's life intended for the broader audience. Ackerknecht's biography is still read by those seeking an introduction to Keller. He had already published a slim volume in 1937, in which he discusses Keller's perspectives on art, education, politics, and life. The volumes complemented one another: Ackerknecht's earlier work provides neither an introduction to the inexperienced Keller reader, nor insightful new interpretations for the seasoned reader. Together, they provide the first readable biography of Keller for a general audience, and some standard interpretations. Most remarkable about both these volumes is that they remained untainted by the German politics of the day.

The Marxist literary scholar Georg Lukács, wrote an insightful article on Keller in 1939, in which he claims Keller to be one of the greatest authors of the epic in nineteenth-century world literature (Lukács, 1939, 147). This study, written during the height of Lukács's Stalinist period, certainly contains political undertones, but is nevertheless an extraordinary example of literary scholarship and the first critique to rank Keller among and above great European Realists of his time. Lukács believes that Keller's unshakable faith in the deeply rooted Swiss democracy sets him apart from his German contemporaries. Whereas Raabe, Reuter, and Storm had turned inward in Lukács's estimation, in effect turning their backs on an economically, socially, and politically backward Germany (150, 155), Keller reached out to his readers and through them sought to further develop, but not to idolize, the long tradition of Swiss democracy (160). Keller is the only German author of the period who did not turn to provincial interests, who refused to assimilate the reactionary mind set of the bourgeoisie and who did not turn inward (164). Keller always remained true to Swiss democracy and sovereignty; he was prepared to take up arms to defend Switzerland should it be threatened by reactionary powers abroad. Yet as much as he believed in Swiss democracy and supported Swiss political unity, Keller was opposed to the concept of a Swiss national literature. He wrote for readers of German at home and abroad. For Keller, literature is political (161). The union of pedagogical and artistic tendencies in Keller's realism constitute the responsibility of the author to transmit to the people the ceaseless advance of culture in a persuasive and convincing fashion (170). Lukács contends that Keller introduced the ideals of German humanism through a realistic portrayal of life. He sees in Keller's "Volkstümlichkeit" (folksiness) the continuation of classical German humanism, which connects high culture with the life of the common people. Keller is an author of the people as well as an artist and teacher.

Through the folk festivals, Keller is able to unite private life (family) with public life (society). This is a central theme in *Der grüne Heinrich*: one who fails to control his private affairs cannot be expected to become a productive member of society. Lukács is clearly fascinated by Keller's successful attempt to write an educational novel (Bildungsroman) in the tradition of Goethe's *Wilhelm Meister* and is particularly taken by Keller's ability to place those same themes, goals, and characters among the common people. In Keller's novel, Lukács sees the direct descendent of *Wilhelm Meister* and he makes many astute observations in his comparison of the two novels. For Lukács, this "Volkstümlichkeit," this ability to portray the significant moments in everyday life, constitutes the cornerstone of Keller's realism (176). Keller's realism is not merely an imitation of life; rather it exhibits a love of Swiss democracy which sought to influence and to preserve, but not to glorify. Lukács sees in Keller's attempts to change society an extension of the ethics of the Enlightenment

Lukács also discusses Keller's humor, which, he shows, is closely bound to the artistic and moral demands Keller places on his art and himself. It makes no attempt to spare individual plights or brighten up awkward situations. Rather, it uncovers certain character-types, revealing their hidden ridiculousness, stupidity, and folly (177). Keller's mockery can be just as cruel as that of Shakespeare, Cervantes, or Moliere.

Keller's realism is also haunted by resignation. While ancient democracies enjoyed the harmony between the private and public sphere, capitalism has shattered this harmony. Keller's resignation stems in part from his inability to fully unite the two spheres in his characters. Whenever he seeks such a union, the fictional characters such as Fritz Amrain and Arnold Salander dissipate into mere sketches. This failure is not an artistic one, Lukács claims, but stems from the inability of bourgeois democracies to resolve a problem whose solution could only be found under communism.

Lukács demonstrates how Keller further developed the German novella, and devotes special attention to the frame-tales and to the novella cycles. He then discusses the two versions of *Der grüne Heinrich* in the context of world literature, contrasting them with the educational novels of Stendhal and Balzac (208–09). He illuminates the similarities between Keller's novel and Goethe's *Wilhelm Meister*. Keller's novel is more modern than Goethe's in that it treats the day-to-day trials and tribulations of economic existence among the common people, while at the same time aspiring to the loftier goals of ethical, political, and social education. Keller remained an author of the common man: he was too much the realist not to portray honestly the moral decay caused by the advance of capitalism; the muse that empowered him to poeticize reality was no longer able to elevate the grim reality portrayed in *Das verlorene Lachen* and *Martin Salander*. Lukács also saw in Keller's novel certain affinities with Tolstoy's *War and Peace*. Keller's way of looking at the world from a perspective deeply rooted in Swiss democracy affords him the ability to create a naïve epic greatness that was shared in the nineteenth-century only by Tolstoy (217). Gorki was able in the context of socialist realism to portray what Keller could not have been expected to portray in his day. Keller's greatness, Lukács concludes, lies in his ability to achieve such sophisticated art in such an unfavorable political and social situation, without becoming provincial (230).

Emil Staiger first published his monograph, *Die Zeit als Einbildungskraft des Dichters* (Time as the Poet's Power of Imagination) in 1939.[5] The book investigates three poems: one by Brentano, another by Goethe, and Keller's "Die Zeit geht nicht." Staiger attempts to demonstrate how a close textual analysis of a single poem can provide a deeper understanding of an author's works. He departs from the assumption that literary interpretation stems from the central question "What is man?," and surveys what earlier literary historians have thought the task to be. Staiger criticizes Wilhelm Scherer's formula for literary investigation: experience (*Erlebtes*), acquired knowledge (*Erlerntes*), and cultural inheritance (*Ererbtes*). Staiger argues, that it does not matter whether we know what an author has read, nor for that matter can we know how he has experienced a given reading. Likewise, the literary historian can only surmise how the author has been influenced by culture. Staiger insists that the literary historian must concern himself first and foremost with the text of the author, with the word for its own sake (Staiger, 11). Staiger believes that to categorize in broad terms such as Dionysian and Apollonian allows the literary historian to organize vast amounts of material, but fails to provide a deep illumination of specific texts. For these reasons he concentrates on the individual artwork. In order to narrow the field of investigation as much as possible, he chooses to concentrate on poems, in this case, three of them. His goal: to understand a single poem as part of the whole work of an author.

The section on Keller focuses on the poem "Die Zeit geht nicht" (Time stands Still), from the cycle "Sonnwende und Entsagung" (Solstice and Resignation). Staiger's interpretation is readable and brilliantly done; however it presumes complete familiarity with Keller's works and life. Could Staiger have made such a brilliant interpretation if he had not already known Keller's oeuvre extensively? Is there not a paradox inherent in this methodology? Drawing upon other works Staiger points to Heinrich Lee, Pankraz, John Kabys, all of whom dream of the future and take considerable time to see the light and to comprehend the present. Staiger shows how the seemingly incongruous lines of the poem dissolve light, time and mind (*Geist*) into one. Every individual who opens his eyes, sees the light, becomes consciously enlightened as did Keller through Feuerbach. Having perceived the light, each individual will abound in the eternal tranquillity of time ("die ewige Ruhe der Zeit") where things "exist" in the truest

---

[5] This essay is the expanded version of the public lecture, the annual Herbstbott of the Gottfried Keller Society, delivered by Emil Staiger in 1937 in Zurich. *Die Zeit als Einbildungskraft des Dichters* was published in 1939 and reissued unchanged in 1953. Pages 161 to 210 pertain to Keller.

sense of the word (169). Staiger shows that the word "Ruhevoll" (tranquil) per-
meates Keller's works. Peace of mind can only emanate from a tranquil state
(*SW,* XVIII,6). He cites Judith in Keller's novel as the embodiment of this tranquil soul, whereas both Manz and Marti represent dreamers driven by greed.
They have lost inner tranquillity and hence their grip on reality, an imbalance
which becomes the source of humor. Manz and Marti, Pankraz, Strapinski, the
Combmakers, and a host of other characters have lost their facility to laugh.
Their goal-oriented lives drive them to live in the future, forcing them to forego
the present. The ability to laugh, which all these characters have lost, is the sign
of a healthy balance. Keller sets up many of these characters (and the reader)
with certain expectations that for various reasons remain unfulfilled or are fulfilled in some completely unexpected manner, thereby creating humorous situations, for the reader at least. Staiger suggests that, in the comical moment when
Keller shatters the reader's expectations, a certain shifting takes place transport-
ing the reader back to the present (186). His laughter is well meaning, an inherent part of man's dignity. Thus what starts off as Staiger's interpretation of one
poem — but soon broadens to bring in a number of other works, which brings
Staiger's stated methodology into question — affords us keen insight into
Keller's humor while shedding light on some central tenets and themes that
permeate Keller's works. By comparing Keller with his German contemporaries
(Droste-Hülshoff, Mörike, Stifter) Staiger reveals how all drew heavily upon the
experiences of their youth. Yet Keller was perhaps the most forward looking
among them. Keller saw himself as one who furthered tradition while keeping
both feet planted in the present. As Staiger reminds us, Keller considered it the
duty of the poet to transfigure the past and to strengthen and brighten the present. He concludes the section on Keller by showing how Keller's works continue
the long tradition of Swiss letters beginning with Niklaus Manuel, Albrecht von
Haller, Salomon Gessner, and Jeremias Gotthelf. All of these harbored an "inherently Swiss" distrust for artists, and in fact all held solid and socially acceptable professions. All had a penchant for the epic, regarded metaphysics with
great suspicion, and contributed to Swiss achievements in ethics, psychology,
and pedagogy. All upheld the notion that *Lebenstüchtigkeit* (ability to cope with
life) was an enduring Swiss virtue.

In *Gottfried Keller als Maler,* Paul Schaffner presents 71 of Keller's sketches,
studies, aquarelles, and oil paintings with an accompanying text that describes
the stages of Keller's development as a landscape artist. It is replete with relevant
letters and journal entries, selected to emphasize the artistic stages of Keller's development.[6] Schaffner discusses Keller's inadequate formal preparation in Zurich, which made the journeyman years in Munich so difficult for the aspiring

---

[6] Schaffner refers the reader seeking greater depth to his two earlier publications:
Der Grüne Heinrich als Künstlerroman (Stuttgart: Cotta'schen Verlag, 1919) and to
Gottfried Keller als Maler (Stuttgart: Cotta'schen Verlag, 1923).

landscape artist. He also discusses those landscape artists who were influential, most notably Karl Rottmann (1798–1850), whose cycle of Greek landscapes particularly appealed to Keller. Rottmann's classical atmospheric landscapes were inspired by the Romantic Caspar David Friedrich's Ossianic landscapes.[7] These depictions of the melancholic Scottish Highlands and coast eventually replaced the idyllic landscapes in vogue at the time. Keller also incorporated such scenes in his paintings and, upon his return to Zurich in 1842, continued to paint Ossianic landscapes, though he eventually moved to idyllic landscapes.[8] Schaffner suggests that Keller could not have become the writer he was, had he not first studied painting; that the profession the young Keller chose on a whim became one of necessity for his future development as an author (1942, 79). The visual images on the written page, the sense of closure and of the presentation of a complete world (the Novella cycles) are but a few of the traits carried over from the visual arts. Comparing Stifter's painting with Keller's, Schaffner suggests that as an author, Stifter remained a repressed painter, while Keller used his artistic training in his writing. In fact, Keller's development as a painter parallels his development as a writer. In painting as in fiction Keller moved away from Ossian, away from the romantic and toward greater realism (75).

Erich Auerbach contributed to the theoretical debate on realism with the publication of *Mimesis* in 1946. Auerbach suggests that no new developments in realism arose from German soil, though a few members of the older generation, mentioning Keller by name, still crafted prose "of cadence and weight" (517). Of all the German realist writers, only the elder Fontane handled contemporary themes well; and despite the fact that he finds Keller a better writer, he holds that Fontane's art, despite the restriction of its setting to Berlin and the Prussian provinces, offers a transition to a less provincial, more cosmopolitan realism. Auerbach finds Keller much more politically inclined than Stifter and much more modern (519). Keller remains on the intermediate plane of seriousness; his endearing charm is his cheerfulness and his ability to wield "benign irony with the most incongruous and repulsive things" (519). Unlike Lukács, Auerbach does not view Keller — or any of the German realist writers with the possible exception of the later Fontane — as serious contenders on the stage of European

[7] The heroic songs of Ossian, purportedly translated from the Gaelic by the Scotsman James Macpherson (1736–96), were published in 1765. Macpherson most likely pieced together Gaelic fragments, muddled bits of history, and ideas of his own imagining to produce the songs. Nevertheless, they had tremendous impact, particularly in Europe and especially in Germany, where they influenced Herder, Goethe, and Schiller: Macpherson had sensed the Romantic impulse of the times.

[8] Several lines in the second part of a poem entitled "Mutlosigkeit" indicate that Ossian was also a literary experience for the young Keller: "Habet ihr des Gälenbarden [Ossian] schöne Lieder nie gelesen . . . ." (G. W. XIII, 201)

Realism. This is an assertion that is taken to task by later literary historians such as Wolfgang Preisendanz, Hartmut Steinecke, and Martin Swales.[9]

Hermann Hesse revised his original 1930 tribute to Gottfried Keller in 1951. Hesse believed that the individual idealism Keller promoted seemed irretrievable in the wake of the first world war. Keller's love for detail and his passion for nature seemed rather grandfatherly in the modern age. The first world war had called not only Keller's, but all beliefs into question. Nevertheless, Keller's fiction and art carry consolation and sustenance in time of need, opening a door to the eternal in the modern age (Hesse, 295). "Why is this so?" Hesse asks. If the ideas presented in a text are no longer applicable to the modern world, then why are they still read? Hesse believes that Keller's secret lies in the mastery over his craft (296). It is neither the fullness nor the originality of the content that gives fiction its longevity, nor is it the strength of the artist's personality. Rather, it is the degree of mastery attained by the artist in shaping his material that may, if he is successful, produce a work that will remain timeless (296). While Hesse agrees that modern psychoanalytical approaches to literature may unveil the author's soul, they remain unable to illuminate the most important aspect of any work, namely the degree to which mastery has been attained. Hesse draws upon psychoanalysis, suggesting that an author driven by his own needs, seeks to overcome inadequacies by perfecting his fiction or poetry. Certainly in Keller we can observe a life filled with distress, resignation, an author who was driven to create a harmony in his own works that was lacking in his own life (297). Indeed, Keller did create well rounded harmonious works that stand in contrast to his own life. Keller's life appears so poor and unexemplary because the biographers can only relate those activities that were not related to creative work: Keller's best hours were devoted to the mastery of his art, and of those we can know little. The long hours spread over decades spent struggling with the muse, this single, lonely, persistent battle to sublimate, to overcome himself in favor of his work, this secret space within the artist's life that makes mastery possible, Hesse designates as tragic. Keller, the crotchety wine-imbiber and bitter bachelor, assumes tragic proportions. Hesse concludes that Keller's prose and poetry, while belonging to a later intellectual era, are intimately entwined with the intellectual and philosophical world of Biedermeier, much like Stifter's fiction and Schubert's Lieder, yet all retain their timeless magical power, despite the outmoded intellectual content, because each of these artists achieved mastery over their craft.

In 1952 Alfred Zäch published *Gottfried Keller Im Spiegel seiner Zeit*, a useful handbook on the reception of the author. Zäch modestly yields the floor to Keller's contemporary critics, showing how they viewed, interacted and judged

---

[9] See: Martin Swales, "Reflectivity and Realism in *Der Grüne Heinrich*" (1991); Hartmut Steinecke, "Keller's Romane und Romanvorstellungen in europäischer Perspektive" (1990); also: Wolfgang Preisendanz, *Wege des Realismus* (1977).

both the author and his works. The first section is devoted to Keller's youth and early poetry. The second encompasses the Heidelberg and Berlin years and in particular includes those original reviews pertaining to *Der grüne Heinrich*. The third section covers those works written between the first novel and the *Züricher Novellen*. The next is devoted to reactions to all those works written during the last fourteen years of Keller's life. The last half of the volume provides an image of Keller as seen through his extensive correspondence. The volume concludes with the centennial celebration of 1919 and demonstrates the growing appeal that Keller's works have engendered. Valuable in this study is the wealth of original materials and documentation painstakingly collected from letters, from such existing studies (Vischer, Brahm, Prutz, Baechtold, and Ermatinger), and also from newspapers and journals of the period. Zäch's volume has contributed substantially to Keller scholarship by providing useful materials that afford the reader considerable insight into how Keller was received and perceived by his contemporaries.

The first extensive study of Gottfried Keller's religiosity was published by W. Zollinger-Wells in 1954, pursues the author's views on church, faith, and God from Keller's origins in Zwingli's Zurich. One third of the study is devoted to Keller's youthful reflections on God. These years are filled with reverence for a higher being, and with a pantheistic view of nature, revealed in such works as "Die Nacht auf dem Uto." At the same time, Keller exhibits a healthy dislike for organized religion, particularly for Catholicism, and for any form of church propagated dogma. Keller's early encounters with the church did indeed lay the foundation for his later beliefs. His fatherless childhood, his expulsion from school provided him with the need and the time for religious reflection. He believed that God helps those who help themselves, and he was an ardent advocate of free-thinking. The word of God was available for all to ponder and, from it, the young Keller drew sustenance and inspiration.

Despite the importance of those early influences, Zollinger-Wells does not deny that Keller's encounter with Feuerbach altered his faith and changed his view of God. He also shows how Feuerbach's new philosophy spoke to Keller's pre-existing thoughts. Influenced by Feuerbach, Keller developed a more profound appreciation for this life once he accepted death's finality. But Zollinger-Wells argues that this Feuerbach stage was only a passing phase in Keller's religious development, which culminated in a mature outlook on God, faith, and death. Zollinger-Wells suggests that Keller did not feel entirely comfortable with Feuerbach, a thesis which he substantiates by analyzing Heinrich's death in *Der grüne Heinrich* through his encounters with Dortchen in the count's castle. Zollinger-Wells ultimately suggests that Heinrich must die because he has lost all hope. Dortchen has robbed him of Divine grace and its consolation; Heinrich realizes that he can never compensate for his neglect of his mother. Unlike Nietzsche, whose pride prevented him from turning his back on a failed experiment, Keller was able to recognize the pitfalls in Feuerbach's philosophy and eventually distanced himself from it. What Keller did learn from Feuerbach, however, was that men must work together to build an increasingly humane community.

Zollinger-Wells turns to Keller's *Bettagsmandate* and to *Das verlorene Lachen* as evidence of his deeply felt religious views. In the former, Zollinger-Wells argues less convincingly that the religious fervor espoused in these speeches was not merely dictated by their form and by the occasion, but was fervently felt by Keller. In *Das verlorene Lachen*, the pastor of Schönau is clearly a caricature of those who promoted the religious reforms of Keller's day. While Keller's message is anti-clerical, and advocates free-thinking, it is hardly atheistic.

Likewise, in *Martin Salander*, Keller takes a stand against corruption, against those with blind ambition, and against those who have forsaken ethics for materialism. Though, references to religion and to the Divine appear sparingly in Keller's last novel, Zollinger-Wells sees in Maria Salander the embodiment of true faith. He suggests that hope also remains, embodied in Arnold Salander, whose educated generation would build a better, less corrupt, moral society of free thinkers. Zollinger-Wells seeks to persuade us that Keller did not abandon his faith; rather he sought to purge society of false prophets and to lay the foundation for a morally correct society. Zollinger-Wells's reading shows that Keller's concept of men helping their fellow man build a greater humanity is grounded in universal Christian love.

Despite the care taken in his examination of Keller's relationship to religion, Zollinger-Wells seems intent in proving that the author remained a believer, which has the effect of minimizing Feuerbach's influence. Problematic in this respect is Zollinger-Wells's decision not to analyze the *Sieben Legenden*. The sheer number of citations, all intending to support the thesis, are actually contradictory and tend to confuse rather than persuade the overwhelmed reader. It becomes clear that Zollinger-Wells is pursuing an active agenda and that, even if his study is more scholarly and thorough, it is less moderate than Ernst Ackert's 1942 analysis, *Gottfried Keller's Weltanschauung* (Gottfried Keller's Philosophy of Life). Those readers seeking a less subjective study might wish to consult Kurt Wenger's *Gottfried Kellers Auseinandersetzung mit dem Christentum*, which is discussed in chapter 6.

In 1958 Wolfgang Preisendanz published a concise critical bibliography of Keller Scholarship from 1939 to 1957 in the *Germanisch-Romanische Monatsschrift*. Preisendanz's bibliography, which evaluates several articles not included in this study, bridges the gap between Zippermann's comprehensive, but uncritical bibliography of Keller's works and Keller scholarship through 1935,and the scholarship of the modern era, which will be discussed in chapters five (Anglo-American tradition) and six (the German tradition) of this study.

Of the available editions of Keller's works published after the comprehensive, critical edition by Fränkel and Helbling (the preferred edition when citing Keller for publication), the three volume critical edition by Clemens Heselhaus (Hanser, 1958) has proven to be the most practical and reliable. The Heselhaus edition re-examines the concept of collected works, which usually refers to the last published edition of an author's oeuvre. This leads to complications with *Der grüne Heinrich* and those poems which went through subsequent revisions. Heselhaus decided to include the original version of *Der grüne Heinrich* and to reprint the revised novel beginning with book III, chapter 9. Likewise, Heselhaus chose to reprint the earlier editions, including Gedichte 1846, Neuere Gedichte 1851 and 1854, rather than to publish the *Gesammelte Gedichte* of 1883, thus reversing Follen's revisions by printing Keller's original texts, and giving the reader a better overview of the development in his poetry. Heselhaus also includes representative dramatic fragments and made the prudent decision to include five of the 33 essays on politics and nine of the 34 essays on literature and art. The selected letters are based on Helbling's critical edition of Keller's correspondence. In a careful examination of *Martin Salander*, Heselhaus attempts to correct mistakes made by the original type-setter which had led to misreadings, and expresses his gratitude for Fränkel's critique of Helbling's editorship, which he re-examined and corrected coming as close as possible to Keller's original manuscript.

Heselhaus is to be commended for his lucid afterword, in which he presents a comprehensive overview of Keller's works. According to Heselhaus, Keller affords consolation to those readers who accept his depiction of a world full of disappointment and disillusionment, and who can learn to appreciate the veil of fantasy that transfigures the whole landscape, bringing consolation to the reader. Keller's poetry is crafted, folksy, and without pretension. It embodies clarity, simplicity, and truth. What Keller particularly appreciated in drama is the pure effect of human passion and internal conflict on the characters. These attributes place Keller firmly in the literary historical period we have come to call poetic realism. The authors of the period, including Keller, sought to unite realistic material, motifs and forms with the classical style exemplified by Lessing, Goethe and Schiller. However, while classicism had appealed to a cultural elite, poetic realism sought to make the aesthetic and esoteric ideals of Classicism available to the people. To this end the German realists placed great emphasis on content and less emphasis on form. Keller's goal, as Heselhaus demonstrates, was to educate people to become responsible members of society, to teach them to live humanely together with their fellow men. Thus Heinrich Lee must fail, because someone who is incapable of controlling his own life and family cannot expect to become a useful member of society. Only in the later stories, the second volume of *Die Leute von Seldwyla*, the *Züricher Novellas*, the *Sinngedicht* and in the revised edition of *Der grüne Heinrich*, are the characters able to control their lives. Keller's primary objective, Heselhaus suggests, is to bring individuals into contact with one another, for only through this mutual exchange will they become rational and responsible human beings. Keller attempts to educate people to help one another, to help them lend their lives meaning. It was the duty of the author to clarify the past, to transfigure the present, and to afford the reader sustenance for the future; a future toward which they would strive and in which they would achieve a greater degree of common sense and responsibility. Keller has been more popular than his contemporaries and hence has enjoyed greater success because he has created characters who tend to show and exemplify rather than to preach. Heselhaus reminds us of Hofmannsthal, who praised Keller's well balanced distribution of *Maß, Zahl* and *Gewicht* (moderation, diversity, and purport) referring to the portrayal of a well-rounded, fully lived human life.

Heselhaus suggests that there is something of the "picassoesque" in Keller's desire for fleeting sketches and his lust for changing and transforming existing material. No other German writer in the nineteenth century was so radical and so unequivocally decided in his critique of the old, while remaining so open and willing to give himself over to the new and untested. Yet it was Keller's poetical genius that enable him to reconcile the old and new with the humane.

Fritz Martini opens his interpretation of Keller's works by comparing the author to Adalbert Stifter. Both sought to capture the whole of reality in visual images; both drew upon their strengths as painters. Both sought to lend traditional values and timeless virtues a sense of permanence in a changing world. Both possessed a strong sense of the ethical and, consequently, both believed in the strength of an individual ethical code that would ultimately lead to a more humane world. Keller and Stifter sought to educate through art. They struggled to overcome the fantastic, the subjective, and the capricious in their writing. Finally, both authors tried to craft a consciousness in their readers in which moral values and individual ethics would thrive.

In contrast to Keller, Stifter's worldview represents the world prior to the revolutions of 1848, whereas Keller reflects a world which begins thereafter. Thus, Martini agrees with Friedrich Theodor Vischer who saw Keller as a mature realist (Vischer, 2, 135). Martini focuses on Keller as a representative of the German realist tradition; he explores Keller's conception of his own poetic license and depicts the author's struggle to overcome subjectivity, to achieve through various uses of frames, cycles, historical material, and not least of all humor a degree of distance from his characters and hence a greater objectivity, which obtains its pinnacle in *Das Sinngedicht*. Martini's study places Keller in the context of his contemporaries and reserves a unique place for him in the discussion of realism.

Keller's political poetry of the 1840s is subjective; its value lies in content rather than in form. Self-reflection and didacticism bind this early poetry to reality. But with the publication of the *Neue Gedichte*, Keller planned to move away from the subjectivity of his political poetry into more objective genres, namely prose and particularly drama. In his essay entitled "Am Mythenstein," Keller envisions dramatic sketches and plays, written for moral, political and civic education. Such plays would include large choral parts and large casts and would be performed at folk festivals across Switzerland, a conception that Martini heralds as unique (282).

The subjectivity of Keller's early poetry is also carried over into his first novel. Keller subjectively imposed his conclusion onto *Der Grüne Heinrich* — a conclusion which does not grow organically out of the work itself. Martini believes that, for Keller, Heinrich's death represents an escape from the illusion of art and its appearance (*Schein*) as depicted in the carnival scenes in Munich. This disillusionment with the aesthetic reveals a changed attitude towards art and life that would become endemic in the second half of the century (571). Despite Keller's noble attempts, art and life become increasingly separated in Keller's later works. According to Martini, Keller remains in the idealist tradition because he believes in the right of self-determination, in moderation, in reflection and in resignation.

Martini believes that *Der grüne Heinrich* exposes the author's struggle with the inherent contradiction between objectivity and subjectivity. The first and third person narrative forms in the first edition provide just one example. The more Heinrich Lee struggles to obtain a practical education, the more thought-laden, abstract, and didactic the novel becomes. This is all the more evident when the episodes in Munich are contrasted to the poetic prose in the story of Heinrich's youth.

Martini sees Keller's humor as the reconciling agent in his struggle for distance and greater objectivity, for instance in the first volume of *Die Leute von Seldwyla* (60). Through humor, Keller is able to reconcile the ethics of middle-class society with a changing reality; in the first volume of Seldwyla novellas Martini detects an underscored didacticism, a touch of the idyllic, and a hint of resignation that would become more pronounced, particularly in the second volume of Seldwyla novellas, the *Züricher Novellen,* the revised *Grüner Heinrich,* and in *Martin Salander.* Keller's irony enables the reader to reflect upon happenings that are frighteningly close to his own experience, to see through Keller's tapestry, and thereby to learn. Martini comments that both Keller and Raabe struggle against a middle-class mentality (*Bürgerlichkeit*) fashioned by philistine provincialism, and advocate instead a middle-class mentality that promotes humane values and social ethics; both authors strive to create an ideal individual ethical mentality that emanates from deep within each of their characters. For Keller, this virtuous middle-class mentality was closely bound to the political and social community, whose potential was represented in Swiss democracy. Martini, like Lukács, accuses Fontane of misjudging Keller's fiction in stating that it was suffused with a "Kellerian tone"; Martini reminds the reader that Fontane also imparted to his fiction a specific Fontanesque hue. He also contends that it is precisely Keller's tone that lends subjective unity to his narrative world.

The historical events of the day also had their effect upon Keller's fiction. Keller's poetic imagination is rendered powerless in the face of reality: conscience, laughter, and love are no longer strong enough to reassemble the fragmentation of reality (Martini, 588). The quiet revolution of 1868–69 in the Zurich cantonal government influenced Keller's views and, consequently, his fiction. It ushered in a more conservative, if mature language that is already recognizable in the second volume of the Seldwyla novellas (586). Martini finds that art and life grow apart in Keller's later works with the exception of *Das Sinngedicht*. In the *Züricher Novellen*, Keller turned to historical figures and situations to seek life's truth, a truth he could no longer find in his own times. This is the source of the resignation evident in many of his works, in which the ideal becomes ever more distant, removed to the providence of hope (598). In the revised edition of *Der grüne Heinrich*, Judith and Heinrich lend their resignation substance by devoting themselves to service in the community. Martini suggests that Keller speaks not of happiness, but of fulfillment and satisfaction through community service. The revised novel has become more unified, but at the cost of the romantic, demonic-fatalistic, erotic, and poetic elements of the original version.

Martini and Vischer view *Das Sinngedicht* as Keller's greatest artistic achievement. In this cycle of novellas, love transcends passion and attains ceaseless giving of the self to another. The inset novellas represent the maturation process in the love between Lucie and Reinhart. Here Keller finds tranquillity in movement, permanence in change, and a style, that he had struggled to achieve in his earliest prose (605).The artistic achievement attained by Keller in *Das Sinngedicht*, this blending of art and life, was Keller's unsurpassed achievement.

In *Martin Salander* art and life separate again. The humor which pervades the Seldwyla novellas has dissipated, and didacticism becomes increasingly transparent. Although Keller went to great lengths to shape his material artistically, he was primarily concerned with exposing corruption in the public sphere. Martini contends that the second volume, featuring Arnold Salander, was never begun because Keller was an ethical and not a political democrat, meaning that he felt estranged and frustrated by those who misunderstood or failed to listen to his moral message (607). The small Salander family unit stands defenseless before shifting social, political, and economic values. Keller's exhaustion and melancholy of those later years as joins that of an entire generation including Stifter, Raabe, Vischer, Fontane, and Meyer. A world vanished with this generation, a world whose humane, social, and artistic worth, had been fashioned, defended and reaffirmed by these authors.

Preisendanz devotes a substantial chapter to Keller in his 1963 study, *Humor als Dichterische Einbildungskraft*, in which he traces the development of humor in nineteenth-century German literature. Beyond analyzing those elements that constitute Keller's humor, he seeks to determine the function humor plays in Keller's depiction of reality. In Preisendanz's estimation, it is this element of humor that makes Keller the most significant of the nineteenth-century authors.

The chapter begins with a summary of existing studies on Keller's humor. Preisendanz shows how Ermatinger set the tone by suggesting that the contrast between essence (*Sein*) and appearance (*Schein*) formed a central theme in Keller's work and hence was closely associated with Keller's humor. Demeter viewed Keller's humor as an isolated individual phenomenon closely bound to his style. Emil Staiger believes Keller's humor to be closely associated with the manner with which he draws his characters, and with the interaction of those characters to their surroundings. For Lukács, Keller's humor assumes the position of judge over the problematic relationship between being and appearance, between subjective imagination and objective reality. Benno von Wiese also interprets Keller's humor as his way of overcoming the dialectical relationship between "Schein" and "sein." All of these interpretations agree that this contrast becomes the central focus of Keller's prose and sets a stage for his humor. All infer that the relationship between fantasy and reality, between imagination and empirical fact become problematic. The conflict between a subjectively designed world and an objective legality provides the blueprint for Keller's stories.

Preisendanz wants to explore Keller's personal tone, which Fontane had critiqued in his famous 1881 letter to Lepel. Preisendanz also builds upon Benjamin's subtle comment concerning the saturation of the narrative and the poetic ("Durchdringung des Erzählerischen und Dichterischen"), which characterizes much of the German writers in the postromantic period, but which attained its zenith in Keller's descriptive prose (Benjamin, 1955, II, 292). Benjamin had in his own words formulated what Keller believed the task of the epic talent or genius to be. Preisendanz suggests that Keller had himself come to formulate this definition of epic talent as he was reading and writing his essays on Gotthelf (Hanser, III, 965). Keller praised Gotthelf's prose for its elements, its Homeric qualities. Keller then architectonically fulfills this tenet of epic writing himself by enabling the appearance (*Erscheinung*) and the happening (*Geschehende*) to fuse and become a whole. Preisendanz believes that Keller achieves in his prose this Homeric classical totality, a state in which man feels comfortable and at home (*heimisch:* 152). Poetic humor is not merely a way of looking at the world, but a means by which communication and understanding is made possible (Preisendanz, 1963, 151). Preisendanz observes a polarity between the objective portrayed and the subjective refraction ("objektiv Dargestelltem and the subjektiver Brechung"), a dualism in perspective that signifies a "humoristische Verinnigung" and reminds us of Hebbel's words: "Humor is duality that perceives itself" (Humor sei Zweiheit, die sich selbst empfindet). Preisendanz insists that this dualism has nothing to do with the conflict between "Schein" and "Sein" but is rather a device used to describe things, objects, happenings and events in an entirely believable manner that enables the reader to see what is portrayed in a new light (154). Preisendanz cites Zwiehahn's encounter with a clothesline in *Der grüne Heinrich:* Zwiehahn tries to prevent the feminine garments from blowing away, but Keller's careful description, his use of polarity between appearance (*Erscheinung*) and the significance of the event (*Bedeutung*), make the reader aware that much more is at stake than the rescue of a few garments, rather the tumult of the wind-swept wash is commensurate with the tumult of Zwiehahn's emotions. The tension between appearance and significance determines the relationship between portrayed and portrayal, resulting from the polarity between imagined objectivity and subjective reflex.

Likewise in a passage from "Die arme Baronin" in *Das Sinngedicht* Preisendanz demonstrates how the carefully chosen vocabulary describes not only the chamber of the baroness but that on a second level the descriptors come to embody the fears of the baroness herself. While the inventory of the chamber is intimately connected to and indeed embodies the state of mind of the baroness, it does not share her state of mind, and this contrast constitutes the play of "humorischer Verinnigung" (160). A situation is humorous when it simultaneously exhibits two different levels of experience and reveals a double meaning. Preisendanz compares excerpts from Flaubert with those from Keller and concludes that Flaubert's descriptions remain descriptions, and lack the added dimension that he detects in Keller's. This added dimension is the "humorische Verinnigung" that Keller associated with the epic totality of Gotthelf and Homer.

Hofmannsthal believed Keller's strength lay in his fine descriptions in which the most banal and trivial are placed next to the monumental. Keller created tension between the banal event and its human significance. Preisendanz cites an example from the end of the third chapter of *Martin Salander* in which the couple, Marie and Martin Salander, are preparing for bed after many years of separation. Martin wonders whether or not Marie will remember his boot jack and he is delighted to find it, just where he had left it years earlier. This seemingly trivial incident becomes a momentous occasion, because it demonstrates the loyalty of his spouse both in word and in gesture. Preisendanz suggests that this seemingly insignificant event is a hallmark of Keller's style, because it is suffused with humor and is also Homeric, in that Martin's return is reminiscent to that of Odysseus.

Keller, as Preisendanz notes, was opposed to what he referred to as eternal preaching ("ewige Referieren"). Keller praised Gotthelf's prose because he drew his simple creations without resorting to one-sided depictions (*GK*, Hanser, III, 966). Likewise, Keller sought to convey the dialectic of the cultural movement (*Kulturbewegung*) with an epic totality. Keller asserts in his discussion of Gotthelf that the task of fiction, including *Volkspoesie*, or popular fiction, is to seek the dignity of man among the people. The writer should not avoid the everyday world, but should draw upon it and incorporate it into his poetic work. As early as in an 1854 letter to Hettner, Keller realized that all the great and enduring characters, conflicts, situations, and plots have been the subject of classical literature. Contemporary writers can no longer hope to come up with original ideas. New, however, is the manner in which these classical topoi come into contact with cultural development. Keller's writing is filled with these classical topoi or in Northrup Frye's terminology, archetypes. Pankraz begs comparison with the returning prodigal son. Romeo and Julia have a host of predecessors, lovers whose love is destroyed by their families. Martin Salander returns like Odysseus. Yet each of these topoi is viewed in a new light, in a new setting, and is bound up in the dialectics of cultural change: hence they are original.

Preisendanz concludes that Keller is less concerned than his contemporaries with depicting human existence in the vertical and more concerned with the horizontal dimensions, meaning the broad epic. Tension, dynamism and humor arise from given situations and from the mediation between the inner and outer, rather than from the spiritual or intellectual depth of the characters (203). Keller thereby places greater weight upon the reciprocal relationship between man and society. Keller's poetic transformation has its foundations in the secrets of his double-edged humor, which creates a double world of constant tension between the internal poetic reality and concrete reality. Preisendanz hastens to add that we should not confuse Keller's double world with that of Jean Paul, Hoffmann or Tieck. For Keller, contrast is no longer a means to strive toward the transcendental, rather, poetic humor is that which embraces and envelops humanity. His specific humor mediates between the "Reichsunmittelbarkeit der Poesie" and the dialectic of cultural change, thus setting his humor apart from that of his nineteenth-century contemporaries.

Rudolf Wildbolz's anthropological approach (1964) attempts to view Keller's oeuvre holistically. Like Roffler (1931), Wildbolz reaffirms the timeless significance of Keller's works which project an image of man that remains an enduring possibility. Keller's fiction is filled with characters who must be unmasked, unveiled, before they can see reality. Some characters such as Martin Salander never do see the light. Martin is so caught up in his illusions that he cannot manage to grasp reality. Wildbolz shows how the eccentric behavior and actions of Keller's characters reveal their estrangement from reality and hence expose the illusions by which they live. The goal of life is to overcome the dangers of middle-class life; the key is not to be overly idealistic but rather to be reasonable and to set attainable goals. Wildbolz identifies six ways in which Keller's characters rescue themselves by becoming self aware and cognizant of reality. Some, such as Heinrich Lee or Wenzel Strapinski, turn to honest work, but Keller does not make the work ethic the alpha and omega of life; rather, it must be balanced with other aspects of life (81). Some characters are returned to reality when their dreams self-destruct. Still others find themselves when they fall in love, such as

Wilhelm, the schoolmaster, and Gritli. Wildbolz sees Keller's humor differently from Preisendanz. There is no healing effect; instead humor appears only after the crisis has been managed. Humor alleviates tension in life's crises in those characters, like Marie Salander and Salomon Landolt, who have by virtue of their reflection come to understand life.

Sociological studies of Keller began with Benjamin's essay in the late 1920s, and continued with Lukács's Marxist study from the late thirties. Roy Pascal's 1956 analysis of *Der grüne Heinrich* is also written from a leftist perspective. Michael Kaiser's *Literatursoziologische Studien zu Gottfried Kellers Dichtung* (1965) is perhaps the first book-length study of Keller's works from a sociological vantage point. Kaiser examines Keller's works in the context of the changing social, political, historical, and economic climate of the nineteenth century. Kaiser's thesis is that, because Keller's education was prematurely terminated, he became more acutely aware of the political and economic transformations than he would have been, had he completed his formal schooling (37). Keller's own family participated in the mass urban migration during the period of industrialization. Keller's father had viewed education as an opportunity to raise the general welfare of the masses, and Keller, like his father, also advocated advancement through education. As an autodidact, Keller firmly believed that ethical rigor would counter selfishness. While it was important to his sense of self-esteem to return from Berlin as an acknowledged and established author, he also wanted to return as a financially solvent one. Kaiser suggests that Keller's later resignation or "stiller Grundtrauer" (quiet melancholy) was due in part to his inability to realize this dream of becoming financially self-supporting until much later. Resignation is also attributed to his failure to become a respected dramatist as well as to his failure to secure domestic happiness.

Keller's reputation as the author of the *Der grüne Heinrich* did allow him to frequent the circles of the intellectual elite in Zurich, such as those that gathered at the Wesendonck home, where he was able to socialize with intellectuals such as the professor of aesthetics Friedrich Theodor Vischer, the Basel professor of art history Jakob Burckhardt, the professor of architecture Gottfried Semper, and the composer Richard Wagner. While these associations sustained and inspired him intellectually, they did not make him a breadwinner. Keller still wanted to live from the proceeds of his writing, but was forced to acknowledge that he would have to seek gainful employment outside the domain of literature, having unsuccessfully attempted numerous times to extract monthly honorariums for regularly submitted work. Keller even turned down several chances for a professorship, in part because he still harbored illusions of sustaining himself from his writing. Kaiser's insight into Keller's financial plight during the 1850s shows why he chose to apply for cantonal clerk. Perhaps more surprising was that he was hired for the position, since Alfred Escher, the statesman and independently wealthy railway tycoon, did not share Keller's political views. Nevertheless, Escher recognized Keller's abilities and offered him one of the highest salaries paid any civil employee in the canton of Zurich. Many of Keller's former political friends came to view him as an opportunist because he had accepted the post.

Kaiser's study provides a fine overview of Swiss liberalism in the years before 1848. Keller remained true to the liberalism of his youth long after it had outlived its time, which leads one to conclude that Keller's understanding of the social and economic forces in transition was lacking because he tended to focus on the ethical and ideal (52). Keller's inability to live from his writing was similarly due partially to his naiveté regarding the literary industry and due partially to his lack of understanding of industrialization. Keller underestimated the increasing economic weight of the middle-class, but he remained a proponent of the *Bildungsbürgertum*, that echelon of middle-class society interested in a classical education, a social group for which he wrote. Kaiser shows how Keller's personal relationship with Escher and the prevailing conditions in the second half of the nineteenth century influenced him enormously. Keller felt the sheer power and weight of Escher's personality, and was all the more aware of his own economic plight prior to assuming the cantonal position, yet he continued to maintain a faith in the role of the intelligentsia in building a democratic state which would lead ultimately to a completely egalitarian society. But Keller was also the alienated, isolated and ultimately powerless intellectual in an industrialized, materially driven society. All these conflicting thoughts, emotions and forces had an enormous impact upon Keller's fiction (72).

Kaiser provides keen insights into the literary industry of Keller's day and also shows how industrialization changed class structures. Indeed, historic and social change ultimately worked to Keller's advantage. That Keller could risk giving up his well paid cantonal position without a retirement pension to devote himself to writing, suggests either that the situation in the publishing industry had changed dramatically or that Keller was optimistically naive. Kaiser attributes the improved book market after 1870/71 to a combination of factors: 1) political stagnation following German unification; 2) the establishment of the *Deutsche Rundschau* in 1870; 3) increased literacy among the general populace, and, ironically 4) the rejection of naturalism in the 1880s by many readers of German, who only then discovered Keller. Keller's increased readership manifested itself in the spiraling sales and multiple editions of his works which appeared in that final decade of his life. Keller's readers consisted largely of upper class patricians in Switzerland and also of civil servants in Germany. Although his popularity grew, Keller's fiction did not sell nearly as well as that of his less literary-minded contemporaries. Nevertheless, Keller was able to live off the royalties from his publications during the last fifteen years of his life and thus realized what had seemed an unattainable dream during the 1850s.

Several studies were published in 1969 commemorating the 150th anniversary of Keller's birth. One such study is Hartmut Laufhütte's seminal book devoted to reality and art (*Wirklichkeit und Kunst*) in *Der grüne Heinrich*. This erudite work is obligatory reading for anyone interested in that first novel. There are no other works prior to this study that explore Keller's art and artistic craft as they relate to the mid-nineteenth-century Zeitgeist. Laufhütte traces the scholarship on *Der grüne Heinrich* in an exhaustive and thorough critical bibliography in the second chapter of his book (32–76), and explains that he chose *Der grüne Heinrich*, because it is the one work that preoccupied Keller for half of his life and therefore represents both his early and mature reflections on art and reality. Laufhütte is guided by a central question that also preoccupied Keller throughout his life: How is an author born after the age of classicism and romanticism to become an independent artist? How was a modern author to avoid becoming an epigone? Indeed, *Der grüne Heinrich* is a work of fermentation which reflects Keller's interaction with the cultural transformation of his time. The products of Classicism were neither able to speak to the issues of the modern age, nor could they address its changing values. Keller did not advocate a break with the past, but sought instead to establish a continuity with that past. His belief in humanity remained a guiding principle and part of that continuum coming out of Weimar Humanism. Laufhütte investigates the degree to which the dialectics of the "Kulturbewegung" influenced Keller's works of art and asks to what extent the "Streben nach Humanität" (striving towards humanity) was realized in Keller's novel. To accomplish this, he must determine how poetic reality is created.

According to Laufhütte, Keller neither saw himself as an epigone of Goethe nor as a romantic, though he respected Goethe and admired Jean Paul Richter. Instead he made it his mission as a writer to capture his own epoch in his fiction. A detailed study of *Der grüne Heinrich* demonstrates where Keller stood in his lifelong struggle with the classical heritage. Such an investigation reveals how he integrated this heritage with the social and artistic problems of his time. Laufhütte shows how Keller, by expanding his understanding of Goethe, formulated a philosophy of art uniquely his own, one that yielded singularly original poetic images of astonishing power.

Heinrich Lee experiences the relationship between life and art, which becomes an ongoing problem of his existence. Pursuing this dichotomy, Laufhütte provides a wonderful interpretation of Heinrich's reading of Goethe, which becomes the foundation for his understanding of the relationship between art and reality: Imagined reality, when transfigured by art becomes more realistic, more genuine, has more content. In the process of transformation, reality is reduced to its barest essentials and the observant reader becomes witness to an event that he would have missed in reality.

While this relationship between art and reality is important to Heinrich and to Keller, it poses a more universal aesthetic problem concerning how art is crafted. In this sense, Laufhütte suggests that Heinrich's Goethe-Reflections are the organizing principle of this novel, because they constitute the foundation for aesthetic appraisal and for the art of portrayal. In his conclusion, Laufhütte asserts that Keller's novel is something other than a *Künstlerroman* (artist's novel) or an *Entwicklungsroman* (developmental novel), that it is neither a Bildungsroman (novel of apprenticeship), nor an *Erziehungsroman* (educational novel); rather, he asserts that *Der grüne Heinrich*, without being didactic, provides a way of looking at the world, an entire philosophy of life, and so is a *Weltanschauungs-* or *Perspektivenroman* (novel that portrays a worldview or perspective). Laufhütte believes that the novel is the *Meisterstück* that preoccupied Keller throughout his life. He believes that, the synthesis between Goethe and Feuerbach, between the classic and the modern, while distancing the Romantic, constitutes Keller's singularly successful contribution to rescuing poesy in modernity. The resulting novel is an original that cannot be compared with any of the novels of German classicism, yet maintains a continuity with the heritage of Goethe.

In a lucid essay in Benno von Wiese's *Deutsche Dichter des 19. Jahrhunderts*, Wolfgang Preisendanz analyzes Keller's narrative technique and explains the role and function of Keller's unusual humor that set him apart from his contemporaries. Many readers refer to "der Charis, der Sonnenwärme" (love, warmth of the sun) when describing Keller's art. Nietzsche describes the emulation of happiness ("Nachahmung des Glücklichen"); Hauptmann refers to the "wundervolle Festivitas aller echten Kunstwerke" (marvelous celebrations of all true works of art); Benjamin the communicability of happiness ("die Mitteilbarkeit des Glückes"); and Bloch to not a reduction but rather an intensification of life ("das nichtreduzierte, sondern potenzierte Leben"). Preisendanz lends these descriptions additional credence by citing Keller himself who, at an early stage in his development, asserts that it was the task of the author, while remaining within the strictures of reality, to create a more beautiful world than the existing one. We may recall Keller's letter to Auerbach, in which he concedes that the author must show the reading public a stronger and more attractive image of themselves. These compliments then enable the author to scold them all the more where they need it most (*G.B.* III/2, 195). In other words, the golden abundance of the world ("der goldene Überfluß der Welt") does not originate in euphoria, rather it seeks to be perceived and recognized as a contradiction (Preisendanz, 1969, 442). Preisendanz's interpretation of Keller's narrative technique and humor shows the process by which Keller accomplishes this goal. The narrative perspective and mode set the stage for transforming objective into subjective and subjective into objective. Preisendanz cites Martini's statement that the narrative mode encompasses the real while simultaneously making the possible come true (Martini, 1962, 443). In contrast to Martini, however, Preisendanz sees in Keller's humor a vehicle not a reconciliation but of contact and understanding between the author and his public. In fact, Keller's humor complements realism; it is the bonding element between the tensions of imagination and experience, between poetic and bourgeois existence, between the play with what is possible and what is given or real. (Preisendanz, 451).

Preisendanz also rejects the hitherto held conviction that reduces Keller's humor merely to the reconciling force between the real and ideal in his writing. Instead, he sees in Keller's narrative style the stage on which the transformation of the objective into the subjective and the reverse takes place; in other words the narrative perspective and the narrative style register and design everyday reality while projecting a better world (443). Preisendanz agrees that Keller's *Erzähl-praxis* is a friendly mirror of the world. He cautions the reader not to confuse humor with irony, but rather suggests that humor is dependent upon the will of the reader to interact with the notion of reality being portrayed in the text. Preisendanz suggests that Keller's humor is much more than a lens. It acts as a bond, as an integrating force between the power of imagination (the author's and the reader's) and the reality depicted in the text. Keller does not view prose and poetry as estranged from one another, rather poetical reality is a dimension of the prosaic (450). Carl Spitteler once wrote in reference to Keller that humor is the poesy of prose (*Poesie der Prosa*). Preisendanz agrees that in Keller's works humor and realism are complementary, because humor acts as the bonding force that retains tension between imagination and experience, between artistic and middle-class existence. Preisendanz's interpretation transcends the cliché of Keller's fiction revealing the eye of the painter. More importantly, he contends that it is Keller's intention to depict reality by raising it to an aesthetic level, thereby lending it a multiplicity of shades and senses of meaning; in Keller's words the appearance (*Erscheinung*) and the occurring event (*das Geschehende*) must converge and become one. Often Keller will intensify his depiction by using outlandish comparisons that conjure up unusual, even grotesque images which rivet the reader's attention. The result is a depiction of reality that can still be read, understood, and appreciated today. Preisendanz proves his point with an example from *Der Schmied seines Glückes* (*S.W.* IV, 347).

The most extensive and thought-provoking study of Keller's early poetry and of his *Neue Gedichte* (1851) is Kaspar T. Locher's 1969 monograph, *Gottfried Keller — Der Weg zur Reife*, Locher shows how Keller used the poetic medium as a vessel for argumentation and reflection. Locher begins with Keller's earliest essays such as "Nacht auf der Uto" in which virtue is identified with naturalness which then is equated with beauty. Beauty is then defined as all that is good and truthful. Already at this early stage art carries the ethical obligation to ennoble man, to make him better serve society. Art should motivate us to question and to reflect, and should help us to spiritual freedom. Locher believes that, while Keller's artistic abilities made great strides in these years, his philosophy of life remained steadfast.

The early poems serve as a forum for problem-solving and for self-reflection. The poetry of the young Keller shows that he was against religious coercion, though it does at times become difficult to separate the anti-clerical from the political. Locher divides the early poems into two categories: those expressing self-doubt and others in which Keller attempts to persuade himself. Keller became a polemical poet in order to preserve his own faith in the goodness in the world (Locher, 1969, 66). Thus it is also difficult to separate the political poems from the apolitical, because Keller's involvement in the politics was also an escape from personal problems. Writing poetry was an act of self-preservation, a medium through which he sought to come to terms with himself and the world.

Locher shows how the personal concerns in the early poems give way in the *Neue Gedichte* (new poems) to broader concerns of humankind. This transformation parallels a similar trend in Keller's prose from the personal struggles in *Der grüne Heinrich* to the first Seldwyla novellas which reveal a transition in focus toward the larger problems confronting mankind. According to Locher, Keller believed that the artist must strive to achieve spiritual freedom (*Unbefangenheit*), purity, genuineness, and truth (72). Art must no longer be legitimized by direct experience, but rather the artist must transfigure the experience, thereby distancing himself from it. An artwork is genuine, when it pulsates with life and its beauty is not merely an empty vessel. Drawing on Keller's critical essays, Locher demonstrates how he came to focus on five concepts which he sought to achieve in himself and in his art: consciousness (*Bewußtheit*); prudence; moderation; presence of mind (*Besonnenheit*); and spiritual freedom (Unbefangenheit). Therefore, it is not surprising that Locher, along with Herbert Reichert, believes that, given Keller's own struggle for spiritual freedom prior to his encounter with Feuerbach, the philosopher merely served to confirm Keller's own carefully-reached and long-held convictions regarding immortality.[10] For Keller, achieving spiritual freedom meant relinquishing his hold on immortality. Most of the *Neue Gedichte* explore the concept and problem of achieving spiritual freedom. Locher's study shows that the poet's struggle for spiritual freedom did not go unfulfilled. Keller's ultimate objective is to maintain spiritual freedom and to liberate the reader's conscience from all partiality. The reader recognizes the distance the poet has achieved from his poetry and can take pleasure in the joy of story-telling itself (183). The resignation (*Entsagung*) which is so much a part of our impression of Keller's worldview is not an end but a beginning. Keller achieves a seldom recognized "joie de vivre" as a result of this resignation, a joy which counterbalances the much celebrated melancholy (*Grundtrauer*). Locher's study concludes by emphasizing that aesthetic form devoid of content meant little to Keller. His objective was to write poetry fulfilling the Horatian poetic axiom "delectare" and "prodesse": poetry that entertains and instructs.

---

[10] See also Herbert Reichert's *Basic Concepts in the Philosophy of Gottfried Keller* (Chapel Hill, NC: U of North Carolina P, 1949), in which he analyzes Keller's concept of freedom. Reichert's text is discussed in chapter 5 of this study.

Its seems appropriate to conclude this era of Keller scholarship with a slender but useful volume on Keller by Hermann Boeschenstein, a selective critical bibliography of Keller scholarship through 1969. It provides a brief biography of Keller that focuses on the most momentous crises in Keller's life and concludes with an extensive list of the Keller biographies. The second section is organized according to genre: the novels, the novella cycles, the legends and poetry. The most significant scholarly literature on each of the Seldwyla novellas is also reviewed. The final section of the critical bibliography is organized thematically. Boeschenstein lists the most important scholarship pertaining to such topics as Keller's humor, his position on Romanticism and Realism, and his philosophy of life. While this biography is now dated, it provides the newcomer to Keller with solid orientation.

Before turning to recent Keller scholarship in the final chapter, we shall turn to Keller scholarship in America and Britain.

Works Cited

Ackerknecht, Erwin. *Gottfried Keller*. Berlin-Lichterfelde: Widukind, 1937.

———. *Gottfried Keller. Geschichte seines Lebens*. Berlin and Leipzig: Insel, 1939.

Ackert, Ernst. *Gottfried Kellers Weltanschauung*. Bern: 1942.

Auerbach, Erich. *Mimesis. The Representation of Reality in Western Literature*. Trans. Willard R. Trask. Princeton: Princeton UP, 1969.

Benjamin, Walter. *Schriften*. Vol. 2. 284–96. Frankfurt am Main: Suhrkamp, 1955.

Boeschenstein, Hermann. *Gottfried Keller*. Stuttgart: Metzler, 1969.

Brahm, Otto. *Gottfried Keller. Ein literarisches Essay*. Berlin: Auerbach, 1883.

Brinkmann, Richard. *Wirklichkeit und Illusion*. Tübingen: Niemeyer, 1957.

Demeter, Hildegard. *Gottfried Kellers Humor*. Berlin: Ebering, 1938.

Demetz, Peter. "Zur Definition des Realismus." *Literatur und Kritik* 16–17 (1967), 333–45.

———. "Über die Fiktionen des Realismus." *Neue Rundschau* 4 (1977), 554–67.

Ermatinger, Emil. *Gottfried Kellers Leben, Briefe und Tagebücher*. Vol. 3, 397. Stuttgart and Berlin: J. G Cotta, 1919.

Fränkel, Jonas. *Dichtung und Wissenschaft*. 84–194. Heidelberg: Lambert Schneider, 1954.

———. *Gottfried Kellers politische Sendung*. Zurich: Oprecht, 1939.

Frye, Northrup. *Anatomy of Criticism*. Princeton: Princeton UP, 1957.

Helbling, Carl. "Gottfried Keller in seinen Briefen." *Jahresbericht der Gottfried Keller Gesellschaft* (1938): 3–14.

Heselhaus, Clemens. Afterword, *Gottfried Keller Sämtliche Werke und Ausgewählte Briefe*, vol. 3. 1315–41. Darmstadt: Wissenschaftliche Buchgesellschaft, 1963.

Hesse, Hermann. *Eine Literaturgeschichte in Rezensionen und Aufsätzen*. Vol. 2, 293–98, ed. Volker Michels. Frankfurt am Main: Suhrkamp, 1972.

Hofmannsthal, Hugo von. "Unterhaltung über die Schriften von Gottfried Keller." *Gesammelte Werke*. Vol. 2, 266–75. Berlin: S. Fischer, 1924.

Hunziker, Fritz. "Gottfried Keller und Zurich." *Jahresbericht der Gottfried Keller-Gesellschaft*. Zurich: Gottfried Keller-Gesellschaft, 1932.

Jahresbericht der Gottfried Keller Gesellschaft 9 (1940), 16.

Jahresbericht der Gottfried Keller Gesellschaft 25 (1983), 25.

Kaiser, Michael. *Literatursoziologische Studien zu Gottfried Kellers Dichtung*. Bonn: Bouvier, 1965.

Keller, Gottfried. *Gesammelte Briefe*. Ed. Carl Helbling. Bern: Benteli, 1950–54

——. *Gesammelte Werke*. 10 vols. Berlin: Wilhelm Hertz, 1889.

——. *Gottfried Kellers Werke*. 6 vols. Ed. Harry Maync. Berlin: Propyläen-Verlag, 1921–23.

——. *Gottfried Kellers Werke*. Kritisch-historische und erläuterte Ausgabe. 8 vols. Ed. Max Nußberger. Leipzig: Bibliographisches Institut, 1921.

——. *Gottfried Kellers Werke*. 5 vols. Max Zollinger. Berlin: Deutsches Verlaghaus Bong & Co., 1936.

——. *Sämtliche Werke*. Eds. Jonas Fränkel and Carl Helbling. Erlenbach/Zurich: Rentsch, 1926–48.

——. *Sämtliche Werke und ausgewählte Briefe*. 3 vols. Ed. Clemens Heselhaus. Munich: Carl Hanser, 1958.

——. *Sämtliche Werke*. 7 vols. Eds. Thomas Böning, Gerhard Kaiser, Kai Kauffmann, Dominik Müller and Peter Villwoch. Frankfurt am Main: Deutscher Klassiker Verlag, 1985–96.

Laufhütte, Hartmut. *Wirklichkeit und Kunst in Gottfried Kellers Roman* Der Grüne Heinrich. Bonn: Bouvier, 1969.

Locher, Kaspar T. *Gottfried Keller. Der Weg zur Reife*. Bern: Francke, 1969.

Lukács, Georg. "Gottfried Keller." In *Deutsche Realisten des 19. Jahrhunderts*. 147–230. 1946; rpt. Berlin: Aufbau, 1952.

Martini, Fritz. *Deutsche Literatur im bürgerlichen Realismus*. 557–610. Stuttgart: J. B. Metzler, 1962.

Preisendanz, Wolfgang. "Gottfried Keller." *Deutsche Dichter des 19. Jahrhunderts*. Ed. Benno von Wiese. 440–62. Berlin: Erich Schmidt Verlag, 1969.

——. *Humor als dichterische Einbildungskraft. Studien zur Erzählkunst des poetischen Realismus*. Munich: Eidos, 1963.

——. "Die Keller-Forschung der Jahre 1939–1957." *Germanisch-Romanische Monatsschrift* 39 (1958): 144–78.

——. *Wege des Realismus*. 104–203. Munich: Wilhelm Fink, 1977.

Roffler, Thomas. *Gottfried Keller. Ein Bildnis*. Frauenfeld: Huber, 1931.

Sammons, Jeffrey. *The Shifting Fortunes of Wilhelm Raabe*. Columbia, SC: Camden House, 1992.

Schaffner, Paul. "Gottfried Keller als Malerdichter." *Jahresbericht der Gottfried Keller-Gesellschaft* (1936): 3–14.

——. *Gottfried Keller als Maler*. Zurich: Atlantis, 1942.

Staiger, Emil. "Gottfried Keller und die Romantik." *Jahresbericht der Gottfried Keller-Gesellschaft* (1937): 3–11.

——. "Die ruhende Zeit." *Die Zeit als Einbildungskraft des Dichters. Untersuchungen zu Gedichten von Brentano, Goethe und Keller*. 159–210. Zurich: Atlantis, 1939. (2nd printing: 1953, 161–221).

Whalley, George. *Studies in Literature and the Humanities: Innocence of Intent.* Kingston and Montreal: McGill-Queens UP, 1985.

Wiese, Benno von. "Gottfried Keller— Kleider Machen Leute." In *Die Deutsche Novelle.* Vol. 1, 238–49. Düsseldorf: August Bagel, 1956.

Wildbolz, Rudolf. *Gottfried Kellers Menschenbild.* Bern & Munich: Francke, 1964.

Zäch, Alfred. *Gottfried Keller im Spiegel seiner Zeit. Urteile und Berichte über den Menschen und Dichter.* Zurich: Sientia, 1952.

Zollinger-Wells, W. *Gottfried Kellers Religiosität.* Zurich: Artemis, 1954.

5: The Anglo-American Perspective

ANGLO-AMERICAN SCHOLARSHIP ON Keller emanates from a methodo-logical tradition different both in its focus and ultimately in its purpose from the German criticism. Whereas both traditions seek to illuminate and ultimately to refine appraisals and our understanding of given literary works, the Anglo-American tradition additionally seeks to acquaint non-German readers with authors writing in German. Moreover, Anglo-American critics (both Germanists and Comparatists) view Keller's works through their own heritage and may even compare his works with American and British as well as other German authors or use other critical approaches. Because they come from an entirely different background, many non-native German readers are liberated from the cultural baggage which burdens native German speakers, thus often allowing them fresh insights that lead to new critical interpretations. This perspective enables Anglo-American literary historians to contribute broadly to German scholarship. The scholarly efforts of Americans, British, Canadians, and many other members of the Commonwealth have established a substantial presence in Keller scholarship both before and particularly after the Second World War.

Gottfried Keller has fared better in Anglo-American scholarly circles than most other nineteenth-century German realists. His stories, such as *Kleider Machen Leute*, were published in English already in 1876 under the title *Clothes Make the Man* and were discussed during the 1880s in British and American journals (Mullen, 30). One respected critic who dealt with Keller's works was Helen Zimmern, who was known for her articles on art and literature which appeared in British, American, German, and Italian journals. She commanded respect in England for her biographies of Lessing and Schopenhauer, and became known as a translator of Nietzsche. Zimmern frequented the London circle of Ferdinand Freiligrath, Keller's trusted old friend, and was thus introduced by Freiligrath to Keller's works.[1] Zimmern published the first essay in English on Gottfried Keller in 1880. The eighteen page essay entitled "A Swiss Novelist" appeared in *Frazer's Magazine* (London) and was reprinted in *Appleton's Journal* and by *Litwell's Living Age* later that same year. The essay introduces Keller and his works, and laments that he is so little known among English readers. Her article concentrates on the 1855 edition of *Der grüne Heinrich* and on several of

---

[1] Zimmern was introduced to Keller in a letter from Ida Freiligrath and Zimmern subsequently corresponded with him (*G.B.* II, 350). Freiligrath wrote to Keller on July 11, 1979; Keller responded on July 13.

Keller's novellas from *Die Leute von Seldwyla*. *Der grüne Heinrich* is described as "a strange work, full of glaring faults of construction, capricious, unequal, an incongruous medley, which nevertheless contains so many beauties that we cannot lay it down unsatisfied, ... it is full of that ineffable youthful fire of a first effort . . . . " (461). She also acknowledges the psychological purport of the novel which she interprets as a serious character study of an artistic soul. Keller wanted Zimmern to discuss the second edition which she agreed to do in a separate article, which was published anonymously in the *Spectator* (G.B. II, 357).[2] Zimmern agrees with German literary historians that the unified narrative structure lends greater harmony to the novel as a whole. Surprising is her reluctance to discuss the deletion of the bathing scene that so many Europeans scholars criticized. She finds the Dortchen episode crudely presented and offensive to one's ethical and artistic sensitivities. She also finds the new edition to be even more shapeless than the original, despite the unified narrative structure, a shapelessness she attributes to the influence of Goethe's *Wilhelm Meister*, which results in a novel lacking in artistic form, a serious flaw that "infests" German novels. She believes the new conclusion to be an improvement over the original, less crude and roughly hewn. Zimmern attributes the clarity in Keller's writing to his Swissness and to his familiarity with the Swiss countryside. However, she comments that Keller's stories grow vague and indistinct as soon as he leaves the Swiss setting where he is concrete, observant, and humorously original. Zimmern had also mentioned in her earlier article that Keller's "most marked characteristic consists in his being a Switzer of the Swiss." Keller took umbrage to this statement in a letter to Ida Freiligrath, for he did not believe in a Swiss national literature (*G.B.* II, 350–51). It is hardly surprising, given the enthusiastic reception of the novellas in Europe, that Zimmern was particularly enamored by the Seldwyla stories and was one of the first in the English-speaking world to acknowledge the pre-eminence of *Romeo und Julia auf dem Dorfe* among Keller's works. Despite this enthusiastic publicity, Keller's work remained little known on the American scene outside of German-speaking circles, because of the paucity of English translations, a lamentable situation that to a degree still persists today.

John George Robertson (1867–1933) was professor of German language and literature at the University of London from 1903 until 1933. Under his leadership the University of London became the center of German studies in England. Robertson's *History of German Literature* (1902) presented the first complete portrayal óf Keller in a German literary history written in English. Hardly anyone took note of Keller in the English-speaking world prior to Rob-

---

[2] Waltraud Kolb has found that the style and repetition of key words of this article are characteristic of Zimmern's writing (42). Her 1992 book is an in-depth study of Gottfried Keller's reception in the English-speaking world until 1920. I am indebted to her thoroughness for a number of obscure, but important references to Keller. Her book will be discussed in greater detail in chapter six.

ertson's literary history. Indeed, most earlier books on the subject concluded their overview of German literary history with Goethe and Schiller. Robertson, a Goethe and Lessing scholar, recognized Keller's stature and refers to him as the "master novelist" of the period. Robertson prefaces his discussion of Keller with a brief biography based on Brahm's and Baechtold's studies, before moving on to discuss the individual works. *Der grüne Heinrich* is "rich in imaginative charm" and is compared to Novalis's *Heinrich von Ofterdingen* "in a realistic nineteenth century setting." Robertson suggests that this novel has many of the faults of the Romantic novels, but that these are "more than atoned for by its vividness as a confession in Goethe's sense" (Robertson, 1902, 484). In fact, Robertson suggests that Keller was the last descendant of the German romantic tradition and *Der grüne Heinrich* was the end or even the "culmination" of the German Bildungsroman. His entry on Keller includes an excerpt from the introduction to *Die Leute von Seldwyla* and he summarizes at length *Romeo und Julia auf dem Dorfe* which he considered to be a fine example of Keller's work, though he considered *Der Landvogt von Greifensee* to be Keller's best work and agrees with most the German critics that *Martin Salander* is a prosaic and uninspired novel about Swiss life.. While Keller is the master of the Novella his forms and the proportion of his stories leave much to be desired. Robertson believes that it is "the personality behind his writing that fascinates us; above all, his genial and never-failing humour" (485). Robertson felt that Keller enjoyed limited popularity beyond German-speaking borders and sensed it would remain for future generations to recognize his greatness. Nevertheless, by dedicating four pages to Keller, as compared with only one page to Fontane and Storm, the Swiss author was awarded prominence and recognition for the first time in British German studies. We will turn later to a much more extensive article on Keller by Robertson which was published posthumously in 1935.

John F. Coar's *Studies in German Literature in the Nineteenth Century* (1903) suggests that Keller would never have been able to formulate the "happy solution of the real and ideal" in his writing, if it had not been for the intellectual freedom of Swiss democracy. Coar's objective was to explore the influence of the Swiss democratic ideals upon Keller's writing, without overlooking the line between the political nature of Keller's Swiss patriotism and literary aspect of his German linguistic prowess. He views Keller as a great German rather than Swiss author, a position which Keller would have appreciated. Coar sees in *Martin Salander* — which he evaluates favorably — the first novel, in which Keller moves away from individual self-absorption to focus on the role of the individual in society. Though Coar's point carries weight, one should not overlook that the same theme of the individual responsibility to society is prevalent in the Seldwyla stories and in the revised (1880) edition of *Der grüne Heinrich*.

In his 1909 book *A History of German Literature*, Calvin Thomas, professor of German at Columbia University, refers to Keller as the "wizard story-teller of

Zürich" whose works are "the very best reading to be found in the whole range of nineteenth-century German fiction" (364). Thomas agrees that Keller was little known even in Germany until about a decade before his death. By the time of Thomas's writing there is a library of books about Keller and he is universally "considered a fixed star of high magnitude." Thomas refers to Keller as "a romantic realist with the soul of a poet, the eye of a man of science, and the temperament of an artist who loves life in all its manifestations" (365). Thomas observes in Keller a didactic moralist in the tradition of Goethe. In fact, he considers Keller to be the greatest German writer since Goethe. According to Thomas, it was Keller's mission to humor his countrymen with descriptions of themselves, so as to enable them to work toward bettering themselves with the aim of "furthering them toward higher ideals of communal life" (365). Thomas correctly acknowledges that Keller tempers his didacticism with humor and offers "not medicine but food — the nourishment of sane and delightful art"(365).

The Canadian Edward Hauch first read Keller as an undergraduate in Toronto. Later, as a graduate student at Columbia under the guidance of Calvin Thomas, he wrote his dissertation and published the often cited study: *Gottfried Keller as a Democratic Idealist* (1916). After discussing various democratic tendencies in nineteenth-century German literature, Hauch reserves for Keller a significant place in the canon of nineteenth-century German literature. Hauch's study is significant for two reasons: First, it is testimony to the fact that Keller had become a canonical author as early as 1916, and was recognized as such even in the United States. Second, it is the first extensive scholarly study of Keller's life and works produced by a North American. Hauch recognizes that three currents of nineteenth-century thought — the romantic, the propagandist, and the realistic — are all represented in and flow simultaneously through Keller's works, but rather he intends to show "more clearly the development of his democratic thinking, and to define and outline his own peculiar type of democratic idealism in its various aspects" as reflected in both his life and works (4). In the first chapter, Hauch discusses Keller's political awakening during the 1840s, his political involvement as reflected in his early poetry and in his activities leading up to the Sonderbund War of 1847. While acknowledging the radical anti-clerical bent of those early poems, Hauch remarks that the *Neuere Gedichte* (1851) already show markedly fewer poems of a "pronounced political tendency." Indeed Hauch demonstrates that Keller quickly developed a strong dislike for extremism. Hauch's study brings some new documentation to light which elucidates Keller's political stance during his years as cantonal clerk and includes discussions of such patriotic pieces as *Das Fähnlein der Sieben Aufrechten* and the essay "Am Mythenstein" which demand that a nation "no matter how well constituted, exists not merely for its own sake, but also for the sake of the good it can do to humanity" (28). The political optimism espoused in *Das Fähnlein* is vastly different from the pessimistic reality of such works as *Das verlorene Lachen*. The difference in tone of these two stories reflects the constitutional changes, the stormy political scenes and ferment in Zurich that Keller witnessed as cantonal clerk. Keller was a staunch supporter of representative democracy, and believed that direct democracy, with its referenda and people's initiatives, was too slow paced to be efficient. Likewise, Keller did not encourage the emancipation of women to the extent that they become directly involved in the political arena which, he believed, belonged to the province of men. Hauch suggests that Frau Regel Amrain's political and civic education of her son was Keller's conception of the proper degree of political involvement for women. Hauch reads *Martin Salander* as a warning against the abuses that the most liberal kind of democratic institutions foster. Increased direct participation in the affairs of government had not achieved a proportionate increase in democratic egalitarianism in Switzerland; quite to the contrary, it encouraged ambition and social aspiration or "Strebertum," which Keller detested. Hauch is the first literary historian to explore in detail the process of writing *Martin Salander* and, as a result came to appreciate Keller's faith in the capacity of the people to work out their own social and political destiny. He shows in this last novel, how Keller raised a voice against all those, who would use politics as a means of acquiring wealth and fame. It is not surprising that Keller planned to oppose the "travesty of democratic thinking" inherent in *Martin Salander* in the proposed sequel, "Arnold Salander"; Keller planned to create a political environment, in which "a guarantee to all of the opportunity to work out their own individual destiny in private well-being, and in harmony with the interests of the community at large" would be realized (38). In contrast to many European critics, Hauch does not detect in *Martin Salander* any marked break in style with earlier works, and he finds Keller's inextinguishable optimism ever present.

Keller's romantic tendencies stem neither from close association with representatives of German romanticism, nor from his readings, but rather from his uncommon and vivid imagination (40). Hauch points to many characteristics in Keller's works that he associates with romanticism. Keller's early propensity to question immortality, his radical political bent against the Jesuits, and his plea for intellectual liberty in religious matters all led him down the path toward realism. Keller rigorously applied his theories of democracy to his views on religion, and insisted on "mutual helpfulness as the essence of true religion" (56). As Reichert would later do, Hauch argues that Feuerbach did not radically change the way Keller viewed the world, but merely reaffirmed existing ideas by providing Keller with an organized system that would accommodate them.

The move toward realism was reinforced by Keller's growing belief that man must serve humanity throughout his life and work (*G.B.* I, 354). Hauch agrees with a host of earlier German literary historians that the original Heinrich Lee must die, because he has failed to care properly for the most precious social unit, his immediate family. Heinrich, in the revised edition, survives because he begins serving society. Heredity, life's experience, and education all play an important role in helping Keller's characters establish this relationship of service to society. Hauch comments that Keller turned first to the study of history to broaden his knowledge. It is hardly a coincidence that Arnold Salander studies history as a means of understanding broader political, social, and economic events. Hauch then compares Pestalozzi's theories of education as espoused in *Lienhard und Gertrud* with Keller's, observing that Pestalozzi included a program of vocational training which emphasized building strong character as a goal of that educational process. Keller, on the other hand, makes character development a prerequisite for all that follows, so that the actual life work may be "more honestly and effectively attacked" (77).[3] Keller's fiction provides us with numerous examples of his belief. In the *Die drei gerechten Kammacher*, for example, one sees where the vocational training can lead when the trainees are devoid of substantive character. The two prosperous peasants in *Romeo und Julia auf dem Dorfe* both know their business, but lack character and are without scruples. Hauch sees in Keller's democratic aims for education two equally important and inter-connected goals: first, the development of the individual for his own sake, second, the development of an individual who will further society (80). Society should expect a properly educated individual to be a humane citizen capable of caring for himself, but also "moral and mentally equipped" to be of service to mankind (82). Likewise, the artist was also obliged to serve society with his art. Keller's admiration for Schiller expressed in the essay "Am Mythenstein" thus hardly comes as a surprise. Though Hauch places Keller in the tradition of Pestalozzi, Gotthelf, and Auerbach, Keller surpassed them, because he was endowed with a greater sense of humor, and shows rather than tells his reader what they ought to think or believe. This is an important observation, but Hauch does not develop it. Keller's art is organic; it hails from life and in turn, acts with vitality upon life, thereby serving mankind. Keller's works exhibit "a sobered and enlightened democracy with sane and sound idealism." Hauch's book is a well wrought, thorough investigation of Keller's democratic thinking, bringing forth new ideas based on information and documentation not readily available to U. S. scholars in 1915, and represents the first extensive scholarly study of Keller in North America.

In 1911, William H. Faulkner read a paper on Keller at the University of Virginia. It was subsequently published in the Humanistic Section of the *Virginia University Philological Society Bulletin* (1912), and bears the title "Keller's *Der grüne Heinrich*. Anna and Judith and Their Predecessors in Rousseau's *Confessions*." Faulkner argues that Heinrich's two simultaneous loves, for Judith and

---

[3] Heinrich Pestalozzi, *Lienhard und Gertrud*, a four volume work, was originally published in 1781 and 1783. It embodies in a barely disguised fictional form Pestalozzi's education ideals. Pestalozzi was one of Switzerland's great educators and a tireless advocate for the poor.

Anna, are unusual and could not possibly have evolved out of Keller's own experience. While Keller suggested that nothing in this first novel was not personally experienced, he later admitted in a letter to his sister that there is much that is made up in the novel, especially Heinrich's love for two women. It is also widely accepted that Henriette Keller, Keller's cousin, who died at age twenty and to whom he dedicated the poem "Das Grab am Zürichsee," was his real-life love and became the model for Heinrich Lee's Anna. Faulkner structures his argument upon Varnhagen von Ense's comment that there is a breath of Rousseau in *Der grüne Heinrich*, a comment which Keller later confirmed in his autobiographical notes. Indeed, Keller was reading autobiographies before and during his writing of his first novel, and he certainly knew Rousseau's *Confessions*. Faulkner discovered in Rousseau's experience as related in the *Confessions* simultaneous loves that the twelve-year-old Jean-Jacques experienced with Mademoiselle de Vulson and la petite Mademoiselle Goton. Faulkner's study of Rousseau's episodes led him to suggest that they might be the model upon which Heinrich's love for Anna and Judith is based. Anna and Judith resemble la petite Mademoiselle Goton and Mademoiselle de Vulson both in appearance and in age. Jean-Jacques and Heinrich Lee experience their respective double loves at the same age. Rousseau's love affair lasted only one year, but Keller's vivid imagination embellished and dramatized this framework substantially. Heinrich's love for both women covers some five years, and Keller provides a much more richly developed account of Heinrich's passion and guilt than is portrayed by Rousseau. Faulkner attempts to show that Keller appropriated ideas from Rousseau, to whom he is indebted in part for the inspiration of this double love.[4] This study is one of the first attempts by an American scholar to do a comparative study of this nature on Keller's works.

In 1920 the British journalist, Marie Hay, published a popular book on Gottfried Keller, in which she emphasizes that Keller is essentially Swiss as opposed to being German, an assertion that may well have been a reflection of the postwar political climate. She portrays Keller's life, punctuated by short discussions of his stories and many anecdotes. The tone of the monograph is chatty and brings nothing new of scholarly or critical purport to light. Hay possessed an unusual sense of what was important. She dedicates an appropriate amount of space to discuss the two editions of *Der grüne Heinrich*, then goes on at length about *Hadlaub* and scarcely treats other more significant works such as *Romeo und Julia auf dem Dorfe*. The book is also marred by inexactitudes and by typographical errors. But to her credit, Hay's is the first book on Keller written in English for a general audience.

---

[4]   In chapter 4 of *Art and Influence of Jean-Jacques Rousseau* (1973), Mark J. Tremmer compares the *Confessions* with *Der Grüne Heinrich*, greatly expanding Faulkner's initial inquiry.

J. G. Robertson's *Essays And Addresses On Literature*, published posthumously in 1935, also contains an essay on Keller. Robertson describes Keller's *Grüner Heinrich* as a "huge, formless, badly proportioned novel, with its irrelevant episodes and often distracting aimlessness," which is the "Dichtung und Wahrheit" of Keller's life, recalling the Goethean tradition that Otto Brahm had long before recognized in Keller's novel; Robertson's essay anticipates Gerhard Kaiser's psychological study, *Gottfried Keller, Das Gedichtete Leben*, published a half a century later (1981). Keller's novel belongs to the grand tradition of the eighteenth-century German Bildungsroman, and Robertson feels that its hero is subjected to a sentimental education in the spirit of Schiller or Sterne. This line of novels, which traces the development of a soul in search of its mission in life, begins with Wieland's *Agathon* and reaches its apex with *Wilhelm Meisters Lehrjahre*. The romantic movement pursued this type of fiction with a long line of "fragmented soul-histories" exemplified by *Franz Sternbalds Wanderungen* and *Heinrich von Ofterdingen*. Robertson includes Keller's novel in this line, lauding Heinrich Lee's tale of his youth, but finding the chapters devoted to Lee's life in Munich a "dull chronicle," commenting that, what should have been more interesting to the reader becomes drudgery, because Keller failed to communicate in prose his experience as an artist in Munich.

Although Robertson acknowledges Jean Paul Richter's early influence on Keller, he believes that Keller's enthusiasm for Richter was short-lived (1935, 71). He cautions that it is misleading to seek similarity between Richter's and Keller's humor, suggesting that Richter's was a combination of the grotesque in the tradition of Rabelais and of sentimental irony in the tradition of Sterne. Keller's humor lay "in the sunny geniality of his outlook on life" and in the "kindly sympathy" he bestows upon the world he creates (72). Keller's *Grüner Heinrich* was first influenced by the author's struggle with his own religious beliefs and, second, by his attempt to work his way through two traditions: the aesthetic education of German Romanticism and the Swiss pedagogical emphasis on a practical vocation. Robertson places Keller on the threshold of transition between the spiritual other-worldliness of Romanticism and the realities of science and industrialization. Robertson makes the astute observation, that Heinrich Lee is "shipwrecked on the ideal he fails to attain," suggesting that "he comes to grief, because the Romantic world in which he had striven to make himself a denizen, had itself passed away before his apprenticeship was at an end" (74). For Robertson, Keller's *Grüner Heinrich* is the last, the "fullest and richest" of all the romantic novels and that, furthermore, it stands on the threshold of a modern world.

Robertson's reception of the first volume of the Seldwyla novellas is complimentary. He declares *Romeo und Julia auf dem Dorfe* to be perhaps the finest novella in German literature describing peasant life. On the topic of the black fiddler Robertson agrees with Brahm that the figure is a remnant of E. T. A.

Hoffmann, out of keeping with the realism of the novella, a last vestige of romanticism. Keller is the legitimate successor to Jeremias Gotthelf, the first European master of the "peasant novel." Keller's realism concentrates only on essential details. Robertson refers to this realism as the essentially national element in Keller's work, and refers to the romanticism as "only the German literary varnish" (78). Robertson is less enamored with the second volume of Seldwyla stories. While he praises the originality of *Kleider Machen Leute*, he laments the relatively poor reception of *Die mißbrauchten Liebesbriefe* and classifies *Das verlorene Lachen* as a mere forerunner of *Martin Salander*.

Of the *Züricher Novellen*, Robertson hails *Der Landvogt von Greifensee* as one of Keller's greatest achievements, because he takes the spare facts of a real biography and embellishes them with his own experience and imagination. Robertson finds *Ursula*, despite its unsatisfactory conclusion, to be the best of Keller's purely historical fiction. He praises the "beauty and delicacy" of the *Sieben Legenden*, and lauds the "genial harmony" which he calls "that most precious quality of Keller's mind" (84). Robertson was surprisingly less enchanted by *Das Sinngedicht*, which he believed had an artificiality that estranged it from reality. Robertson criticizes the cycle of stories as too exotic, having little of that personal empathy that makes the Seldwyla stories so compelling. Yet, he refers to the artificial romantic conclusion as "delightful." Robertson confesses that the foreign reader may find it difficult to have any real sympathy for *Martin Salander*, and blames the bankruptcy of Swiss liberalism in 1869 for Keller's dismal outlook in this final novel. It is surprising that an English scholar of Robertson's renown, should fail to understand Keller's objectives in *Das verlorene Lachen* and again in *Martin Salander*. It is accepted that both these works contain far less poetry, but they do reflect the monumental social and economic transitions that Keller witnessed during his life. He calls Keller the "greatest colorist" among the writers of novellas. What Keller had failed to put on canvas he had expressed in "pristine freshness" in his writings. Comparing Keller to his famous friend and countryman, Arnold Böcklin, Robertson writes that both men "possessed the power of captivating the modern mind, in spite of its leanings toward a drabber naturalism; both form a bulwark of the romantic spirit in Europe in an unromantic age" (88) Robertson does however admire Keller's ability to stand in the materially-minded present, to recognize the aspirations and transitions of his own time, and to wrestle with the spirit of the past and "conquer it anew" for his contemporaries.

Charles Zippermann's bibliography (1935) offers a comprehensive if uncritical view of all the literature on Gottfried Keller through the end of 1934. Zippermann lists everything that has ever been written on or by Keller, and incorporates Baechtold's original *Gottfried-Keller-Bibliographie* (1844–1897), as well as Bayard Quincy Morgan's Keller bibliography (part of Morgan's *Bibliography of German Literature in English Translation*).

Keller's penchant for composing cycles of stories and poems has secured him a unique place among his European contemporaries. Priscilla Kramer investigates Keller's predilection for novella-cycles in her carefully wrought study, *The Cyclical Method of Composition in Gottfried Keller's Sinngedicht* (1939). She applies the term cycle in the strictest form as "a course of operations returning into itself" and suggests that this definition separates the *Sinngedicht* from Keller's other novella series such as *Die Leute von Seldwyla* or the *Züricher Novellen*, tales that share a common frame but are not intrinsically intertwined. Rather, in the *Sinngedicht*, Keller leads his readers along a spiral route around a central idea, which is embodied in Logau's epigram.[5] While this idea is neither fully revealed nor realized until the cycle has been completed, it is implicit in the epigram: the suggestion that an idea is unfolded by degrees through the process of story-telling until a complete, unified, and radiant personality is achieved. For Kramer, the insistence on simultaneous blushing and laughter in response to a kiss suggests cooperation between the senses and the spirit. This duality in every human being is paralleled by the duality of sex. Kramer suggests that if women are more sensitive than men, and that men are more spirited than women, then harmonizing this feminine and masculine duality would reconcile the conflict, thereby leading to the ideal human being. The realization of this epigram thus embodies Keller's conception of ideal humanity. The courtship, which does not begin consciously between Lucie and Reinhart, progresses through several stages of dueling in the form of story-telling that temper and thereby cultivate their individual personalities until a degree of harmony is achieved, making an ideal marriage between the two possible.

Kramer's study renders a sophisticated interpretation of the whole. Six of thirteen titled chapters are separate stories told by either Lucie, Reinhart, or the uncle, yet as Kramer reveals, each inset story is a stage in the progress of the main story. While most of the subsidiary stories are negative, they shed positive light upon the main story; both Lucie and Reinhart develop and mature until they can solve the problem posed by the epigram. Reinhart was initially dismayed to discover that the scientist in him had come to dominate his personality; he had lost contact with all that was purely human. Thus Reinhart sets out to test the epigram (not to seek a spouse) and eventually encounters Lucie. Lucie is a strong willed scholar in her own right, who has been emotionally hurt and subsequently hardened by events in her past; therefore, she vows to nurture her intellectual abilities so as to stand independently. Reinhart is initially put off by

[5] Friedrich von Logau (1604–1655) was one of the greatest of the seventeenth-century German epigrammatists. The epigram that forms the centerpiece of Keller's *Sinngedicht*, and from which its action proceeds, reads: "Wie willst du weiße Lilien zu roten Rosen machen? Küß eine weiße Galathee: sie wird errötend lachen" (How will one transform white lilies into red roses? Kiss a white Galatea [nymph]: she will blush while laughing). Gottfried Keller, *Das Sinngedicht* (Frankfurt am Main: Deutscher Klassiker Verlag, 1991) vol. VI, 100.

Lucie's bluestocking qualities. She likewise rejects his initial conception of marriage as little more than amiable companionship. Lucie is very much aware that Reinhart's stories imply a critique of her personality. The epigram becomes for Reinhart the precise formula for the perfect woman: she must possess the freedom of spirit to laugh and must be sufficiently in touch with her feelings and instincts to be able to blush. If by laughing she shows herself to be a human being, by blushing she proves that she is capable of womanly feeling. While the epigram applies primarily to women, its implications for men become clear. The man is more inclined to laugh, whereas the woman is more inclined to blush, but each must possess the capacity to do both. This exchange of stories in the *Sinngedicht*, centered around Logau's epigram, becomes Reinhart's and Lucie's education for marriage. By reacting to one another's stories, each individual personality transforms him/herself. Lucie loosens her grip on the conventions of her day and retreats a little from her fiercely won independence; she learns to laugh. Reinhart learns to become more sensitive. He has learned to blush. Both individuals have achieved a greater, more well rounded degree of humanity, which makes their union a more ideal marriage.

On a larger scale Kramer sees the *Sinngedicht* as tantamount to an exposition of the proper relations between the sexes; one which emphasizes their interdependence (43). On another level Kramer explores the social problems that permeate the work and are connected to nature and culture. Influenced by Feuerbach, Keller believed that nature is truly moral. Lucie and Reinhart represent both worlds: the inherently moral nature and the consciously moral world of culture. Initially Reinhart possesses too much natural freedom; Lucie teaches him greater respect for the world of conventional morality. Reciprocally, Lucie is imprisoned by her conventional morality; Reinhart enables her to achieve a greater degree of freedom to allow for the development of the natural, which she is inclined to suppress (72). The objective of marriage becomes the development of the personality in its dual forms, both feminine and masculine. Logau, Kramer suggests, has guided both Lucie and Reinhart through his epigram toward the light of a more perfect humanity. The enlightenment of Lucie and Reinhart is the process through which they acquire a complete, unified, and radiant personality. This personality embodies the achievement of self-awareness of a vivid consciousness and of the power to estimate things according to their essential values as well as to view them in the proper perspective (80). Kramer embellishes this ideal personality with the ability to blush and to laugh, combined with the radiance derived from self-knowledge and consequent self-control. The laugh represents the freedom of spirit and the blush reveals the recognition of the senses; both must be simultaneous, so that they testify to a perfect balance of qualities. The epigram thus implies a definition of a perfect humanity composed alone of the harmony of the spirit and of the senses. Education toward a more refined humanity, we will recall, was Keller's objective, and remains the most sacred duty of mankind — man must continually seek his higher self. Therefore Lucie's and Reinhart's enlightenment constitutes a stage in this self-knowledge and hence progress toward a greater humanity. In discovering each other, they find themselves, echoing Goethe's "Werde, was du bist." Kramer clearly and eruditely demonstrates how the complex cyclical structure of the *Sinngedicht*, Keller's most refined artistic achievement, leads the reader and the two main characters through a spiral round about an epigram to an understanding of just how they and mankind can achieve an ever more refined form of humanity.

Herbert W. Reichert's *Basic Concepts in the Philosophy of Gottfried Keller* takes on all previous significant studies on this topic. Whereas earlier scholars, such as Edward Hauch and Hans Kriesi, saw Keller primarily as a political personality, espousing a democratic philosophy, others, such as Hugo von Hofmannsthal and Ricarda Huch, maintained that Keller was a religious person whose political interests were secondary. Still others, such as Hans Dünnebier and Emil Ermatinger, believed that Keller was a proponent of German Romanticism in his younger years and that he later became a disciple of Feuerbach. Max Hochdorf ultimately saw him as a determinist, and Ackerknecht, writing during the Nazi period, considered Keller's political philosophy to be based on a philosophy of cultural nationalism. Jonas Fränkel, trying to refute German propaganda of the day, goes to great length in *Gottfried Kellers Politische Sendung* to differentiate between Keller's understanding of "Volk" and race, maintaining that Keller's ideas were in place before he met Feuerbach. Reichert's study further develops Fränkel's conviction, demonstrating that Keller's philosophy of life remained constant throughout his life, and merely underwent refinement after meeting Feuerbach in 1849.

Reichert maintains that nature, "the purposefully-ordered world" and "Freiheit," or "moral freedom based on enlightenment" form the cornerstones of Keller's worldview. For Keller, nature is a "dynamic monism resembling Herderian pantheism" (Reichert, 10). Reichert shows in Keller's pre-1848 writings as well as in his later prose, the extent to which he continues to revere nature, even as he begins to lose his faith in a higher guiding force, while conceding that Feuerbach was the force behind Keller's acceptance of mortality. Nevertheless, he hastens to add that Keller's earlier poems already refer to death as "an impersonalized sleep in nature" (Reichert 59). Feuerbach was someone who corroborated Keller's thoughts on immorality and on God; he lent Keller a framework for pre-existing ideas. While Keller did adopt Feuerbach's concept of the organism, he believed that the organism possessed a moral center out of which free will developed. According to Keller, moral law was the natural law of mankind, the one motivating force in all man's doings and also contains a "kernel of free will." Keller believed that the enlightened individual acquired free will gradually. Absolute enlightenment would bring about happiness and an end to evil. Free will implies moral conduct based upon enlightenment; this is essentially Keller's ideal of intellectual freedom prior to meeting Feuerbach in 1849. The new aspect presented in Reichert's interpretation is that man becomes his own driving force in determining moral action, whereas formerly man was guided by Divine Law. Keller refers to the individual who has acquired free will through enlightenment as one possessing a firm, tranquil equanimity ("eine feste ruhige Gleichmut") and cites *Der grüne Heinrich* and *Frau Regel Amrain* as examples of such equanimity. Reichert argues that Keller wrote *Der grüne Heinrich* to pursue the development of a young person from subjectivity to objectivity, "from spiritualism to enlightened materialism, from romanticism to realism" (70). He then demonstrates that this conception of free will remained fundamental for Keller. In this context the *Sinngedicht* becomes an "apotheosis" of intellectual freedom and is the "most complex" and most "profound" of Keller's works (71). Reichert recognizes the importance of the *Sinngedicht* in terms of Keller's intellectual and artistic development, and reveals how Keller uses this work, on one level to discuss his views on marriage and the sexes, and on another how Keller weaves into the story his views on determinism and idealism. Reichert believes that Reinhart learns decorum in the course of events and he regains his belief in the moral law. Lucie for her part retains her natural feminine feelings and her belief in the natural law. Both Lucie and Reinhart come to understand themselves as creatures of nature, possessing a law of their own and, through the events in the story, both come to possess the moral freedom to act in accordance with that law. Their marriage is a fusion of determinism with moral idealism, of a belief in moral law with a belief in natural law, thereby realizing Keller's conception of intellectual freedom (75).

There is much of Schiller in Reichert's analysis, indeed some of these thoughts are echoed in Keller's "Prolog zur Schillerfeier" held in Bern in 1859. The "Prolog" is a tribute to Schiller's conviction that ideal beauty alone would lead to morality.[6] Beauty prefers to dwell among moral people and clear thinkers. Moral conduct is safeguarded by beauty, and beauty is akin to intellectual clarity. Keller once again affirms his belief that intellectual clarity alone leads to moral freedom and that enlightenment preserves that freedom. Reichert believes that all the stories in *Die Leute von Seldwyla* are concerned with intellectual freedom, for instance Justine and Jukundus in *Das verlorene Lachen*, Salomon Landolt in *Der Landvogt von Greifensee*, Judith in the revised version of *Der grüne Heinrich*, and Arnold in *Martin Salander*. Reichert believes that *Das Sinngedicht* represents Keller's attitude in 1881 as well as his attitude from the 1850s, since a changed attitude toward life would have been reflected in both *Das Sinngedicht* and in the

---

[6] Those wishing to explore Schiller's thesis that beauty alone would lead to morality and a greater humanity are referred to his treatise *On the Aesthetic Education of Man*, edited by Elizabeth M. Wilkinson and L. A. Willoughby (Oxford: Clarendon Press, 1982).

revised edition of *Der grüne Heinrich*. *Martin Salander* expresses the same firm hope that intellectual freedom will one day remedy the ills of mankind.

Reichert is the first to argue persuasively that Keller's early conception of freedom was influenced more by Schiller than by any of the romantic writers. Keller shared Schiller's conviction of the importance and goodness of natural law throughout his life. Already in his youth Keller had conceived of Freiheit (freedom) as obedience to natural law. Thus, this ideological bond that Keller shared with Schiller demonstrates for Reichert "consistency" rather than change in Keller's Weltanschauung. However, Reichert is honest enough to admit that the crisis in Keller's life·and in Swiss politics, not to mention his association with Feuerbach, played a significant part in developing his intellectual worldview. But Reichert has indeed made a convincing argument that certain tenets of Keller's philosophy, such as his concepts of nature and freedom remained essentially unchanged throughout his life. Nature remains tangible and refers to the "apparent order of her forms." Freiheit remains the "goal toward which man was traveling, to the freedom to act in a necessary way and be oneself, to the moral discernment which came with enlightenment"(91). Reichert demonstrates how these two concepts of nature and freedom influenced Keller's ideas on ethics, aesthetics, politics and social relations.

Roy Pascal devotes an illuminating chapter in *The German Novel* to *Der grüne Heinrich*. His objective is to discover what makes novels good, by examining their aesthetic qualities. He believes it necessary on occasion to explore the social environment of the authors and their outlook. In his preface, he quotes Keller to define realism: "a respect for the right and significance of every thing" (ix). Pascal believes that Keller extends moral responsibility in the social world to every member of the community. Indeed, his essay is an early sociological study of *Der grüne Heinrich* viewed from the political left.[7] He sees it as the first novel that truly assimilates the theme and form of *Wilhelm Meisters Lehrjahre* without being a "glib imitation." He refers to Keller's novel as the story of the growth of a child to manhood; as the story of an unsuccessful artist, who discovers that his true calling is to be found in service to society. Heinrich's death in the original version forces everything into the parameters of the fate of one individual. In the revised edition of 1880 the vitality of a fruitful life in service of society makes Heinrich a representative man. The novel illuminates the internal development of an individual. According to Pascal, this novel is the fruit of Keller's whole wisdom, his entire experience, and represents Keller's search for the "fundamental structure of human life" (35) Keller's account of Heinrich's youth is depicted as far worse than that portrayed in *David Copperfield*, *Great Expectations* and *Jane Eyre* in two ways: "the child is more contaminated, his moral growth more en-

---

[7] Pascal's sociological essay on *Der grüne Heinrich* was published in 1956. In 1965 Michael Kaiser published *Literatursoziologische Studien zu Gottfried Kellers Dichtung*, which encompasses all of Keller's works. See chapter four.

dangered," while he through his experience acquires a social representativeness (Pascal, 39). Heinrich's shy nature forces him to turn his back on the church and his "irregular" education challenges him to raise unorthodox questions. He is an acute observer and perceives and experiences social injustice; he comes to interpret the Divine in terms of republican freedom and personal self-determination. Pascal understands Heinrich's struggle between "reality and imagination," between "nature and the ideal," and between "community and isolation" as embodied in his love for Judith and Anna. Anna comes to represent the ideal, the imaginative, the frail isolation of an innocent, pure young maiden not destined to survive this world. Judith represents the real, worldly, natural, and socially well adapted young woman. Likewise the two festivals (Wilhelm Tell and the artist's festival in Munich) represent the two forces of art: vigorous and social versus empty and vain. At the Wilhelm Tell festival Heinrich learns from the sheriff that a vigorous community cannot exist on altruism and renunciation; it requires the energetic interest and dedication of its members. This festival is seen as enhancing the villagers social consciousness as manifested in the communal flood control effort. Heinrich learns of the importance of social integration and social consciousness at the Tell festival. The carnival scenes in Munich, by contrast, re-enact the Germany of Dürer, an era of remarkable homogeneity amongst the different classes of society — a homogeneity no longer present in the society of Heinrich's time. The festival itself, with its elaborate costumes, is not based in modern day reality; Pascal asserts that the "idle purposelessness of the Carnival is emphasized by the outcome for Heinrich and his friends" (43). The message Keller wants to convey, according to Pascal, is that art divorced from reality and from the community becomes empty and desolate. Pascal criticizes what he perceives as the lack of spatial and atmospheric precision in Heinrich's Munich years, a precision that is so prevalent in the story of his youth. He finds the long dream that introduces Heinrich's decision to return home inadequate, the whole episode at the count's mansion to be forced, the return home, the acceptance of social duty in the second edition to be lacking in detail. Heinrich has become a mere "shadow" of himself; Judith, a mere abstraction. We have some sense of Heinrich's development, but no clear conception of the society into which he has become integrated. Heinrich's childhood and youth are fraught with his own internal conflict waged between reality and imagination, between the public and private self; Pascal asserts that these events give an "undertone" to his life as an artist and ultimately help him to return to the real world of his youth and to become an integrated and responsible citizen (45). It would have been impossible to have treated Heinrich's past in the same detached manner as Goethe treats Wilhelm Meister's childhood. Thus the unity of form in the 1880 version of *Der grüne Heinrich* is thematically central to the text.

Keller presents Heinrich's youth through the eyes of a mature individual who is able to recapture through memory and creative imagination the world of the child. This perspective lends form and shape to the experiences which contribute to the education of Heinrich. Pascal cites Heinrich's fabricated tale to account for the origin of certain oaths he had learned; he shows how Heinrich spins a yarn which includes more knowledge than a child of that age could possibly possess. Pascal demonstrates how Keller's style presents this story as an example of how events both past and present are portrayed in mature, well reflected, digested form, and when combined with mature wisdom, serve one another. Heinrich becomes so engrossed in his own story that he exchanges the fiction he has created for reality; his deed leads to injustice for others that he does not rue. Perceptively, Pascal notes that this "incident embodies the whole theme of the book": namely the narrowness of the elders, the misuse and abuse of the imagination and the resulting disharmony and dislocation, which make the imaginative world more palatable than the real world (50). Keller has through this imaginary incident been able to criticize the real world. Thus Pascal asserts, "The theme of the book, the discovery of the poetry of what is living and reasonable, is not only Heinrich's spiritual development, but also the development of the social reality to which he learns to devote himself" (50). Keller's faith in Swiss democracy led him to try to improve it. Thus Keller's humor, which "fuses his sympathy and his criticism" is never sentimental, because he believes that social wrongs can be corrected, that the society in which he lives can be improved. Society, like Heinrich, can be educated toward more humane values. Pascal contends that the affirming critical realism in this book contains not only the social message of the work, but is also "the secret of its poetic quality" (51).

Victor J. Lemke's "The Deification Of Gottfried Keller" (1956) surveys the many interpretations and misinterpretations of Keller's humor. Many earlier critics regarded tragedy to be a higher, more profound literary form than comedy or satire, therefore Keller's humor was often viewed as eccentric and amusing, but rarely as profound. Echoing Calvin Thomas and Victor Lange, Lemke asserts that Keller's humor is what makes him a great author. Lemke defines this element of humor by drawing upon Johannes Volkelt's *System der Ästhetik*. Volkelt severs the comic from the tragic and the sublime, and juxtaposes it to the serious or non-comic, claiming that when the comic becomes humor, it is just as profound as the tragic. Successful comedy is humorous when it "presupposes a feeling of freedom and individuality, as well as a profound, significant, harmonious view of life" (Lemke, 121). Successful humor must also contain a bit of pessimism, which allows the humor to expose life's contradictions. In Keller, Lemke sees the optimistic humorist who reveals a loving, benevolent and gracious attitude toward nature and the whims of fate, exemplified in *Der grüne Heinrich*. Lemke explains that the benevolent attitude characterized by Keller's goodnatured mood and cheerful serenity came to be viewed as an "indispensable" component of his humor. Humor may use all forms of crude or subtle comedy, satire, wit, irony, but can also dispense with them. Indeed, according to Lemke, German humor need not actually be funny; it suffices to have an all pervasive sunny or benevolent mood. Some readers, Lemke contends, feel uncomfortable with the more cruel elements of Keller's humor and try to explain away such elements as the result of an irresistible subconscious urge. While for others, great humor must have a moral basis.

Lemke observes a problem in the attempt by critics to reconcile Keller's apparent godlessness with his humanistic worldview that embraces Christian ethics in a secular age. Huch attempts to solve this dilemma by making Keller's adherence to this world (his *Diesseitigkeit*) his religion. Lemke demonstrates Keller's atheistic inclinations by using various well known excerpts from his letters and prose, citing in particular the famous testimony in *Das verlorene Lachen* (123–24). But *Das verlorene Lachen* was not Keller's last word regarding a higher being and is properly viewed as being written during the agnostic period in his life. Lemke also wonders how anyone could suggest that Keller was a "God-like individual who had a great love for mankind and all of nature" (124). Lemke finds too much evidence to the contrary. He also questions Keller's objectivity: those characters who share his outlook enjoy his benevolence; those characters who do not, such as the Kammacher, are brutally punished. Some of Lemke's ideas are worth pondering, but many of his assertions are overstated. While Keller did become what may well be called agnostic during the middle phase of his life, he never denied the existence of God or declares himself an atheist, and there are many examples in his later poetry that clearly document just how much he was preoccupied with the existence of God.

In the chapter titled "Realism and Tolerance: Theodor Fontane" from his book *Re-interpretations* (1964), J. P. Stern discusses Keller's *Grüner Heinrich* and *Die Leute von Seldwyla* because they are exceptional stories and outstanding representations of German poetic realism. In his essay Stern compares specific aspects of Keller's works to concrete examples of works by Keller's European contemporaries. Stern refers to *Der grüne Heinrich* as "perhaps the most original work in German" to have been directly influenced by the Goethean tradition (302). Keller's novel represents a compromise between the gradual development of human potentialities embodied by the sense of "becoming" in Goethe's *Wilhelm Meisters Lehrjahre,* and the civic responsibilities expected of one in society. Stern finds Keller's keen moral insight as striking as his much-noted psychological insight. In Keller's novel, Heinrich is unveiled layer by layer until his self-indulgence emerges with startling clarity. He is able to acknowledge and accept his wrongdoings and to learn from them, allowing them to shape his nature, a process that constitutes an elevation of the Goethean prototype (304). Keller's novel brings to light the moral implications that remain hidden in Goethe's novel. Keller's is a most engaging novel because of its honesty, because Keller refuses to allow Heinrich Lee to become a successful artist.

Yet *Der grüne Heinrich* cannot live up to the greater standards of European literature. Stern contrasts Keller's novel to Stendhal's *Le rouge et le noir* and shows how almost every one of Stendhal's characters have "tremendous vitality." Julien

Sorel, the book's chief protagonist, is incomparably more ambitious than his counterpart, Heinrich Lee. The discussions of road planning and civic duties that teach Heinrich to become a responsible citizen pale in comparison to the political intrigue in which Julien becomes involved in Paris. Sorel must fight for whatever he wants, and the passion he displays in his struggle affords Stendhal's novel a dimension entirely lacking in Keller's novel. Keller's concept that society will yield before the hero's weakness, as it does in the last section of Keller's novel, is as alien to Stendhal as it is to life itself. The moral values suggested by Sorel's transgressions have far greater impact than Heinrich's lengthy and languid "tussle" with art. Stendhal's task is to show the inseparable elements of world and self that "determine the course of events and shape the novel" (307). Sorel is "unscrupulous and attractive, intelligent and vain, calculating and reckless" and above all passionate in all things; these attributes constitute both life and an intimation of values in the novel. It is this kind of passionate engagement with human strife — engagement that provides enduring images that speak directly to the human condition — that is sorely lacking in Keller's novel.

Keller's strength lies in the smaller genre, the novella. Stern views Keller's mania for telling each story to the end, one of the negative aspects of his first novel. Self-contained episodes in *Der grüne Heinrich* become self-contained novellas. Stern finds Nietzsche's comment on "petit genres" appropriate in this context. Nietzsche had attacked Wagner's conception of the total artwork because Nietzsche believed that only small works could be truly well crafted and thereby maintain integrity (308). Nietzsche praised Keller's prose, but he focused his praise on the novella cycles rather than on Keller's novel. Seldwyla, an imaginary provincial Swiss village, provided Keller with a unified setting, which as Stern shows, is further drawn together by a single but broadly varying *idée fixe* around which each novella is structured. For example, the *idée fixe* of the first novella centers on the drastic cure for sulking (Pankraz), while the next plays on the Romeo and Juliet theme. Stern demonstrates how the narrative tone is determined by the idée fixe, for example the tale of sulkiness is told in the tone of a child's voice. Keller's tones are remarkably broad and include wit, lighthearted irony, farce, burlesque, and caricature. Keller's criticism can be opaque and direct, it can range from tragedy to harsh satire and the grotesque. Stern finds that caricature turns up most because it is the most direct expression of the constrictions of life (309). The grotesque provides insight into the morality of *Die Leute von Seldwyla* where the morality is implied through a satirically inverted set of values. Indeed, when Keller positively asserts certain values, as he does in *Frau Regel Amrain und ihr Jüngster*, he does so unconvincingly; the values become flat and conventional; satire is his most effective tool. Keller's social realism is at its most boring, according to Stern, when he begins to preach social responsibility, for which Lukács has lauded him. Stern believes Keller is unable to provide a convincing picture of positive social values behind his satirical scheme, a predicament that he shares with his fellow European realists such as Dickens. What gives Keller's work a European quality and relevance is that his provincial milieu— the Seldwyla folk with their inbred morality— are a European phenomenon (315).

J. M. Lindsay's *Gottfried Keller, Life and Works* (1968), remains the most complete introduction to and interpretation of Keller and his oeuvre available in English. Lindsay begins with a one hundred page biography of Keller. He provides a clear and concise overview of Feuerbach's teachings and assesses their influence on Keller (37–41). Lindsay explores all aspects of Keller's literary output, often offering keen insight into his novels, novellas and poetry. His introduction to the poetry is particularly insightful, and he does not hesitate to differentiate between good and mediocre works. Keller's forte is in his images and effective use of vocabulary, while his technical prowess, his use of rhythm and meter is lacking in originality. Keller's strength as a poet lies "in the genuineness of his feeling and the complete integrity of his thought" (107).

Lindsay's discussion of *Der grüne Heinrich* includes a plot summary and a good character analysis. He is critical of the novel, because Keller had not allowed sufficient time to pass in order to digest the experiences that he incorporated; they were too immediate. While the story of Heinrich's youth is beautifully written, the prolonged stay at the count's castle seems improbable, and Feuerbach's arid creed rests uneasily upon Dortchen Schönfund's shoulders. But Keller is capable of writing realistically, even of assimilating distant times and places with which he is unfamiliar. Although Heinrich is an artist, Keller never allows him to be the typical artist hero so prevalent elsewhere in German literature; Keller's artist is not essentially different from the average member of society: he is not placed on a pedestal. As a Bildungsroman *Der grüne Heinrich* fairs better than as an artist's novel (*Künstlerroman*). Lindsay believes that Keller's novel is the last of the great Bildungsromane to show that the confusions and uncertainties of life really can be solved by a man of good character and perseverance. In the revised edition (1880) Heinrich tackles and solves his own difficulties, never losing faith in life. He tends first to assume that he has made an error, rather than to assume that the world is in error or that the world has wronged him in some way. When the count calls him "ein wesentlicher Mensch" (a significant individual) he has summed up the essence of *Der grüne Heinrich*, for the novel tells the story of a real man of good will, intelligence, and discrimination (139). Lindsay's interpretation of this novel includes a comparison of the two editions. While conceding that the 1880 version is an improvement over the original, because of the first person narrative and because the protagonist lives, he still finds it ungainly and shapeless, because it lacks a constructed plot. The novel contains the raw material, but it is not well enough fashioned to become great literature. The style of the novel is not consistent. Although a master of prose is clearly in command, one is reminded that he needs training and rigor.

One admires Keller's novel for its "excellent character portraits and for individual stylistic excellences, single brilliant chapters, occasional good images, the feeling that here is an author with something to say and the gift of frequently but not always being able to say it memorably" (143).

In his introduction to the Seldwyla stories, Lindsay demonstrates how much Keller loves the old Seldwyla which represents for him an attitude toward life rather than a geographical entity. Keller's stories are written using the most suitable genre for his abilities, namely the novella. Lindsay provides a brief summary and a solid interpretation of each of the stories, including *Romeo und Julia auf dem Dorfe*, which he finds the most "absolute and uncompromising" of the novellas in its assertion that life should be lived to its full intensity (148). Keller's ability to take the characters from a newspaper report and transform them into Sali and Vrenchen, two believable innately good and wholesome young people, is a tribute to Keller's talent and creative genius. Keller persuades us that the tragic death of these two characters is justified, because a life without love would be unthinkable for them. In *Die drei gerechten Kammacher*, Keller has shown that the blind pursuit of money and ambition can lead to disappointment. Stylistically Lindsay finds the work typical of Keller, with its detailed objects and the highly ironical verbal illustrations. In particular, Lindsay praises the skill with which Keller confronts the transition from grotesque to tragic, commenting that Keller displays "a disciplined sense of form, acute moral perception, rich humor and that awareness of tragic overtones which is an essential constituent of the best comedy" (157).

Moving on to the *Züricher Novellen*, Lindsay agrees with the general consensus that *Der Landvogt von Greifensee* is the best in this collection. Keller clearly admires the historical figure, Salomon Landolt, for his renaissance qualities. He is a "paragon of manly virtues" and a man "not insensitive to aesthetic delights" (199). With these novellas, Keller made the transition from the individual morality espoused by the characters in Seldwyla and has begun to focus on the community and society at large.

Das Sinngedicht represents for Lindsay the artistic high point of Keller's career. He demonstrates how Keller, the confirmed bachelor, explores the relationship between the sexes based on Logau's epigram "How will you make white lilies into red roses? Kiss a white Galatea; blushing she will laugh," as discussed earlier in this chapter. Lindsay finds the cycle as a whole to be remarkable for its organic unity. He discusses each of the inset stories and finds Lucie's stories, although more directly tendentious, "rather trivial and lacking in emotional intensity" than Reinhart's. Linday believes that Lucie sees issues too clearly and simply; he tends to side with Reinhart's arguments. Ultimately, Lucie is swayed by Reinhart's stories. In the closing pages, Keller is able to draw all the threads of his narrative together, making the *Sinngedicht* the most rounded, the most artistically complete and the most beautiful, Lindsay believes, of Keller's works. *Das*

Sinngedicht embodies a conception of life in which each of the sexes has a separate, but equally important position. The construction of the cycle is somewhat artificial: that a young man goes off into the world in search of the right woman, based on an epigram, and that the two would-be partners sort out their opinions on love and marriage by exchanging stories resembles an intellectual exercise rather than life. However, this tightly woven set of novellas, Lindsay asserts, is Keller's best constructed creation (228). The frame story, which constitutes Reinhart's and Lucie's courtship, is deepened by each of the inset stories. These *Novellen*, Lindsay contends, "help to enlighten and purify the lovers' understanding of one another and of the respective functions of man and woman in marriage" (225). Beyond the relationship between the sexes, Lindsay suggests that *Das Sinngedicht* represents Keller's most mature thoughts on how life should be lived. The cycle copes "with the element of free choice in human conduct, with the deliberate cultivation of attitudes and activities which make life as fully as possible, what it can and ought to be" (225). Clearly, Keller wrote here of life not as he had known it, but as he would have wished it to be. For its artistic achievement, for its breadth of perception and psychological finesse representing the mature artist, Lindsay holds *Das Sinngedicht* to be Keller's masterpiece.

Lindsay acknowledges that *Martin Salander* was an attempt at a new kind of novel, but, he contends, "it is a dull book about dull people leading dull lives" (232). In Lindsay's reading, Keller appears to be out of sympathy with his age. He believes that Keller's reading of Flaubert and Zola influenced *Martin Salander*. Lindsay suggests that the conflict between the romantic and realistic which pervades all of Keller's work has been resolved, but at too high a price. Nevertheless, Lindsay does find the characters interesting, although Maria Salander is rather a stock figure; other literary historians tend to view Maria as a strong woman in the tradition of Frau Amrain, Frau Meyenthaler, or have even compared her to the old Stauffacherin in Schiller's *Wilhelm Tell*. The warm humor, the tolerant understanding, the human failings, the laughter, which suffuse Keller's other works, have been replaced with satire and general disillusionment. Lindsay finds this work to be a failure, because it lacks that inner truth which is the hallmark of great works of art.

Lindsay concludes by reasserting his belief that the *Sieben Legenden* and *Das Sinngedicht* represent the apex of Keller's artistic activity from the formal point of view. While the inset stories told by Reinhart and Lucie are neither better nor worse than Keller's other novellas, the total achievement of this cycle surpasses anything else Keller has written; no other European writer has written such a formally distinguished cycle of stories on love and marriage. Lindsay then examines Keller's style, his use of metaphor and simile, the *Kanzleistil* [burocratese] in his later writing and his humor stood out among his fellow German Poetic Realists; he possessed a natural genius and exhibited a broader range of interests than any other German writer of his day. Keller's profound conviction that life is good and has meaning was welcomed by his readers. He came to represent not just the Bernese spirit as Gotthelf did, or the Zurich elite as C. F. Meyer did, but rather the whole of German-speaking Switzerland. Keller became "the literary spokesman and the guardian angel of the entire country" (247).

John M. Ellis's *Narration In The German Novelle* discusses the relationship of the narrator to the story and the importance of this relationship for the interpretation of the story. Keller's *Die drei Gerechten Kammacher* is one of eight nineteenth-century German novellas chosen for this study. Keller's narrator comments on events and renders judgment through his narration without interpreting the story for the reader. Keller's narrator transforms what appears to be the narration of a superficial anecdote into a powerful vehicle for discussion of serious themes concerning the goals individuals set for themselves. This discussion promotes the establishment of worthy goals and the need to situate those goals within a rational framework in which one can accept achievement or defeat while maintaining a balanced perspective on life. Ellis shows us how Keller used the narrator to transform a seemingly simple story into a powerful literary masterpiece, in which the narrator's perspective becomes an important operational mode for the reader's understanding and ultimately for his interpretation of the story.

In *The German Bildungsroman from Wieland to Hesse* (1978), Martin Swales devotes an illuminating chapter to *Der grüne Heinrich*. Swales's study is a thoughtful, clearly written explanation of this peculiarly German genre aimed primarily at an English speaking audience. For Swales, *Der grüne Heinrich* depicts the conflict between potentiality and the constrictions of practical social living. As the episode with the count and Dortchen Schönfund make clear, Heinrich is incapable of voicing his feelings, leading to the failure of that relationship. In both versions of the novel Heinrich's vivid imagination, which counteracts the drab reality of his childhood, continues to color reality throughout his life. Drawing upon Pascal's observation that Heinrich's unbounded imagination has untold socio-psychological ramifications, Swales claims that particularly in the revised (1880) edition the reader is not merely confronted with the dialectic of imagination verses reality, but also with a "dialectical interaction and interpenetration" (90). Imagination, Swales asserts, can serve as an escapist compensation, but it can also be a vital medium through which the "contingent facts of a social environment are rounded out into the density of an embracing human reality" (90). Heinrich Lee has with this story produced a fiction that is more interesting than his own reality. In the story that led to his expulsion, Heinrich finds himself rather by accident, as a ringleader of a loosely organized student operation, that has come to harass a disliked teacher. This time Heinrich is again unable to assess correctly the gravity of the situation. His desire to be accepted by his schoolmates was stronger than his sense of propriety and the consequences of irrational behavior. Swales postulates that Heinrich's psychological dislocations are symptomatic of the social uncertainties embedded in bourgeois idealism (93). Heinrich's dualistic relationship to reality is manifested in his love for the ideal Anna and in his love for the sensual Judith. His idealistic image of his love for Anna makes it impossible for him to overcome his love for Judith. The imperfectly understood relationship between his imaginative hopes, desires, and claims, and the demands of the social world result in a double impoverishment. His ideals become unfocused, making him unable to express his love for Judith. Swales alludes to a host of themes that inquire into the dynamic between an individual's creativity and practical living. Swales suggests that these issues, which are rooted in the vital intellectual issues of bourgeois society, are at the heart of the Bildungsroman as a genre (96). Heinrich cannot possibly accept, much less love the world as it is, or Judith as she is, or for that matter be loved as he is, because he has lived so long in a state of mind, in which the real can only appear woeful when measured against the created ideals of his imagination. Thus, Heinrich, unable to overcome his ideal of love epitomized by Anna, must repudiate Judith. Indeed, Heinrich never overcomes this dualism in his character. Thus, Keller's work is part of the critical debate in the novel tradition that tends to cherish the potential rather than the actual, inwardness rather than outward self-realization. Swales reads *Der grüne Heinrich* as an integral part of the Bildungsroman tradition, because even if the protagonist loses his way, the novel itself does not (104).

Lee B. Jennings's 1983 "The Model of the Self in Gottfried Keller's Prose" is the most modern and thorough psychoanalytical examination of Keller's works available in English. Jennings's study was written shortly after Adolf Muschg's Kindler biography of Gottfried Keller, in which Muschg employs both Freudian and economic principles to examine Keller's lifelong sense of guilt.[8] When Jennings submitted his article, Gerhard Kaiser's *Gottfried Keller: Das gedichtete Leben*, an extensive psychoanalytic interpretation of Keller and his works, was not yet available. In his introduction, Jennings differentiates between the intrinsic and extrinsic models of the self. In the extrinsic, or Freudian model, the essence of the self is largely confined to ego-driven consciousness. This self matures often by following role models and learns to adapt to social requirements. Continued growth is not an issue. By contrast, in the intrinsic model (Jungian) the essence of the self is sought within the mind, in an unconscious core of the personality; this entity corresponds roughly to the idea of the soul. This soul contains not only the potentialities of the whole individual or self, but exercises a guardian function as well. It is the ultimate arbiter of right and wrong. The soul is driven by intuition. Development / maturation is not linear, but proceeds in stages, remaining open-ended. Goethe's concept of "werden" (becoming) repre-

---

[8] See also Muschg's biography *Gottfried Keller* (1978) and Gerhard Kaiser's extensive study: *Gottfried Keller: Das gedichtete Leben* (1981) discussed in chapter six.

sents the intrinsic model of the self. The intrinsic model of the self also flourished under the German Romantics. Jennings comments that Keller, while inheriting much from the age of Goethe, also sought to interpret the historical times in which he lived. While Keller's "lingering" idealism and his "incident" realism have been much discussed from an ideological viewpoint, Jennings wants to examine empirically the model of the self that emerges from Keller's prose in order to achieve a "clearer demarcation" of Keller's position in cultural history.

Indeed, Jennings in this adeptly written analysis examines all of Keller's prose works, exploring the model of the self that emerges. He investigates Keller's concept of the soul, asserting that this term is not inconsistent with Feuerbach's teaching which, while disclaiming the soul as a separate entity from the body and thereby attacking immortality, never denied the existence of the soul. In Keller's works, soullessness becomes a sad depiction of the inner self. The soul serves as the seat of the conscience and of higher instincts. The soul must continually distinguish between acceptable and unacceptable instinctual desires while serving to further the well-being and maturation of the individual (Jennings, 203). After exploring this role of the soul in various prose works, Jennings concludes that "Keller's intuitive grasp of unconscious processes is largely expressed in terms of a 'soul,' which accounts for the depth, humaneness, and essential individuality of the character" (209). Jennings also discusses the impact of vanity and the role of free will and guilt on the model of the self, believing that a free decision stemming from the heart, soul, or total being remains an elusive goal in *Der grüne Heinrich*. Keller has portrayed characters in other works who manage to act swiftly, even forcefully without sacrificing their spiritual integrity, but Keller fails to convey persuasively how they became that way (225). Keller's insight, Jennings suggests, ranges from the "preconscious" to the "subconscious," but he is still under the influence of idealistic philosophy in assuming an uncorrupted inner counterpart to the ego and a reservoir of innate moral values. The soul remains the essence of the individual, but it is rarely the mainspring of action. The intrinsic model of the self is surprisingly strong, but in the gap between thought and action, gives way to the extrinsic model. Keller's insistence on a productive social place in society mirrors the belief that one becomes what societies says one is. Happiness, he suggests, becomes both inward fulfillment and outward status. Missing in Keller's works is the will, which acts as a bridge between the intrinsic and the extrinsic self. Jennings concludes his impressively compact study by acknowledging the author's "considerable psychological acumen," particularly when it came to unveiling "self-serving motivation and self-deception or when reason is contaminated by passion" (225).

In *Reflections of Realism* (1985) Robert C. Holub reopens the discussion of realism with some reinterpretations. His thesis is that texts, which have been considered realist, are most revealing when they begin to reflect upon the precarious nature of their own poetics. Holub endeavors to reinterpret canonical texts to disclose the ideology and paradoxes informing the realist enterprise. His

is a noble and thought-provoking undertaking, which offers an intriguing interpretation of Keller's *Romeo und Julia auf dem Dorfe*. Holub raises the question of
ambiguity (not a lack of realism) surrounding Vrenchen's and Sali's inability to
remain happily together. Holub cites the usual justifications: their social status in
particular Sali's hopeless origins, honor or values associated with the bourgeois
world, and Sali's role in the injury of Vrenchen's father. Holub carefully dis-
counts each of these explanations for their suicide. An examination of the language used to describe the relationship leads Holub to conclude that Sali's and
Vrenchen's love is portrayed "as a force beyond the control of the two lovers"
(113). This force is incest. Holub interprets Marti and Manz as a parental unit,
which would then draw Sali and Vrenchen into the same family and help to explain their mutual attraction, their odd behavior toward one another, and their
demise by mutual consent. Holub suggests that this pattern can best be described as the structure of an incestuous desire. Holub's interpretation offers new
perspective on troublesome questions for the consenting believer.

Scholars have long observed the subtle but ever-present didactic presence
in Keller's fiction. My 1988 monograph *Gottfried Keller: Poet, Pedagogue and
Humanist* explores this all-pervasive aspect in his prose — namely, that literature is a vehicle for disseminating knowledge and has the power, at least in
theory, to transform society. The study includes a two-part biography of
Keller that focuses on the role of education in Keller's life and extrapolates his
reflections on education from essays, correspondence and other materials, before investigating education in his fiction. Keller used the original 1855 edition of *Der grüne Heinrich* to come to terms with his own past and as an exercise in writing prose fiction. After the completion of his first novel, Keller became increasingly aware of the obligation of the artist to use his talent for the
good of society. He was a firm believer in eighteenth-century German Idealism, hence he maintained the view that man is basically good and has been
endowed with reason, and as such is inclined to work for the common good of
mankind. This conception of man and his world sustained his faith in working toward an ever more humane humankind. Keller's fiction has always concerned itself first and foremost with the formation of individual character and
integrity for the purpose of serving society. While writing *Der grüne Heinrich*
was largely a venture in self-education, Keller swiftly began to focus on the
role of the individual in middle-class society. In *Die Leute von Seldwyla* he
lures the reader into a dialogue about the people of this imaginary village.
Keller's humor and irony gently stroke the reader, enabling him to scold all
the more harshly by helping the reader to see himself and his life mirrored in
the folly of the Seldwyler themselves (Cf. *G.B.* III/2, 195). Certainly, in *Das
Fähnlein der Sieben Aufrechten* Keller depicts a Swiss world in which family
values and social ethics appear to be intact. His essay "Am Mythenstein"
praises Schiller's conception of freedom and beauty as a means to an aestheti-

cally driven moral education, and envisions using massive folk productions and choirs to stage performances for the purpose of political and social education of the common people. Keller recognized the extent to which the industrial revolution in Switzerland had rent the traditional social fabric, and he was forced to acknowledge that man, despite his basic goodness, was endowed with free will and was materially driven to follow his own primitive instincts of self-preservation. His *Bettagsmandate* illustrate his awareness of a society in transition. Keller also struggled under the influence of Feuerbach to create a system of ethics for the modern, increasingly post-Christian era. Keller's *Sieben Legenden* are former religious tales transformed for the secular age. The tone set by the introduction and the stories in the second volume of *Die Leute von Seldwyla* (1874) reflects the radical changes of a society in transition, which had not been evident in *Das Fähnlein*. *Das verlorene Lachen* exhibits the darker side of Keller's didacticism, revealing his increasing resignation concerning the ability of fiction to direct or transform society. Jukundus must find his way by seeking answers within himself.[9] Neither the church nor faith, neither family nor tradition seem able to provide comfort and solace in the industrial age. Although Martin in Keller's last novel *Martin Salander* declares "Knowledge is power," one is less convinced by his hollow exclamation, despite the emphasis the novel places on education. While Keller never abandoned his belief in man's goodness or changed his views on education, one detects a tentative resignation regarding the ability of fiction to transform society and to prepare the way for a more gracious humanity.

Other Keller scholars such as Gail Hart have raised questions regarding his belief in the didactic impact of fiction. In her highly original study, *Readers and Their Fictions in the Novels of Gottfried Keller*, Hart explores Keller's fictional readers for the first time. In so doing she challenges the long held view of Keller as a consistently didactic author and questions his faith in fiction as a medium of education. Her study begins with an historical overview of the archetype of the reader-hero, whose uncritical reception of literary fictions leads him astray. She sets up the theoretical frame, using Uwe Japp's thesis that fictional readers help to distance the "real" reader by reinforcing his consciousness of the untruth of fiction. The "real" reader of these books (about books) encounters an image not of reality but of himself. She then draws upon Girard's study, *Deceit, Desire and the Novel*, in which he identifies the workings of "metaphysical desire," the impulse that drives fictional characters away from the self in favor of imitation of literary models. Hart sees in Feuerbach's influence upon Keller, the link between

[9] My lecture at the International Gottfried Keller Colloquium held in Zurich in 1990 explored Keller's ethical views as they are presented in selected works: the ensuing essay "Gottfried Kellers Ethik im Zusammenhang mit ästhetischen, religiösen und historischen Aspekten seiner Kunst" is discussed in chapter 6, and was published in *Elf Essays*, ed. H. Wysling, 61–76.

Keller's "representation of fictional readings" and Girard's findings. Hart ascertains that both Girard's contemporary theory of metaphysical desire and Feuerbach's earlier attack on metaphysics in general rest upon the same perception, "that of a prevalent cultural tendency to affix the self to an Other and to live in the shadow of this Other, who is nothing more than a self-generated fiction" (8). Hart then traces the development of Keller's fictional characters from the earliest stories, in which he suspiciously views his central characters as "mediators and manipulators" of desire (Heinrich Lee, Pankraz, Sali and Vrenchen, Jacques) to his later more playful and sophisticated attitude toward fiction in the *Sinngedicht*. Reinhart (*Sinngedicht*) falls into the same trap as his predecessors — he tries to enact the text (epigram) he is reading and consequently meets Lucie. The courtship between Lucie and Reinhart's consists of storytelling and, like the storytellers in the *Decameron*, Lucie and Reinhart are one step removed from worldly strife. Social reality is not an issue. Keller "consciously maneuvers" to exclude social reality from this example of "pure" fiction, and constructs a "hermetically" sealed "ultraliterary" world in which poetry thrives, allowing the irresponsible imagination to roam without the shackles of social reality and moral didacticism (113). Hart challenges Keller's statements of didactic intention through an analysis of Keller's "conscious" creation of fictional readers who misread and misuse their readings.

The Theodor Storm scholar David Jackson applies his clear insight and wit to demonstrate how Keller's *Kleider Machen Leute* combines *Trivialliteratur*, specifically the drugstore romance, with elements of Greek classicism to convey the serious themes of the poetic realists. While Classical images, allusions, and meter were in vogue at the time, and the Helvetian Confederation preferred to see itself as a modern day Greek state, Keller sought to address both his educated readers and the general reading public without reducing his art to *Trivialliteratur*. Thus Keller hoped, despite his increasing disillusionment with the political trends in Switzerland, that stories, such as *Die Leute von Seldwyla* could still serve an "educative humanitarian function." According to Jackson, Keller knew that he could no longer portray contemporary Swiss reality in Homeric terms, rather the fairy-tale was a means of masking and of parodying classical categories, of conveying ethical notions that would lead to greater humanitarian values. *Kleider machen Leute* intentionally parodies scenes from penny romances and mocks classical Homeric elements. Jackson suggests that Keller's deceptive romance would make the biting socio-economic critique more palatable to a larger reading public than if it had been written in a direct, moralizing tone. Later Keller would write *Martin Salander* in just such a direct style which was misunderstood and broadly rejected by his readers. Jackson suggests, that it is precisely the very implausibility of the tale, in which a penniless foreigner is wed to the daughter of a wealthy *Amtsmann* (civil servant), that enables Keller to make his radical humanitarian message acceptable. Many high- and middle-brow middle-class writers, while despising the low-brow romances, provided their self-congratulatory middle-class readers with the fiction of self-deception that they wanted. Keller's stylistic achievement in *Kleider machen Leute* implies that those writers who deceptively depicted modern capitalist society as a supportive community that espoused true happiness and human fulfillment for all only fostered illusions. Jackson asserts that Keller used the spicy romance as a means to stimulate critical insight into the nature of contemporary reality and, by doing so, had devised a vehicle by which socially critical and ultimately humanitarian ideals could be communicated to the general public while maintaining literary integrity.

It would seem appropriate to conclude this chapter on Anglo-American Keller scholarship with a brief overview of the topics Keller scholars are currently pursuing. There is a blend of traditional and contemporary approaches covering a broad spectrum from historical, social, economic investigations to ontological and aesthetic questions as well as specific interpretations of Keller's use of allusion, the restrictions of nineteenth-century middle-class society and the influence of the Viennese Volkstheater. On May 29 and 30, 1990, a symposium was held at the London Institute of German Studies to commemorate the centenary of Keller's death. The lectures were edited by John L. Flood and Martin Swales and published in a single volume *Gottfried Keller 1819–1890 — The London Symposium 1990*. The collection contains a surprising number of overlapping topics, themes, approaches and interpretations of narrative technique and style that mirror current issues and directions in Keller scholarship. Martin Swales's essay, "Reflectivity and Realism" and Erika Swales's essay, "Dead End(ing)s in Keller" are discussed in their respective German versions in *Elf Essays* edited by Hans Wysling in chapter 6 of this study. Likewise, David Jackson's essay, "Literary Outfitters by Appointment to the Muses or to the Paying Public?" (also included in Swales's and Flood's volume) was discussed above.

Karl Pestalozzi of the University of Basel leads off the collection with a magnificent essay, "Kellers Gedicht 'Rosenglaube,'" in which he demonstrates how this isolated poem in its various transformations comes to reflect central tenets of Keller's Weltanschauung. Pestalozzi traces the refrain of each stanza in the poem, "So lange eine Rose zu denken vermag, ist noch nie ein Gärtner gestorben" (In the living memory of a rose, a gardener has never died) back to Bernard de Bovier de Fontenelle (1657–1757) whose works were popular in his day because he made metaphysical and scientific phenomena understandable through fiction — his *Entretiens sur la pluralite des mondes* (1686) enjoyed 33 editions in the author's lifetime, and Keller may well have read Gottsched's translation of the *Entretiens* (Pestalozzi, 14). Keller's poem is grouped together with several others under the rubric "Aus dem Leben" (1849), which recalls Keller's sojourn in Heidelberg, where he met both Ludwig Feuerbach and Hermann Hettner. It is possible that Keller had learned about Fontenelle through Hermann Hettner, whose lectures he attended and who later published his *Geschichte der französis-chen Literatur im 18. Jahrhundert* (1860). Pestalozzi is interested in why Keller found this refrain so fascinating. In it, the roses believe that the gardener lives forever, because from the perspective of their shorter existence, he seems forever present. The young child in the first stanza comes to comprehend her biblical God in terms of the gardener, who like the rose is also subjected to the transito-riness of life. In the second stanza the gardener has become gray and is simply portrayed as the caretaker of the flowers. He realizes that even the ephemeral beauty of a rose is subject to the transitoriness of all things. This confrontation between two life spans and their opposing perspectives echoes strains of Goethe's "Erlkönig" and C. F. Meyer's "Der Marmorknabe" (19). The final stanza ushers in an intensification of the tone, nature is vibrating with life, or-chestrating a finale. The fullness of nature approaches a crescendo, manifesting the affirmation of life. Feuerbach's teachings had persuaded Keller, that immor-tality does not exist; thus, the finality of death enhances the meaning of life. Fontanelle's rose becomes a symbol in the third stanza for this intensification of life as a consequence of death's finality. The shorter the life span, the closer life and death come together, the more intensely life is lived (21). Keller included the poem in his 1883 collection, but his reference to Fontenelle was eliminated and the poem was titled: "Rosenglaube." Indeed, Pestalozzi demonstrates the extent to which Dortchen Schönfund embodies the "Rosenglaube" in her tolerance to-ward all faiths and in her acceptance of death without fear. "Rosenglaube" is a spiritual poem without God; it is a creed to which the count, Dortchen and Heinrich all subscribe. In his comparison of the poem to a particular scene in *Der grüne Heinrich* (*SW* XIX, 280–91), Pestalozzi shows how the intensification of life, heralded in the poem, also harbors a seed of resignation. Keller did even-tually place the poem under the rubric: "Sonnwende und Entsagen." Pestalozzi shows how the single poem "Rosenglaube" comes to embody central tenets of Keller's philosophy of life (death's finality, the transitoriness of life, resignation); themes that later became manifest in his fiction.

Michael Minden's contribution to the collection, *"Der grüne Heinrich* and the Legacy of *Wilhelm Meister,"* is initially concerned with the construction of the bourgeois subject as it appears in the Bildungsroman. He begins by com-paring the similarities between *Der grüne Heinrich* and Goethe's *Wilhelm Meister*. Referring to Kaiser's book, in which the death of Heinrich's father plays a central role, Minden compares this to Wilhelm's distant father and the tower society. He reminds us that Goethe placed aesthetics above both the philosophical and the social. Minden bases his approach on Terry Eagleton's recent book *The Ide-ology of the Aesthetic* in which the aesthetic provides an ideological home for the lonely soul of the modern bourgeois. He also refers to Böschenstein's argument that Goethe is the operative paternal force in *Der grüne Heinrich* and that

Goethe's legacy is the ideology of its aesthetic.[10] Minden argues that Heinrich's death in the first version produces circularity, "an aesthetic pattern of reassuring return," such as one finds in the *Lehrjahre*, and which comes to exemplify the genre of the Bildungsroman (31). But the story of the failed artist must somehow be converted to a success, and it is the authority of the aesthetic that saves the day, for art triumphs over autobiography. The state of being fatherless denies one the introduction to socialization, and it enhances the attachment to the maternal. Keller's text according to Gerhard Kaiser is written about the mother, as an aesthetic overcoming of the attachment to the mother (34). Ultimately, Minden realizes that his argument is drifting in a conventional direction: He has come to emphasize the difference between the two Bildungsromane, and he is suggesting that Keller is more realistic than Goethe. While Minden does not want to deny either of these conclusions, he does want to focus on Keller's struggle with the threat of Kitsch "which begins to make itself felt here in the stylistic hesitation about woman figures" Minden has just tried to describe" (35). The high aesthetic ideals of Goethe and Schiller had degenerated into kitsch in the nineteenth century, which affected Keller and all those writing in Goethe's wake. Minden hastens to assure us that he is not accusing Keller of producing kitsch, and asserts that Keller is able to defend himself against the threat of kitsch in his shorter works through the artistic "Wahrung freier Bewegung in jeder Hinsicht" (Preservation of free movement in every respect) as Keller describes it in a letter to Emil Kuh (*G.B.* III/1, 163). *Der grüne Heinrich* is much more of a problem in this regard because Keller is bound to subjectivity through the autobiographical form and bound culturally to Goethe's *Meister* as a model. Minden then demonstrates the process by which Keller handles the potential threat of kitsch in both versions of *Der grüne Heinrich*, and assesses the degree to which Keller is successful.

Brian A. Rowley, in his essay, "Views of Society implied in *Die Leute von Seldwyla*" demonstrates how Keller uses various narrative techniques to inform the reader of his social views. Keller shows rather than tells. Keller's characters do not openly discuss social and political issues; nevertheless, Rowley shows that they are implicit in the text. Keller, Rowley asserts, was primarily concerned with cultivating character; he is a humanistic ethicist (53–4). Keller does not present us with a utopian society, but we may be able to deduce from his stories the society he sought, by imagining a society quite different from the one portrayed in the Seldwyla novellas. The paradoxes inherent in a "wonnig" and "sonnig" (blissful, sunny) Seldwyla depicted in idyllic terms are fraught with problems that require cautious judgment on the part of the reader. Rowley shows how Keller uses prefigured incidents, objects, and settings to convey messages, leitmotifs,

---

[10] Renate Böschenstein, 1981, "Der Schatz unter den Schlangen. Ein Gespräch mit Gerhard Kaisers Buch *Gottfried Keller: Das gedichtete Leben*," *Euphorion* 77 (1983): 176–199.

even animal imagery and conclusions that summarize the fate of his characters as a means of conveying or "showing" his view of society. According to Rowley, form becomes meaning (64). The model society envisioned must be extrapolated from Keller's treatment of the characters in these stories. Harmony must be cultivated between the individual and society; society must be so conceived that it will allow the individual to fully unfold, cultivate and develop their humanity; in other words society exists for human beings. Keller's humanistic view of man allows the individual to make mistakes, provided that these mistakes arise from unintentional error, from sincerity. Indeed, Keller rescues those characters who deserve to be rescued such as Pankraz, Wenzel, John Kabys, and Fritz Amrain. Rowley demonstrates that the severity of ethical offense can be measured by the reconciliation Keller offers in the end. He suggests that Keller's utopian society might well include the survivors of his Seldwyla stories.

T. M. Holmes urges caution in his essay, "Romeo und Julia auf dem Dorfe — The Idyll of Possessive Individualism," in which he demonstrates how Keller's idyll conjured up in the language of the opening paragraphs is undercut by a character's avarice and desire for economic gain. The farmers who exploit the black fiddler are not alone in their actions. The farmer, who buys two acres from Manz is capitalizing on another's demise; his purchase is sanctioned by middle-class society. Keller's language is devoid of social comment: he shows, rather than explaining. The idyllic setting "masks" the economic struggles that have taken place to amass wealth. Holmes shows how Sali and Vrenchen are also caught up in this desire for gain, this individualistic desire for possessions. Those who lose (Marti, Manz), and the dispossessed (the black fiddler, Vrenchen and Sali) have no place in this idyllic setting. While they belong to the society of the dispossessed, Sali and Vrenchen refuse to join, preferring instead to reconstruct the idyll they remember from their bourgeois childhood. Ultimately, the lovers are forced to move beyond society to find space for their love (74–5). Even in idyllically portrayed nature, the well ordered fields directly represent private economic gain. Yet the lovers unite with nature in the concluding paragraphs and their feelings blend harmonically with nature. Holmes argues that this unity of the lovers in nature constitutes Feuerbach's concept of unity of man and woman (*Gattungsleben*) which embodies the universal experience of life. "To discover the 'Gattungsleben' Sali and Vrenchen have not only to go beyond the idyll, which is the secular idealization of possessive society, they must also discount the eternal life which is the transcendental analogy of that society's egoism" (77).

In her essay, "The Art of Allusion in Keller's Fiction," Margaret Jacobs defines allusion as "a covert, implied indirect or passing reference to a form of words, a passage or a work which originated outside the text containing the allusion" (97). She distinguishes between four different types of allusion which Keller employs in his comic narrative, helping him provide a sense of irony and the mock-heroic. The first type is a brief or passing allusion within a section of text. The ten-year-old Heinrich Lee sleeping at the foot of Gretchen following the performance of *Faust* suggests this element of play: the young boy as the knight and protector of Gretchen. The second type constitutes a continuous code or network in a given passage, consisting of a series of allusions. Jacobs' example is from *Das Sinngedicht*, in which she deftly compares Reinhart to Faust. The third type is an allusion to a model or an archetype or a series of the same, which create a theme for a work of fiction. Drawing again upon *Das Sinngedicht*, Jacobs shows how Reinhart's approach to Lucie is labyrinthine and recalls elements of the fairy-tale. The fourth kind is a network of allusions which lends support to the thematic and structural purport of the work. Jacobs demonstrates how a series of fairy-tale elements in *Kleider Machen Leute* enable Keller to create "an artful manipulation of a conspiracy between fantasy and reality" (104). She reveals how the allusions to the fairy tale afford the reader the contrast between reality and illusion, thereby providing space for Keller's irony to unfold. Likewise, she demonstrates how these allusions support the structure of comic plot in the novella. Keller's application of allusions, while setting him apart from those masters of comic novel he so admired, enabled him to integrate the ironic, playful, mocking tone we have come to admire in his fiction.

Also focusing on comedy in her essay "'Göttlicher Unsinn und unbeschränkter Mutwillen': Keller And The Concept of Comedy," Louise Adey reveals Keller's appreciation of and indebtedness to the Viennese popular stage, namely, to the Volkstheater, particularly to Nestroy's *Lokalposse* (farce). Keller appreciated the popular theater because it spoke directly to its audiences, inviting them to participate directly and thereby reap the benefits of such interaction (110). Adey confines her exposition to the stories which make up *Die Leute von Seldwyla*, because they lend themselves well to the rubric of *politische Komödie* (political comedy). With evident humor, she demonstrates how Keller's relationship with the Viennese popular theater and particularly his admiration for Nestroy is key to understanding his own humor. Keller wanted to focus on political comedy and recognized the importance of maintaining a reference to the times while also transcending them. He particularly admired the use of allegory by the Viennese comedians. Keller bases the Seldwyla stories on topical issues. He enters into complicity with his readers in the two introductions to the two volumes, in which he and the reader are discussing the people of Seldwyla, the neighbors, who are always easier to criticize, because we are criticizing another, rather than ourselves. Adey observes that the majority of the stories are not about the people of Seldwyla. She suggests the reason is that "the Seldwyla ethos is much more effective as a foil than as a focus" (116). The Seldwyler come away looking better when they are contrasted with their neighbors in Ruechenstein or Goldach. Of course, Keller satirizes heavily those misfits in the stories that do take place in Seldwyla. The popularity of the Seldwyla stories reveals that Keller's readers were amused by the sense of humor that distinguishes these

merry, undisciplined Seldwyla folk; they most probably did not see themselves as
being portrayed by them. This may explain why the Seldwyler play a tangential
role, except when Keller is really taking them to task. Adey contends that their
role as the perpetrators and accomplices of jokes is one of their most important
functions. She believes that the marginalization of the Seldwyla people is a
manifestation of that "freier Willkurs in der Ökonomie."[11] Caprice will play
down the biting satire and provide for a brand of humor that is more universally
acceptable. By promising to focus on the misfits in his introduction to the Seldwyla novellas, Keller informs his reader that he will avoid painting the *Lebens-
bilder* [portraits of life] so prevalent in Biedermeier, and will at the same time
provide a focus for the novella cycle. Adey demonstrates how Keller adapts the
use of arabesques, which he borrows from the romantic tradition, to celebrate his
unbounded fantasy and its ability to transcend mundane reality. She shows how
the arbitrary and inconsequential, the role of chance and the unusual names of
Keller's characters all contribute to Keller's unique sense of humor. Adey reveals
how much Keller may have drawn upon the Viennese popular theater to transcend banal reality and thereby rejuvenate political comedy.

Eve Mason sheds light on Keller's conflicting views of "Bürgerlichkeit" in
her essay, "Two Views On 'Bürgerlichkeit' in Gottfried Keller's *Die Leute von
Seldwyla*." While many of Keller's characters manage to achieve a degree of independent thought and develop a sense of civic responsibility, Mason finds his
stories rarely provide models of concrete success, citing Heinrich Lee in the revised edition and Pankraz. She suggests that these less than satisfactory conclusions represent "the reflexion of the artist on his life experience" (Mason, 128).
Keller believed in the integrity and goodness of man espoused by eighteenth-
century enlightened humanism, but also recognized the dilemma of the modern
liberal state which, in guaranteeing individual freedom, ultimately obstructed the
full development of the individual in the name of that same freedom (129).
Keller's skeptical view of life enabled him to acknowledge the positive and negative sides of *Bürgerlichkeit*. With this in mind, Mason questions traditional
readings of *Frau Regel Amrain*, which argue that she is an educational model and
a paragon of middle-class values, suggesting rather that Keller was never deluded
by this form of educational program (133). He realized that Frau Amrain's well
meaning education greatly restrains Fritz's personal freedom of development. In
Romeo und Julia auf dem Dorfe, Mason demonstrates how the two lovers are so

---

[11] Adey writes: "'Willkur' is an impossible term to translate satisfactorily into English,
since neither 'whimsy' nor 'arbitrariness' comes anywhere near capturing that delight
in the free play of the imagination which characterizes the term for Friedrich
Schlegel and the Romantics. The meaning of the word nevertheless comes across
quite clearly in the example I have just been discussing, for what could be more
'willkürlich' than to call a collection of stories Die Leute von Seldwyla and then to
announce in your preface that the focus of these stories is going to be exceptions
(*Abfällsel*)." 117–18.

restricted by middle-class morals and virtues, that they can only express their desire for freedom with a mutual suicide. While Sali and Vrenchen have the integrity and ability to overcome the restrictions inherent in bourgeois society, they refuse to live without one another and refuse living with resignation. The young lovers are trapped in the web of middle-class mentality (Bürgerlichkeit), whose adherents transgress the very virtues they uphold (139). Likewise, Mason questions the unsatisfactory conclusion of *Das verlorene Lachen* in which Jukundus and Justine find one another but fail to establish themselves as responsible citizens. Keller repeatedly questions the ability of individuals to maintain ethical standards in a world driven by material greed.

The great economic and social upheavals in the mid-nineteenth century made an indelible imprint on Keller's prose and on his mission as a writer. In her recently published, *The Poetics of Scepticism*, Erika Swales focuses on those tensions which inform Keller's narratives and which lend those narratives their uniqueness. Swales's study is particularly striking because the fractures, fragments and dissonances inherent in Keller's writing are not interpreted (as they have been heretofore), "as a conciliatory balancing act, but rather in terms of a sustained dialectic" (14). Earlier critics have recognized these same dissonances, most notably Hofmannsthal,[12] who evaluated them as a strength of Keller's writing, as well as Fontane,[13] who lamented Keller's overbearing tone (what Swales refers to as Keller's unique texture). Swales's ontological, historical and aesthetic interpretation suggests possible reasons for these inherent ideological and stylistic contradictions. Swales investigates three areas of Keller's skeptical deliberations: 1) his lifelong preoccupation with the ontological value of human achievement; 2) his concern with the specific temporality of the mid-nineteenth century with its material and spiritual conditions; and 3) his sense of unease, which writing in the age of transition precipitates (16). Swales's argument examines Keller's dual view of humanity; specifically, his conception of the traditional eighteenth-century view, in which men and women, having been endowed with reason, sustain his faith in working toward an ever more humane humankind. Juxtaposed with this hope is the depiction of the real world, the deterministic conception, in which human beings, endowed with free will and love of their fellow humans, are viewed as insignificant materially-determined creatures, who follow primitive instinctual principles of self-preservation (22). This dual conception of humanity permeates Keller's works; the debate between free will and chance, as Swales demonstrates in the Seldwyla novellas and be-

---

[12] See chapter three for a discussion of Hofmannsthal's essay on Keller. Hugo von Hofmannsthal, "Unterhaltung über die Schriften on Gottfried Keller," In: Hugo von Hoffmannsthal, *Gesammelte Werke*, Berlin: Fischer, 1924, vol. 2. 226–275.

[13] See the discussion of Fontane's views on Keller discussed at the end of chapter two. Theodor Fontane, *Sämtliche Werke*, Munich: Nymphenburger Verlagshandlung, 1963. Vol. 21, 1. 262.

yond, can be observed in all of Keller's writing and remains unresolved. Swales cites spinning as a reoccurring theme in Keller's works, and shows how it evolves into a strong ontological argument. The spider will continue to spin its web anew, regardless of how often it is destroyed; continuity of being outweighs all of questions of meaning or purpose (24). Likewise, in Swales's interpretation, the *Tanzlegendchen* annuls the Feuerbachian harmony achieved in the first six legends. The muses are banished from heaven — the state of paradise is no longer attainable — "ontologically humanity has been exiled" (25). Keller's depictions of humanity are rife with his profound doubts of the worth of the human world.

These fears, misgivings, and doubts have evolved as a result of the social, economic, and cultural transitions Keller both witnessed and experienced. Swales asserts that Keller's conception of human worth is dependent on the moral aspect; Keller's view of history banks on the affirmative potential of humanity to envision and to work toward a better age. His view of history sways between hope and despair. She suggests that Keller's understanding of his social world is much more subtle and sophisticated than many critics have realized. Keller's works have always concerned themselves with the formation of the individual within the social system. Swales contends that Keller (and Feuerbach) always viewed literature as the guardian of enlightened humanity.

Many critics have shown that Keller began his writing career believing in the educative function of art. Swales, while not disagreeing with this assertion, tempers it considerably by revealing the degree to which his skepticism increased throughout his career due in part to the transitional age in which he lived. Keller's doubts increased, Swales contends, as the historical changes, particularly the rise of speculative capitalism made themselves felt. She clearly demonstrates how carefully Keller constructed the Seldwyla cycle and how it reflects his maturing views of man and society. *Pankraz, der Schmoller* illustrates a drab world and suggests that egoism and selfhood be subordinated to the betterment of the commonweal. Contrasting sharply to this, *Romeo und Julia auf dem Dorfe* promotes the integral being, the unconditional love which binds Sali and Vrenchen. Theirs is a love bound by the dictates of their bourgeois conscience. This tragedy is juxtaposed to the strict didactic regimentation of *Frau Regel Amrain und ihr Jüngster*, a tale devoted to iron discipline and order. The next tale, namely *Die drei gerechten Kammacher*, carry this sense of regulation and duty to an extreme. Thus this "process of self-relativisation," reaches its apex in the middle of the cycle (191). The next four stories address the issue of fictionality by pondering the "interdependence of the material and the aesthetic order" (191). *Spiegel, das Kätzchen* counters the materialist argument by exposing the web of deception in which humanity is engulfed. *Kleider machen Leute* concerns itself with the fiction of social dress and the accompanying language register. *Der Schmied seines Glückes* reveals the need of those living in the Gründerzeit to create tradition as a means to legitimation. *Die mißbrauchten Liebesbriefe* expresses Keller's concern with the massive production of novellas by would-be authors. *Dietegen* sways between brutality and the hope of paradise. *Das verlorene Lachen* is replete with inherent tensions and friction. The conflict between moral and economic necessity remains and likewise poetic expression and prosaic vision continue to be at loggerheads. Thus these stories both individually and by virtue of their interdependence enact "the principle of relativisation" acknowledging "the conditionality of its own being and seeing" (192). Keller never banishes the concept of the undivided being and maintains that "it is humanity's inalienable obligation to work toward socio-political and economic conditions that would warrant the flourishing of both the individual and the community" (45). Keller's misgivings concerning the ability of fiction to overcome the problems of the day are expressed in the introduction to the second volume of the Seldwyla stories and rest largely on the prevailing materialism which threatens poetic pursuits. However, Keller did not believe that socio-political engagement should be asserted at the expense of aesthetic value.

Many critics have noted the stylistic instability of Keller's works. Hettner once suggested that Keller perhaps lacked talent as a writer. Swales argues that the reasons are far more complex. There are the purely biographical factors, such as the lack of a good formal education and the lack of a comfortable (financial) existence, which would have perhaps set the stage for stylistic harmony and would have facilitated complete stability. There was also the pathological procrastination intensified by the literary industry of the day which imposed deadlines on Keller that may have forced him to sacrifice artistic integrity for efficiency. Finally, Swales suggests, there is the cultural argument with an increasing production of epigonal works. These rough-hewn transitions and fragments alert the reader to Keller's specific texture, an imperfection that constitutes the unique "eloquence" in his works (53). This poetic empathy and alienation, this profound skepticism about the merit of the aesthetic undertaking went hand in hand and remained with Keller for the rest of his life. It is fitting that we close this chapter on Anglo-American scholarship with Swales's superb study, because her multi-leveled critical approach serves rather like a weathervane, showing the direction Keller scholarship will take in the 1990s and beyond.

Works Cited

Adey, Louise. "Göttlicher Unsinn und unbeschränkter Mutwillen: Keller and the Concept of Comedy." In *Gottfried Keller 1819–1990 — London Symposium 1990*. 109–126. Stuttgart: Hans-Dieter Heinz, 1991.

Coar, John F. *Studies in German Literature in the Nineteenth Century*. 270–302. New York: Macmillan, 1903.

Eagleton, Terry. *The Ideology of the Aesthetic*. Oxford: Oxford UP, 1990.

Ellis, John M. "Die drei gerechten Kammacher." In *Narration in the German Novella*. 136–54. Cambridge (UK): Cambridge UP, 1974.

Faulkner, William H. "Keller's *Der grüne Heinrich*. Anna and Judith and Their Predecessors in Rousseau's *Confessions*." *Virginia Univ. Phil. Soc. Bulletin*. Humanities Series 1, no. 2 (February 1912), 51–57.

Flood, John L. & Swales, Martin. eds. *Gottfried Keller 1819–1890 — London Symposium 1990*. Stuttgart: Hans-Dieter Heinz, 1991.

Hart, Gail K. *Readers and Their Fictions in the Novels and Novellas of Gottfried Keller*. Chapel Hill: U of North Carolina P, 1989.

Hauch, Edward F. *Gottfried Keller as a Democratic Idealist*. New York: Columbia UP, 1916.

Hay, Marie. *The Story of a Swiss Poet: A Study of Gottfried Keller's Life and Works*. Bern: Wyss, 1920.

Holmes, T. M. "Romeo und Julia auf dem Dorfe: the Idyll of Possessive Individualism." *Gottfried Keller 1819–1890 — London Symposium 1990*. 67–80. Stuttgart: Hans-Dieter Heinz, 1991.

Holub, Robert. *Reflections of Realism*. 101–32. Detroit: Wayne State UP, 1991.

Jackson, David. "*Kleider machen Leute:* Literary Outfitters by Appointment to the Muses or to the Paying Public? " *Gottfried Keller 1819–1890 — London Symposium 1990*. 81–96. Stuttgart: Hans-Dieter Heinz, 1991.

Jacobs, Margaret. "The Art of Allusion in Keller's Fiction." *Gottfried Keller 1819–1890 — London Symposium 1990*. 97–108. Stuttgart: Hans-Dieter Heinz, 1991.

Jennings, Lee B. "The Model of the Self in Gottfried Keller's Prose." *German Quarterly* 56 (March 1983), 196–230.

Kolb, Waltraud. *Die Rezeption Gottfried Kellers im englischen Sprachraum bis 1920*. Bern: Peter Lang, 1992.

Kramer, Priscilla M. *The Cyclical Method of Composition in Gottfried Keller's Sinngedicht*. New York: Ottendorfer, 1939.

Lemke, Victor J. "The Deification of Gottfried Keller." *Monatshefte* 48 (1956), 119–26.

Lindsay, J. M. *Gottfried Keller: Life and Works*. London: Oswald Wolff, 1968.

Mason, Eve. "Two Views on Bürgerlichkeit in Gottfried Keller's *Die Leute von Seldwyla*." *Gottfried Keller 1819–1890 — London Symposium 1990*. 127–44. Stuttgart: Hans-Dieter Heinz, 1991.

Minden, Michael. "*Der grüne Heinrich* and the Legacy of *Wilhelm Meister*." *Gottfried Keller 1819–1890 — London Symposium 1990*. 20–40. Stuttgart: Hans-Dieter Heinz, 1991.

Mullen, Inga E. *German Realism in the United States*. New York: Peter Lang, 1988.

Pascal, Roy. *The German Novel*. 30–51. Manchester: Manchester UP, 1956.

Pestalozzi, Karl. "Kellers Gedicht 'Rosenglaube.'" *Gottfried Keller 1819–1890 — London Symposium 1990.* 11–28. Stuttgart: Hans-Dieter Heinz, 1991.

Reichert, Herbert W. *Basic Concepts in the Philosophy of Gottfried Keller.* Chapel Hill, NC: U of North Carolina P, 1949.

Robertson, John George. *A History of German Literature.* London: William Blackwood & Sons, 1902; reprint, 1966.

———. *Essays and Addresses on Literature.* London: Routledge, 1935.

Rowley, Brian A. "Views of Society Implied in *Die Leute von Seldwyla.*" *Gottfried Keller 1819–1890 — London Symposium 1990.* 53–66. Stuttgart: Hans-Dieter Heinz, 1991.

Ruppel, Richard. R. *Gottfried Keller: Poet, Pedagogue and Humanist.* New York & Bern: Peter Lang, 1988.

Stern, J. P. *Re-Interpretations: Seven Studies in Nineteenth Century German Literature.* 301–47. New York: Basic Books, 1964.

Swales, Erika. *The Poetics of Scepticism. Gottfried Keller and Die Leute von Seldwyla.* Providence, RI & Oxford: Berg, 1994.

Swales, Martin. *The German Bildungsroman from Wieland to Hesse.* 86–104. Princeton: Princeton UP, 1978.

Thomas, Calvin. *A History of German Literature.* 389–390. 1909; rpt. Port Washington, NY: Kennikat.

Zimmern, Helen. "A Swiss Novelist." *Frasers Magazine,* April 21, 1880, 459–76.

Zippermann, Charles C. *Gottfried Keller Bibliographie 1844–1934.* Zurich: Rascher & Cie, 1935.

6: Modern Directions in Keller Scholarship: The Last Twenty-Five Years

KELLER HAS REMAINED AN EVERGREEN in the canon of nineteenth-century German literature. While his works have yet to become well known among non-German-speaking readers, they continue to prove fertile ground for new scholarly investigations. Perhaps the most innovative critical direction in Keller scholarship of the last few decades has been marked by the psychoanalytical studies of Adolf Muschg, Gerhard Kaiser and Lee B. Jennings. Their efforts have been matched by the socio-economic-historical studies of Heinrich Richartz, Adolf Muschg and Erika Swales who have greatly expanded the sociological studies of Roy Pascal and Michael Kaiser in the preceding decades. Wolfgang Preisendanz has provided an investigation of Keller's encounter with the scientific revolution in the nineteenth century, particularly Darwinism, in *Das Sinngedicht*. Both Kurt Wenger and Karl Fehr have reinterpreted Keller's religiosity, arriving at different conclusions. Kaspar Locher has provided a thorough study of Keller's ethics. Jörg Zierleyn unveils the most comprehensive investigation of Keller's debt to Goethe and to Weimar Classicism. Both Karl Fehr and Hans Wysling explore Keller's debt to the ancients and reveal his extensive use of myth and archetype. Bruno Weber has furnished an updated assessment of Keller as landscape artist, the first since Paul Schaffner's in 1923. Rätus Luck has provided a comprehensive study of Keller as literary critic. Renate Böschenstein attempts to define happiness in Keller's works and Karl Pestalozzi explores the techniques that Keller uses to transfer this happiness to the reader. Both Martin Swales and Hartmut Steinecke assess Keller's novels, particularly *Der grüne Heinrich*, in terms of European Realism. Peter von Matt, Adolf Muschg and Erika Swales have begun to explore and expound upon the rumors that haunt Keller's biography and the paradoxes and incongruities in Keller's prose and poetry. The new historical-critical edition of Keller under the editorship of Thomas Böning and published by Bibliothek der deutschen Klassiker attests to Keller's abiding reputation at the end of the twentieth century. Surely the international colloquia in Zürich and London in 1990 marking the centennial of Keller's death constitute a tribute to Keller's popularity and to the enduring relevance of his works.

Keller scholarship in the last quarter of a century was launched in 1970 by Rätus Luck's informative and voluminous book *Gottfried Keller als Literaturkritiker*, a study which has proven particularly helpful and insightful in preparing various stages of this study. Luck provides an overview of Keller's prowess as a literary critic while divulging what Keller thought of his critics. The volume opens with an overview of literary life and literary criticism in the nineteenth century as seen from Keller's perspective. This chapter, when read in tandem with Alfred Zäch's *Gottfried Keller im Spiegel seiner Zeit* and Peter Uwe Hohendahl's *Building A National Literature. The Case of Germany 1830–1870*, provide a thorough understanding of the literary industry in Keller's day.

Luck's text dedicates substantial energy to the dialogue between Hermann Hettner and Gottfried Keller over drama and dramatic theory. Specifically, their correspondence pertaining to Shakespeare, Lessing, Hebbel and Richard Wagner's dramatic theories and works are discussed. Luck examines Keller's criticism of Friedrich Theodor Vischer, particularly Vischer's aesthetic principles. He then investigates Keller's fundamental aesthetic and critical principles and seeks to determine the originality of Keller's criticism. He also explores Keller's knowledge of the ancients and of German Classicism and takes a close look at Keller's analysis of literary genres, specifically the lyric and the theory of the novella. Luck investigates Keller's comments on a Swiss national literature. The final section is devoted to Keller as an essayist. Throughout this study Luck makes astute observations, draws well weighed conclusions, and offers gracious objective carefully annotated commentary.

Kurt Wenger's *Gottfried Kellers Auseinandersetzung mit dem Christentum*, (1971) is an attempt to analyze Keller's lifelong struggle with his relationship to a Supreme Being, the church, faith and immortality. Wenger's study is divided into three sections. The first shows how Keller portrayed Christianity as a threat to the natural man, that faith in immortality and in a personal God disrupted, even hindered the natural development of man. In the second Wenger argues that Keller's worldly piousness (*Weltfrommigkeit*) is juxtaposed to Christianity assumes pantheistic rather than purely Christian implications. The final section of the study discusses Keller's creative polemic in the *Sieben Legenden*, which transposes Christian legends into stories that embrace secular humanism. Section three also examines Keller's dialogue with the reform theology of his day that infuses *Das verlorene Lachen* and, to a lesser degree, *Martin Salander*. Perhaps the greatest difference between reform theology on the one hand and Keller, Feuerbach and later Strauß on the other, is that reform theology was founded upon Schleiermacher and Hegel, who superimposed the Christian religion (*das Christliche*) on everything human (*das Menschliche*), whereas Keller, influenced by Feuerbach, viewed the joy found in human existence and Christian aspirations as irreconcilable opposites. Emanating from this debate is a clear decision in favor of the modern secularism (*Weltlichkeit*) which allows Wenger to conclude that Keller came to understand himself not as a Christian, but as a secular humanist. Wenger's study draws a different conclusion from that of Zollinger-Wells's 1954 study.

Karl Fehr's *Gottfried Keller: Aufschlüsse und Deutungen*, is a collection of essays resulting from some three decades of continuous scholarly endeavor. These essays discuss the entire range of Keller's art. While they lay no claim to comprehensiveness, they collectively reevaluate many of our long held convictions, while offering profound interpretations of Keller's poetry and fiction. This collection of interlocking thematically arranged essays may be read individually or as a monograph. Fehr's essays concentrate on themes in Keller's poetry, but not to the exclusion of his prose. In an enlightening and persuasive manner Fehr discusses the themes of life and death in Keller's early poetry. He shows how Keller at an early age came to accept death as an integral part of life's cycle. Fehr discusses Keller's early Weltanschauung and religious beliefs, labeling him an "Apostat," one who has fallen away from the Christian faith. Fehr begins a reinterpretation and reevaluation of Keller's belief system, which is not the central theme of this monograph, but does constitute the recurrent strain which permeates many of these essays. He compares the reflections contained in Keller's seventeen Ghaseln to similar thoughts in Pindar's poetry, conceding that Keller's direct knowledge of ancient Greek philosophy and the ancient poets was minimal. However, Fehr does find many shared thoughts between Keller and Lucretius: both exude the same passion and love for the empirical world, both believe that the individual must find himself in a community of family and friends. The poems, "Im afrikanischen Felsental" and "Siehst du den Stern im Fernsten blau" are visions, in Fehr's interpretation, of the poet's soul.

Fehr's essay on *Der Landvogt von Greifensee* demonstrates Keller's ability to transform and adapt historical material for his own purposes, as he did the in *Sieben Legenden*. In the first of two essays on *Das verlorene Lachen*, Fehr studies Jukundus Meyenthal as the upright young lad, who must resort to soul-searching in order to find himself. A second essay views the novella — which has made the transition from Biedermeier to Realism — as one that confronts bourgeois, democratic Swiss society and examines those forces that lead to the separation of Justine, Jukundus, and to the collapse of the family in this novella (150). If the *Sieben Legenden* reveal Keller's poetic freedom, then this novella depicts Keller's engagement with the social, economic, and theological questions of his day. Various trials transform Jukundus from a carefree upright individual introduced as the much heralded festival singer into a serious upright Swiss citizen. Jukundus professes a pantheistic religion which corresponds to Keller's own belief in nature (*Naturglaube*), replacing the church dogma he had rejected. Fehr's sensitivity for Keller's language detects a subtle change in the tone of Jukundus's belief system from that of *Der grüne Heinrich*. Keller has, according to Fehr, not rejected God completely, but has come to see Him embodied in the natural world. In a forested natural setting, Jukundus and Justine end their separation on a Sunday morning with distant church bells ringing; in Fehr's interpretation the novella closes in reverential, God-fearing tones. Fehr argues that this subtle change in Keller's religious perspective remains consistent with his monotheistic view of the world (Fehr, 160). Keller's religious creed has assumed the fervor of a religious seeker in pursuit of a God, whose actions and deeds influence and govern all things. The allusions which grace the concluding scenes of *Das verlorene Lachen* manifest themselves again in the stark biblical language of the poem "Die öffentlichen Verleumder." Fehr also points to the timelessness of Keller's wisdom, for this poem allegedly inspired Thomas Mann during his exile in Zürich, and served as inspiration to the members of the famous German underground student resistance movement in Munich, the White Rose (162, 172). Fehr concludes with an analysis of Keller's *Ursula*, in which he returns to a subtle reading of Keller's religious views. In Fehr's interpretation, Keller demonstrates his reverence for Zwingli by portraying him as a hero of the people. He alludes to a softening in Keller's negative position toward Christianity and this would seem substantiated by his eloquent and erudite interpretation of a late poem, "Abend auf Golgatha," which for Fehr becomes the embodiment of Keller's mature religious views. Fehr's study of the musicality in Keller's poetry (*Klangsprache*) is unprecedented. Likewise his examination of the element of play (*Spielelement*) in Keller's works is also groundbreaking. These essays portray Keller as an empirically oriented, witty, Biedermeier-bourgeois realist, who found his equilibrium in the passionate search for and in the rejection of various belief systems, caught as he was between the lonely artist's life and the fervent search for a communal ethic.

In his monograph *Literaturkritik als Gesellschaftskritik* (1975), Heinrich Richartz provides an insightful investigation of the political and didactic purport of the Seldwyla novellas and in particular *Romeo und Julia auf dem Dorfe* and *Kleider Machen Leute*, in an effort to demonstrate the extent to which Keller employed fiction as a vehicle to strengthen democratic thinking as well as a medium for exposing attitudes and behavior that undermined the democratic process. Richartz is less concerned with Keller's democratic and political views which have been explored primarily by Edward F. Hauch (1916), by Hans Max Kriesi (1918), by Jonas Fränkel (1939) among others. Nor is Richartz concerned with the broader aspects of employing literature as a vehicle of education in the whole of Keller's works. Rather, Richartz concentrates on Keller's political goals for his fiction and his methods for achieving them, as they are revealed in the Seldwyla novellas. In Richartz's reading, Keller's fiction is an open dialogue with his epoch, in which Keller lauds the positive and exposes the negative aspects of his time. Keller's awareness of the enormous political, social, and economic changes of his era, enabled him in an enlightened manner to rise above the fray and portray a society in transition. Keller believed that the individual, when properly educated, could make a difference. Keller viewed highbrow literature as a vehicle for inciting change (Richartz, 16). The old classics (Goethe, Schiller, Tieck) could no longer serve as an orientation for the contemporary reader. The modern writer must fulfill the practical and theoretical needs of the modern era. Art is to be shaped by its ability to promote humanity and it will be judged by its impact upon the historical changes of its time (181). Richartz shows the manner in which Keller's conception of art expresses itself in the projection of a narrative on a well-known literary model such as *Romeo and Juliet*. This familiarity raises certain expectations that are then altered or even dashed when measured against the demands of the democratic present. By providing a twist in the narrative, Keller disrupts the expectations of the reader which, as Richartz deftly shows in *Romeo und Julia auf dem Dorfe*, vaults the literary model into the present, a process which unveils certain flaws in democratic behavior and attitude.

Richartz demonstrates how Keller takes his narrative and superimposes it upon Shakespeare's *Romeo and Juliet*. The title reminds the reader of the original story, but the "auf dem Dorfe" sets a new stage for the Shakespearean material, by placing it in the context of a nineteenth-century Swiss village. This setting initially recalls aspects of Goethe's idyllic epic, *Hermann und Dorothea*. Drawing upon Keller's essays on Gotthelf, Richartz shows that Keller placed greater emphasis in his fiction on the ethical-political position than on formal aesthetic criteria. The beauty of any artwork was dependent upon its proportions, its relationship to reality, its ability to introduce political truths (98). Richartz then shows how Keller's choice vocabulary (*Bezirksrat* [regional council], *Pacht zahlen* [to pay leasing fees], *Kanzlei* [chancellery], *Pachtzins* [rent], etc.) sweeps the reader away from the idyllic and into the nineteenth-century bourgeois arena (84–85). Likewise, the lyricism of *Romeo und Juliet* is replaced by simple dialogue. The lovers' emotions are expressed in the sayings on the gingerbread they purchase for one another at the parish fair. In terms of ethical democratic action, the two farmers are clearly not interested in justice. They pretend not to know who owns the fallow acre; their attitude embodies the spirit of the community they inhabit (54). Sali and Vrenchen become the victims of social conditions that warrant transformation. The couple's dependence upon their surroundings becomes the new cloak for the old fable. In Richartz's reading, the entire community become responsible for the death of the lovers. The ironic twist in the closing lines of the story reveals that the community prefers to blame the death of the young couple on moral deficiencies and uncontrolled passions. Richartz demonstrates that these lovers were helplessly entrapped by the bourgeois values of a society that they dearly wanted to join, but which had rejected them. If contributing to society constitutes the foundation for a fruitful existence, then the retreat from and or rejection by society destroys the very foundation on which democracy rests (64).

Thus in Richartz's reading, Keller developed a method of storytelling that would enable his readers to become cognizant of the historical changes, of flaws in society, and in the democratic process; Keller accomplished this by superimposing his narrative upon a literary model (myth, motif, symbol) familiar to his readership, or by transforming that model in a manner that would awaken his readers by making them more conscious of reality (102). He expected the reader to become cognizant of reality, to repossess it and to change it for the better. In this regard he shares with Rousseau the optimism that the education of the individual can influence others in society and contribute to a growing circle of enlightened individuals (194).

The most innovative study published in recent years has been Adolf Muschg's literary portrait of Gottfried Keller. Much more than a revised and innovative biography, Muschg's book offers a plethora of ideas and inspiring reflections that have broadened the horizons of Keller scholarship, and inspired innovative interpretations (Jennings, G. Kaiser, and E. Swales). Muschg's literary portrait is not an introduction; rather, it is a re-encounter for those who know Keller and his oeuvre well. It is Muschg's intention to rejuvenate our image of a well known, but no longer familiar author. Thus, under Muschg's examination, Keller's life consists of melancholic toil (*Trauerarbeit*) and literary work. In his attempt to overcome the myth of Gottfried Keller, thus paving the way for a new evaluation of the author and his works, Muschg discusses Keller in the greater context of nineteenth-century Zurich and its Zeitgeist.

Guilt is the driving force in Keller's life according to Muschg. Keller's own productivity defined his worth in the face of ever present and unresolved guilt. Using the Freudian psychoanalytical approach, Muschg postulates that Keller's guilt stems from the Oedipus complex, the wish for the death of the father, so that he alone could possess his mother. His expulsion from school, no matter how unjust, increased this feeling of guilt and sowed the seeds of a quiet but all pervasive "Grundtrauer" (melancholy). Understanding Keller's unique relationship toward his mother (and eventually toward his sister, who fulfilled the maternal role in the Keller household after his mother's death) helps us understand *Der grüne Heinrich*. Having misjudged their talents as a landscape painter, both Keller and Heinrich feel increased guilt toward themselves and their respective mothers; both mothers encouraged their sons with financial and moral support, making them both guilty of complicity. This personal failure forced Heinrich Lee to perish in the original (1855) version of the novel, enabling Keller to terminate his failed past and begin anew. Guilt drives Keller and Heinrich Lee of the revised edition (1880) to seek employment in service of society, but even a successful career in service of society cannot ease their consciences (148–49). The conclusion to the revised edition is ambiguous at best; Heinrich resigned in love and in his position as an Oberamtsmann, an unproductive white collar position, is unable to assess his individual worth.

Indeed, Keller's self-effacing relationship to women in general presupposes a certain inadequacy. All of Keller's women, even when they are reaching out to him, are behind glass (Muschg, 77). Keller's humor in this context can be understood as a means of self-conquest and ultimately of self-defense. The male, who cannot actualize his masculinity, cannot expect to win the graces of the female sex, and must therefore accept that he can only become an honorable knight.

Keller's guilt toward his mother has an economic as well as a Freudian component. Neither mother nor son were brought up to understand the meaning of money. Handling money meant spending it wisely and not extravagantly. Keller, as the only surviving son should have become the breadwinner in his deceased father's place. Instead he exploited, without malicious intent, his mother's naive innocence in financial matters to pursue his ill-wrought goal of becoming a landscape painter. Keller's dependence on his mother's financial and moral support indebted him to her which increased both their individual and collective guilt: she for not giving her son the professional direction he so needed, and he for deceiving them both in pursuit of an illusion. Their mutual economic plight was further intensified by industrialization which both mother and son failed to comprehend (147). Frau Keller gave up any hope of accumulating sufficient capital to support her son. She withdrew into her boarding house, lived from the rent she collected and the cloth she could weave. Keller, given his preparation in Zurich, was doomed to fail in the urban landscape of Munich. Likewise Keller's fictional creation, Heinrich Lee, is at one stage reduced from would-be Swiss landscape artist to painting flag poles; he thus learns the meaning of money and work. Individual worth in the industrialized age is based upon wealth rather than character. Self-induced poverty becomes social condemnation. Thus, Muschg contends, *Der grüne Heinrich*, is about the memory of hope for success in art and in love — a hope which is lost and leads ultimately to despair born of guilt; this guilt led to the quiet melancholy that became part of Keller's being.

Mushg's reexamination of Keller's political views is the most original since Richartz' study in 1975. At the time of Keller's return from Munich, Switzerland was a center of economic and political liberalism comparable only to the USA and England. Keller sought acceptance through political and social involvement during the forties. Muschg attempts to define Keller's political attitudes by exploring his background and personality: a rural and urban mentality, a petit bourgeois (*Kleinbürger*) and social climber, a worker and an artist. A close study of Keller's ambivalent relationship to Alfred Escher, the great statesman and railway tycoon of Zurich, reveals much about Keller's attitude toward the social, economic and political events of the day. Although Keller's faith in the republic swayed between extremes, Muschg argues that *Das verlorene Lachen* and *Martin Salander* remain literary testaments to Keller's Swiss patriotism (278). Keller's political views oscillated between faith and despair, and between hope and disillusionment; between the euphoria of *Das Fähnlein* and the darkness of Salander's Münsterberg. Driven by a sense of guilt, a sense of a debt owed to his countrymen, Keller served Switzerland as cantonal clerk. His service was impeccable and his esteemed integrity enabled him to survive a transition in governments. Muschg suggests that this position as cantonal clerk is much that of the

Oberamtsmann that Heinrich Lee becomes in the 1880 edition of *Der grüne Heinrich*. Both positions express a loss of self-respect. Both author and character cannot be sure that they are serving modern society, because they do not produce consumables, but rather are civil servants who will never be able to assess whether or not they actually earned their wages, hence the resignation (185–86). The purpose of life (and of government) was to lend life worth, to give life value. Thus his personal melancholy (*Grundtrauer*) reflects the encroaching darkness, political twilight, exemplified by the failures of the Swiss republic as depicted in Keller's last novel *Martin Salander*. In this novel Keller attempts to rescue, whatever is still worthy of preservation. Keller interpreted the sullen reception of this novel as a sign of just how unsalvageable the Swiss republic had become.

A final but important component of Muschg's study is the role death plays in Keller's philosophy of life. Death has three meanings for him. First, it makes life earnest; man is forced to take life's ephemerality seriously, to make something of himself in the life span given us. Second, death is the silent participant and companion of melancholy. Third, death influences the way we live. Together, guilt and death are the driving forces in Keller's life and consequently in his work. These forces generate the all-pervasive melancholy inherent in Keller's work. For Muschg, Keller's literary works constitute "reflections," which conjure up contemporary issues and concern themselves with the question of the significance of art. This melancholy, this resignation, Muschg suggests became for the Keller the inspiration of an entire lifetime.

Just three years after Muschg's biography, Gerhard Kaiser published the most thorough and insightful book on Keller's fiction in recent decades, *Gottfried Keller: Das gedichtete Leben* (1981), which interestingly is dedicated to Adolf Muschg. In contrast to Muschg's biography, Kaiser specifically concentrates on Keller's fiction, poetry and drama; he also accentuates the economic perspective far less than Muschg. Such psychoanalytical approaches to Keller's works are not new. Eduard Hitschmann wrote the first such extensive analysis already in 1919. The spinning and weaving of fiction and reality in Keller's works are in Kaiser's interpretation inseparable. Kaiser's goal is to make Keller's poetic process of spinning and weaving vividly clear and visible (*anschaulich*) to the reader rather than making it conceptually comprehensible (9). The text is a dormant series of events which come to life with each (re)reading. Kaiser wants us to read Keller's cycles with him, to become encircled by them and to experience the cathartic power of the text (654). Keller wove the events of his life into his fiction to the degree that the distinction between them blur; they become one. Certainly, in *Der grüne Heinrich*, Keller's life became the novel and he came to live his fiction (20). Kaiser demonstrates at length just how intertwined Heinrich's fantasy is with Keller's reality. The imbalance in composition, the long story of Heinrich's youth, the diverse episodes and digressive escapades, the wealth of artistic material, the unnatural and imposed conclusion all make *Der grüne Heinrich* unique.

This underscores the authenticity of a novel that fictionalizes its author's life; Keller published himself (30). Kaiser emphasizes that Keller's novel, if read as a confession, takes on a meaning vastly different, than *The Confessions* of St. Augustine or those of Rousseau. While Keller's language and style may well be read with Goethe in mind, his *Grüner Heinrich* cannot be read in the tradition of the Bildungsroman (despite many affinities with *Wilhelm Meister*) in the way that Stifter's *Nachsommer* can.

One third of Kaiser's book is devoted to an analysis of Keller's first novel, which Kaiser believes forms the foundation for all of Keller's later work. He begins with a careful analysis of the relationship between Heinrich Lee and his mother, a relationship that comes to embody the Oedipus myth (56). In Kaiser's reading, Frau Lee persuades Heinrich that his childhood is abnormal because he was fatherless. Guilt plays a central role in this matriarchal family, where Frau Lee struggles to fulfill both the mother's and the father's role. According to Kaiser, the mother embraces nature, emotions, harmony, and poetry, whereas the father embodies intellectual pursuits, dynamic energy, civic responsibility, and prose (56). Frau Lee is clearly overwhelmed by her inability to compensate for the paternal role. Kaiser shows how the mother spins her web, in which Heinrich remains trapped. Heinrich is further influenced by such female figures as Margarete, Anna, Judith, Hulda, and Dortchen.

Heinrich hopes to gain acceptance into society through the back door, by becoming a landscape painter, an occupation that was just barely acceptable by middle-class standards of the day. Heinrich is encouraged if somewhat skeptically (and ultimately financed) by his mother to pursue an occupation, for which he has questionable talent. The men, who act as potential fathers (God, Oheim, schoolmaster, Haberstaat, Römer, Josef Schmalhöfer and the count) all fail to fulfill the fatherly role. Driven by his imagination, encouraged by his mother and misguided by a host of surrogate fathers, Heinrich is doomed to fail as a landscape painter. The neglect he feels toward his mother constitutes a guilt so immense that it becomes the driving force in this novel. Entrapped in his mother's web, Heinrich cannot accept the professional success the count extends to him anymore than he can conceive of the happiness that a potential marriage with Dortchen might bring. Heinrich, as a mother's darling (*Muttersöhnchen*) cannot seek fulfillment or happiness in Dortchen, a potential lifelong partner, because he is instinctively drawn to his biological mother, Frau Lee. Consequently, Heinrich, who is guilt-ridden by her death, cannot hope to rebuild a life for himself. Kaiser suggests that the conclusions to both editions are similar: in the original edition (1855) Heinrich returns to his biological mother and in the revised edition (1880) he returns to his ideal mother, Judith (97). Both returns are imbued with resignation. At the time of writing, Keller was living the fiction he wrote and wrote the life he led. The fictionalized or poeticized life (*das gedichtete Leben*), as Kaiser coins it, reflects an interwoven patchwork of fiction and fact, of fantasy and experience that are inseparably, inextricably bound up in one another.

Keller's preferred genre was the novella which he viewed much in the same way as Goethe had defined it in a conversation to Eckermann of January 29 1827: a novella is nothing more than a story centered around an unprecedented happening (unerhörte Begebenheit). In his discussion of the Seldwyla novellas Kaiser emphasizes the shift from writing to storytelling, from fictionalizing his own life, to writing a fictionalized account of life for a readership. Heinrich Lee writes a monologue whereas most of the novellas have a narrator, thus the novella has the potential to appear less subjective. Despite these formal changes, Kaiser maintains that *Der grüne Heinrich* with its myriad of characters and themes remains the foundation from which all of Keller's works emanate. In fact many of the novellas were conceptually created as he wrote *Der grüne Heinrich*. Kaiser wants people to read these novellas as though they were the fictionalized life of Keller, which he believes they are (277). Seldwyla is not a paternal village, but a maternal one (*Mutterstadt*), and as such, it recalls the mother-son complex in *Der grüne Heinrich* (279). Kaiser insists that all the Seldwyler are siblings of Heinrich Lee; they are well meaning good-for-nothings. For example, Fritz Amrain is under the dominance of Frau Regel Amrain who controls not only her son, but Seldwyla as well. Likewise, Pankraz is a brother to Heinrich Lee. Similarly, the Seldwyla novellas contain many of the central themes of *Der grüne Heinrich*, such as maternally directed education, happiness attained through swindling, deception or lying, and death as a result of love. Particularly interesting is Kaiser's paradigm of just how these Seldwyla novellas are thematically arranged (283). The all-pervasive guilt that drives Heinrich Lee back to his mother also prevents Sali and Vrenchen in *Romeo und Julia auf dem Dorfe* from imagining and ultimately creating a life together. Kaiser reveals how Sali and Vrenchen have much in common with Heinrich and Anna and with Pankraz and Lydia, however without the narcissistic element (311). The couple agrees that Sali's action against Vrenchen's father could never become the foundation for a solid marriage (308). Both Sali and Vrenchen are caught in a web of bourgeois ethics from which they cannot escape. This novella, read against the backdrop of *Der grüne Heinrich* and against the backdrop if its time, reveals the extent to which Keller was aware not only of his own fictionalized life, but of the social, political and economic changes of his day.

All this becomes even more obvious in Kaiser's interpretation of *Das verlorene Lachen*. There, the three strong maternal figures, Frau Meyenthal, Frau Glor (die alte Stauffacherin!) and Justine control Jukundus. When Jukundus fails to succeed professionally on any level, he is taken in and initially cared for by these women. Justine must also overcome trials such as the death of her mother, the bankruptcy of her family's firm and of her pastor's faith, and ultimately the bankruptcy of her own faith, before she has matured sufficiently to rejoin Jukundus. While the reunification of Jukundus and Justine bespeaks hope for (marital) happiness, the same cannot be said for the social, economic and religious fabric of society that disintegrates in the course of the work. Keller was unable to integrate the happiness of the reunified couple into a society in disarray (387). Kaiser points to the deterioration of society exposed in *Das verlorene Lachen*, where Keller criticizes the capitalistic exploitation in the textile branch, lays bare the lack of business ethics and exposes the inability of religion and faith to offer individuals sustenance and guidance in the modern age.

Particularly striking in Kaiser's interpretation of Keller's work is his ability to make vividly clear the organic wholeness of Keller's works. Even *Martin Salander*, which has been traditionally isolated because it possesses a different stylistic stamp and tenet from Keller's earlier work, is drawn convincingly into the opus of Keller's production. Kaiser succeeds in helping us to read Keller's works as his fictionalized life, and has shown convincingly that there is much continuity among the diverse works. Kaiser has achieved, through his clear reference to Keller's biography following Muschg's example, a broad new vision of Keller's works; at the same time he has justifiably transgressed the trend in modern critical approaches to exclude the author's biography from the interpretation of a literary text. It should be noted that in his *Gottfried Keller — Eine Einführung* (Artemis, 1985), Kaiser did reassess his efforts in response to Renate Böschenstein's extensive critique of Kaiser's earlier book.[1] While Kaiser is not the first scholar to interpret Keller's works from a psychoanalytical perspective, his study is undoubtedly the most comprehensive and the most work-oriented — as opposed to biography-oriented — in this vein; moreover it illu-

[1] Renate Böschenstein offers her critical response to Kaiser's 1981 book in her article "Der Schatz und den Schlangen" *Euphorion* 77 (1983): 176–99. Part of Kaiser's response to that criticism follows: "Es ist unmöglich, des biographischen Ausgangsmaterials habhaft zu werden, und ebenso unmöglich, das poetische Produkt vom biographischen Hintergrund völlig abzutrennen; es würde dadurch verflacht. Auch wenn, wie in den letzten Jahren häufig, das Instrumentarium der Psychoanalyse zur Werkerschließung verwendet wird — ich habe daran mit meiner umfangreichen Monographie teilgenommen —, muß gesehen werden, daß es ein wesentlich anderes Anwendungsfeld hat als Triebstrukturen, Triebenergien und deren Transformation im Subjekt. Statt biographische Prozesse im Subjekt zu rekonstruieren, deren Relevanz im Biographischen bleibt, geht es darum, sich einem Werk anzuvertrauen, in dem Biographisches im Blick auf öffentliche Bedeutung bearbeitet ist."

"Von welchem Lebensangriff ich denn ausgehe, war für mich die Kernfrage einer umfangreichen und tiefdringenden Rezension, die Renate Böschenstein dieser Monographie widmete . . . . Dieser Besprechung war ein Glücksfall, denn sie veranlaßte mich dazu, die Voraussetzungen meiner Gottfried-Keller-Interpretationen noch einmal zu überdenken und zu revidieren. Meine Selbstrevision betrifft das Verhältnis von Biographie und Werk und die Relation pyschoanalytischer Deutungsschemata zum Text" (Kaiser, *Gottfried Keller* [Munich, Artemis,1985] 87, 141).

minates a number of far-reaching thematic and symbolic constructs that afford us new critical perspectives on Keller. Lastly, the study must be applauded for its readability and stylistic clarity.

In 1984 Hartmut Steinecke edited a volume of essays titled, *Zu Gottfried Keller*. Although unfortunately out of print, this carefully orchestrated study covers most of Keller's major works and includes essays by such notable Keller scholars and nineteenth-century authorities as Hartmut Laufhütte, Josef Kunz, Martin Swales, Roy C. Cowen, Benno von Wiese, Gert Sautermeister, Arthur Henkel, Fritz Martini, Wolfgang Preisendanz, and Adolf Muschg.

Steinecke's essay "Der Erzähler Gottfried Keller" re-examines Keller's transfiguration of reality as his artistic objective. Keller's term "Reichsunmittelbarkeit der Poesie" is usually understood to mean a refusal to pursue current popular trends in his writing, insisting rather on his autonomy as a writer. Steinecke expands our understanding by suggesting that Keller chose at times to pursue current topics and ideas, but did so because he wanted to and not because he felt the external pressure to do so. Keller's characters interact with the transitional society of their day, they are not *Taugenichts* (good-for-nothings); occasionally there are a few outsiders. Steinecke argues that while objectivity was the goal of realistic writers, subjectivity was Keller's mode or means of portrayal. His narratives are suffused with irony and satire. It was Keller's goal to present a "genuinely truthful portrait of contemporary society" (*G.B.* III/1, 190). Steinecke concludes that it was Keller's goal to apply his wit and humor so as to depict reality in an entertaining manner, but one that did not sacrifice the content or impact of his message.

Martin Swales's essay, "Gottfried Kellers Romeo und Julia auf dem Dorfe", breaks new ground by unveiling the social subtext of this novella. Swales reveals the impact of social proprieties and norms upon the individual characters. Both Marti and Manx allow themselves to be governed by greed, by the inherent social pressure to increase one's wealth. In Swales's interpretation, Sali and Vrenchen are also condemned by their attachment to the social norms that lend their lives structure. Their sense of right and wrong, dictated by their bourgeois conscience, holds them captive to a society that renders their union impossible and ultimately condemns them. The way of "good" society — marriage, profession, and social respect, along with cleanliness and order — as opposed to untamed, unruly degeneration epitomized by the black fiddler and his followers, prescribes the only route Sali and Vrenchen can follow; they are captives of these social norms, and they perish because of them. Similarly, the black fiddler is a social outcast because he cannot prove his identity, and thus forfeits his legal right to possess the disputed acreage. All the characters in this story are victims of social norms. The novella closes with a newspaper clipping that interprets the young couple's suicide as the result of uncontrolled passion; in Swales's interpretation, Sali and Vrenchen's love is not degenerate, but rather the last confession of bourgeois law and order.[2]

Fontane's famous criticism that Keller's entire oeuvre is suffused with a "Kellerscher Ton" is taken to task in Roy C. Cowen's contribution, "Spiegel und Widerspiegelung: Zu Kellers Märchen *Spiegel, das Kätzchen.*" Cowen explores the narrative techniques and examines the two narrators as well as the style and choice of words in this fairy-tale. He examines Keller's vocabulary, explores his use of adverbs and adjectives, and concludes that Keller's adverbs carry more weight than do his adjectives. Often the adjectives seem inappropriate or unusual. Although this is a fairy-tale Keller does not allow Spiegel to speak in a fairy-tale tone. If Spiegel lies, then truth is only to be had in the fairy-tale, for only in the fairy-tale can one express the transitoriness and ambiguity of the world. Adverbs convey this sense of fleeting time. If an author allows his characters and things to have a voice and language all their own, then he cannot be held responsible for the truth. Cowen deduces that Keller believed realist writing can only be objective, if it capriciously employs subjective language. It is through this subjective language that Keller ironically fulfills Fontane's axiom, that realist writers must strive for objectivity.

Fritz Martini's essay "Gottfried Keller: *Hadlaub* oder Falschklang der Kunst und Wahrhaftigkeit der Liebe" demonstrates how Keller transcends the usual historical genre of the period by interweaving the historic, poetic and didactic material into a social fabric that depicts the end of feudalism and the onset of a new historical age. Recalling the frame, Herr Jacques's godfather tries, through a series of stories (*Züricher Novellen*) to persuade his charge that one cannot aspire to become an original. The godfather builds upon the citoyen-term which suggests that the original is something of a model citizen, one who deserves to be emulated. While the godfather is certainly aware of the citoyen moral, it is no longer current in the 1820s when this story is taking place. Herr Jacques represents the unease of the *Gründerzeit* generation (the first generation of the industrial age). He is taught something that he cannot be given, but must acquire or achieve on his own (Martini, 126). The two ensuing Manesse stories that the godfather relates to his charge are replete with the themes of transitoriness, of growing and developing, and of decay. The feudal families represent the transition from feudalism to a bourgeois middle-class society. Hadlaub hails from simple origins, encounters an able master who helps him immerse himself in the *Minnesang* manuscript he is composing. He becomes an epigone and loses himself and his identity to his work. Fiedes, the daughter of aristocratic parents, feels that she cannot trust Hadlaub as long as he is caught up in his role as an epigone, because she does not know who he is. He has made the language of Minne his own and she cannot tell what is real and what is appearance. The danger of art is clearly exposed, for Hadlaub risks losing himself behind the

[2] See also: Richardt, *Literaturkritik als Gesellschaftskritik*, (1975), 51–122.

mask of literature. Fides draws Hadlaub out of this mode orchestrating a test (dragon-slaying), upon which Hadlaub's life depends. Fides successfully liberates Hadlaub and a new historical epoch begins that is symbolized by the marriage of Fides and Hadlaub. The Manesse manuscript is complete; there will not be any more Minnesänger. Moreover the antiquated art of the Minnesänger, while preserved for posterity, has lost its value in the Gründerzeit. The marriage has united a commoner with an aristocrat, thereby breaking down the feudal class structure and becomes a harbinger of the new age. The conflict from which both Fides and Hadlaub emerge triumphant is not merely a conflict between two lovers, rather, between an antiquated society and a new way a life with a new set of traditions, laws and art (136).

Wolfgang Preisendanz's "Gottfried Kellers *Sinngedicht*," asks whether *Das Sinngedicht* is a reaction to the scientific theories of the day and in particular to Darwin. The title and the opening sentence in *Das Sinngedicht* refer to Darwin, whose *On the Origin of Species by Means of Natural Selection* (1859) appeared the next year in German translation. Neither Emil Ermatinger's nor Priscilla M. Kramer's interpretations have convinced Preisendanz that moral and natural law, freedom and attachment between man and woman, so central to the main plot, also serve as the motif for the internal stories. Rather, they come from those thematic relationships which one can find in all of Keller's other works from the first novel to the last, namely the relationship between being and appearance, between the core (*Kern*) and the mere shell (*Schale*), between true characters (*Gestalt*) and masquerade (*Vermummung*), and between factual reality (*faktische Wirklichkeit*) and the imagined world (*Vorstellungswelt*). Preisendanz fails to see the central theme of the main story reflected in the internal stories, which Reinhart and Lucie exchange with one another. Both partners ultimately find their true love in each other, although their stories have little to do with their own reality. Thus, Preisendanz ponders the significance of the relationship between the internal stories, which can be read independently, and the main story. Returning to the Darwin reference in the first sentence, Preisendanz reminds us that Darwin also wrote *The Expression of the Motions in Men and Animals* (1872), published that same year in German. Referring to the Logau axiom, we are reminded that laughter and blushing can be understood as purely physical functions. However laughter and blushing can also be interpreted as the external manifestation of the inner life, dictated by moral codes. As Reinhart discovers, the Logau recipe that he sets out to prove cannot be scientifically proven, because it encounters appearance rather than fact. Preisendanz suggests that Keller wanted to show that some truths cannot be proven through scientific means. The truth we experience in a narrative cannot be arrived at scientifically — it can only be arrived at through narrative. Thus *Das Sinngedicht* in Preisendanz's interpretation becomes a parable of the "Reichsunmittelbarkeit der Poesie" insofar as it demonstrates the dimensions of the moral world over which a work of fiction (and not scientific methodology) may hold sway (157).

Walter Baumann's slender volume, *Auf den Spuren Gottfried Kellers,* offers the lay reader and specialist bold insights into Keller's life. Baumann is well known for his intimate knowledge of Zurich's architectural history. The resulting study, chronologically organized, strives to correct numerous misunderstandings and to correct various myths surrounding Keller's life, that decades of scholarship have transformed into truths. Baumann does not restrict himself to Zurich, but pursues the author's travels to Munich, Heidelberg and Berlin, applying the detective skills and healthy skepticism of an excellent sleuth. The reader will learn much about Rudolf Keller's apprenticeship to the famous Viennese master turner Johann Düno, under whose tutelage Keller's father not only honed his talent on the lathe, but acquired a cultivated taste for theater which, as we know, was not lost on his son. Baumann introduces us to Keller's godfather, the Junker von Meiss, who sat on the Obergericht (high court) during Keller's childhood and, as such, could have had significant influence upon Keller's expulsion from school. Baumann accuses Frey of exaggeration when the latter asserts that Keller's ministerial documentation as cantonal clerk would fill some two hundred volumes. While Keller was certainly diligent and faithful to the duties of cantonal clerk, says Baumann, he was hardly innovative (84–85). Baumann also illuminates the circumstances surrounding the mysterious death of Keller's fiancée Luise Scheidegger and his relationship to his faithful, if difficult sister Regula. Baumann's examination of Keller's biography leads again and again to corrective reassessment and to new understandings of Keller's life.

The most recent study of Keller's ethics is Kaspar T. Locher's *Gottfried Keller: Welterfahrung, Wertstruktur, und Stil* (1985). This book, Locher's second on Keller, is the culmination of a professional career dedicated to the study of Keller and his oeuvre; it is meticulously researched and well written. Locher's second Keller study emulates the methodology of the first. It is the responsibility of art to provide guidance in a chaotic world; art consoles, provides fortitude and direction in times of need.

Locher shows how Keller's characters pass through three phases of development in their perception of the world. The naive child is unselfconscious (*unbefangen*) and hence uninhibited as a result of his inexperience in the world. This state of innocence is quickly lost as the child gains experience and interacts with others. The goal of life which Keller assigns his characters is to recapture this unselfconsciousness, which enables the individual to remain spiritually free and independent (78). As the youngster becomes self-aware, he seeks to define himself and his place in the world around him. The ultimate goal of Keller's system is to achieve and maintain *Weltoffentheit* — the intellectual freedom to filter and to develop an independent position vis-a-vis all ideas and concepts, be they social, economic, political, theological, or philosophical. *Befangenheit,* or self-consciousness, is an escape from freedom and responsibility into some form of deceptive security (1985, 51). Locher cites three forms of Befangenheit: namely, chronic sulking, vanity, and unbridled imagination (57). The social, economic, and political turmoil through which Keller lived all served to intensify Keller's concept of the individual's search for unselfconsciousness and integrity. Furthermore, the process of remaining unselfconscious and uninhibited, once attained, must be continually renewed and sustained. Locher divides those who are not intellectually independent (*befangen*), into two large groups: the emotionally and morally insecure, and those who have become disciples of an ideology or a religion. Keller's works provide an array of such self-satisfied, self-righteous and self-confident characters who are not free thinkers. Many of his characters such as Heinrich Lee are caught up in their own false view of reality; others, such as Ursula, have acquired a false sense of who they are, or have been lured into false ideologies. Still others, like Martin Salander, have become caught up in the mania of accumulating profit. *Befangenheit*, this lack of spiritual freedom, is intolerable because it prevents recognition of the self and inhibits the way to the self; it also imposes upon the individual a skewed sense of reality. Keller does not limit this problem to individuals, but has shown that entire social systems can be "befangen," because they are based on false assumptions. Thus it is the responsibility of each individual to liberate himself from his *Befangenheit*. Failure to recognize this responsibility constitutes guilt. Therefore, the attainment of *Unbefangenheit* becomes a moral duty, and in Locher's estimation an ethical problem.

The unselfconscious, uninhibited individual knows that he does not live in a world of constant values, rather, he is responsible for making sense of the ideas he encounters. Thus the challenge remains to nurture and maintain freedom, integrity and the resulting harmony between self and world.. Prerequisite for this harmony is an attitude that embraces a larger vision of world events: one which recognizes the interdependency of ideas and movements. Such harmony requires a mindset capable of profound reflection and one that espouses the understanding that in society, everything is in a continual dynamic state of transition.

Finding harmony in a world of transition constitutes becoming a good, productive member of society. Intelligence, reason, reverence, respect, and lifeworthiness (*Lebenhaftigkeit*) are all characteristics which enable one to achieve and maintain harmony. In seeking solutions to problems, reason (*Vernunft*) dictates that one search the self before turning to the external world. Keller's happy characters are intelligent; the others, though not necessarily unintelligent, fail to think in large parameters and never acquire an all encompassing vision of their world; they remain "befangen." The individual must be capable of change. Harmony in a changing world can only be sustained through flexibility. Integrity and flexibility are not mutually exclusive in Keller's philosophy of life. In fact the dialectic that arises from contradictory opinions and ideas creates a dynamic process; this conflict encourages dialogue and drives society through the interaction between individuals to strive for an evermore perfect and self-perfecting humanity.

In the final chapter, Locher shows that Keller's style must necessarily be ironic, because Keller refuses to use his text to escape into an idyll. Self-irony was Keller's means of self-distancing. Likewise, Keller's correspondence often uses self-irony, as a means of preserving his integrity, his unselfconsciousness and uninhibitedness. Self-irony enabled Keller to distance himself from Heinrich Lee and brought a heightened awareness of the self, a measure of independence, and opened a channel to critical reflection (138). Keller was a moralist and believed that the well being of the individual and ultimately of society was less dependent on the perfection of institutions than upon the ethical values of individuals. Keller's conception of a dynamic society would be achievable only if each individual would strive to attain and to maintain a heightened awareness of the self (*Unbefangenheit*). Locher provides a masterfully composed, eminently readable study that offers some of the most erudite and profound reflections on Keller's ethics in recent years.

In 1985 Gerhard Kaiser published a slender volume entitled *Gottfried Keller* as part of the Artemis series of introductions to great authors. This densely packaged text is however hardly an introduction to Keller such as Bernd Breitenbruch's Rowohlt edition. With the exception of three illuminating readings of the poem "Augen, meine lieben Fensterlein" and of plot excerpts from the frame in the *Züricher Novellen* "Herr Jacques" as well as a scene from *Kleider machen Leute*, this "introduction" assumes an intimate knowledge of Keller's life and works. It is hardly surprising that Kaiser's introduction is also predominately indebted to the psychoanalytical approach. The psychoanalytic approaches to Keller have enabled Kaiser to realize that psychoanalysis as a means of interpretation has a much broader field of application than inner drives and their effect upon the subject (1985, 87). Inspired by Renate Böschenstein's insightful review, Kaiser rethought the premise of his 1981 study, *Gottfried Keller — Das gedichtete Leben*, and integrated those revisions that evolve around the relationship between biography and the fictional text as well as the relationship of psychoanalytical interpretative models (*Deutungsschemata*) to the text into this introduction to Keller. Kaiser claims that his earlier book on Keller was a necessary step, even if he is now forced to recognize that he had not understood Keller's works in terms of his biography, but rather that he came to understand Keller's biography from his works. In this volume he sought to give a corrective perspective without resorting to extensive close readings which would duplicate the efforts in the original work (Kaiser, 1985, 142). With this new assessment, Kaiser hopes to have diffused any trace of heavy-handed arrogance that may have resulted from his belief that he could interpret all of Keller's works through the author's lifelong suffering, rather than view them as the lifelong achievements that they are.

The closing section, "Keller, seine Epoch und wir" (Keller, his epoch, and us), eloquently places Keller in his own time and bridges the gap with our own. The monograph concludes with a useful, annotated modern critical bibliography and with a chronology of Keller's life and works.

Jörg Zierleyn's study, *Gottfried Keller und das klassische Erbe: Untersuchungen zur Goetherezeption eines Poetischen Realisten* (1989), represents a carefully researched and an informative examination of Goethe reception in the nineteenth century as it relates to Keller. Zierleyn introduces his book with a comprehensive review of previous studies in which he discusses the reception of Weimar Classicism by Keller and his contemporaries. Zierleyn illuminates Keller's image of Goethe and his position vis-à-vis the Weimar classics. For the purposes of this study he draws primarily upon the original edition of *Der grüne Heinrich*, upon the first volume of the Seldwyla novellas and most importantly upon *Das Sinngedicht*. Heinrich Lee's first encounter with Goethe's works made a lasting impression upon him, for they unite spirituality and reality as well as poetry and prose in an exemplary fashion. Zierleyn views *Das Sinngedicht* as that work which best represents the Goethean tradition, because Keller comes closest to attaining the "Reichsunmittelbarkeit der Poesie," in other words he achieves a tension between the real and the ideal that allows him to transcend reality achieving a timeless classicism (267). Keller learns from Goethe that mere imitation of reality (mimesis) is not sufficient; the artist needs to distance himself, to become more objective, so as to be able to transfigure that reality. The material becomes refined and purified (*veredelt*) without becoming untrue (*unwahr*). However, Zierleyn asserts that, although Keller admired Goethe, he was neither inhibited by his admiration for Goethe, nor did he consider Goethe above criticism. Far from viewing his own work as a mere imitation of Goethe, Keller preferred to think of his art as a modern continuation of the Goethean tradition. He viewed his own artistic career as one that had moved beyond Goethe, so that he saw himself rather as the executor of Goethe's literary estate (279). Zierleyn's helps to clarify Keller's relationship to Goethe on the eve of the centennial anniversary of Keller's death.

The centennial tribute to Keller's death in 1990 was marked by colloquia and other festivities both in Zurich and in London.[3] The three-day International Gottfried Keller Colloquium in Zurich, organized by Hans Wysling was a splendid gathering and the culmination of several weeks of festive activities which remembered and paid tribute to the celebrated author of Zurich. This commemorative year and the colloquia predictably occasioned numerous books, articles, and exhibitions, including a new historical-critical edition.

---

[3] The volume containing the lectures of the London Symposium on Gottfried Keller, held on May 29 and 30, 1990 at the University of London's Institute of Germanic Studies and edited by John L. Flood and Martin Swales, is discussed in chapter five of this volume.

Wysling edited a volume in large format entitled *Gottfried Keller 1819–1890*, which introduces the contemporary reader to Keller's world. This volume attempts as few have heretofore to capture Keller and his works in the context of the nineteenth-century Zurich through eminently readable texts, hundreds of pictures, graphics, and maps, innumerable letters and sundry documentation. Wysling has succeeded in creating an all-encompassing vision of Keller and his world. He explores Keller's childhood and provides a wealth of information that expands our understanding of Keller's fatherless formative years and of the forces that led Keller to misjudge his potential talent for landscape painting. Two chapters are devoted to Keller's student days in Heidelberg and to his difficult but highly productive years in Berlin that proved to be the incubator, the breeding ground for many of his later works. Other essays in the volume include those by historian Peter Stadler, who offers an overview of Zurich history, including the political ferment of the 1840s that captured Keller's interest and inspired his early poetry. In addition Stadler provides new information on Keller's position as cantonal clerk while also furnishing insights into the political turmoil of the 1860s and 1870s, the period during which Keller held that position. Art historian Bruno Weber reevaluates Keller as a landscape artist by placing him in the context of nineteenth-century art history.[4] Wysling provides interpretations of the novella cycles augmented by much documentation, including a particularly intriguing interpretation of the *Züricher Novellen*. He discusses the major revisions in the 1880 edition of *Der grüne Heinrich* and shows how Keller was influenced by his correspondence with his contemporaries during the revision process. The closing chapters provide fascinating documentation on Keller's admiration for Gotthelf and his intimate friendships with selected contemporaries such as C. F. Meyer, Theodor Storm, Paul Heyse, Richard Wagner, and Friedrich Nietzsche. The volume concludes with much supporting documentation pertaining to Keller's later years.

Wysling also edited *Gottfried Keller — Elf Essays*, which contains the essay versions of the eleven public lectures held in tribute to the author at the International Gottfried Keller Colloquium commemorating the centenary of Keller's death. Most of the essays in this volume provide us with some indication of the direction Keller scholarship has been taking in the last decade of this century. Both Martin Swales and Hartmut Steinecke discuss Keller's novels in the context of European realism. Likewise, Steinecke argues that the individualism and subjectivity in *Der grüne Heinrich* need not stand in opposition to society or reality. Hartmut Laufhütte reevaluates Keller's last novel, *Martin Salander*. In his reading this novel is not a mere depiction of corruption in society, rather it becomes an admonishment about the dangers of illusionary thinking in a time

---

[4]   For the most recent reevaluation of Keller as a landscape artist, see Bruno Weber's *Gottfried Keller: Landschaftmaler Zürich* (Zurich: Verlag Neue Zürcher Zeitung, 1990).

when accurate analysis of reality is imperative. Gerhard Kaiser traces Heinrich Lee's character back to the stock figures of Sturm and Drang era and compares Keller's protagonist with Faust, citing their shared yearning for nature and their mutual imprisonment in their respective situations. Hans Wysling reaches further back in time, exploring Keller's repeated use of myth and archetypes. Adolf Muschg, Peter von Matt and Erika Swales all focus on incongruities in Keller's fiction and poetry. All three question standard interpretations and convictions about Keller and his work. By exploring the contradictory paradoxes (Muschg), the rumors (Von Matt) and the incongruities (E. Swales), these Keller-scholars have produced illuminating interpretations. Both Renate Böschenstein and Karl Pestalozzi examine Keller's concept of happiness (*Glück*). Böschenstein endeavors to understand what Keller meant by happiness and Pestalozzi seeks to understand how Keller conveys this happiness to the reader. Finally, my own contribution to this collection attempts to examine Keller's conception of an individual ethic.

Martin Swales's "Das realistische Reflexionsniveau: Bemerkungen zu Gottfried Kellers *Der grüne Heinrich*" considers Keller's novel, particularly the revised edition, to be an "unforgettable" example of just how a highly reflective and self-reflective novel can also be a realistic novel in the tradition of European realism (M. Swales, 1990, 9). *Der grüne Heinrich* exhibits two types of novelistic discourse: the Bildungsroman and the realistic novel. The blend of these two and their interaction achieve a dialectic of reflectivity and mimesis (10). This psychological and conceptual reflectivity underscores a critical discussion of realism. Heinrich, as both aspiring visual artist and as narrator, is continually reflecting on how art conveys the "extra-literary and extra-painting experience." Such reflection includes a critical engagement of the social world. The reality that we as human beings experience is not merely composed of facts, but rather of facts that have been informed by reflection and interpretation (11). The artistic medium and the text interact with the extra-textual reality. Swales stresses three aspects that Keller uses to thematicize the artistic and mimetic processes. First, Keller explores art as a social product, a commodity in this novel. Second, the novel explores the role of symbolism and fiction in the social sphere (the *Wilhelm Tell* performance and the carnival scene in Munich). Third, Swales shows how the discussion of art in the novel is suffused with certain religious and philosophical themes (12). Swales distinguishes between Heinrich, the failed artist, lover and son, whose life is imbued with melancholy and who increasingly separates the world of imagination from the world of practical living, and the narrating Heinrich, who exalts the interrelationship between the imagination and practical living and who fully comprehends the interplay between these two realms reflected by the degree to which he exploits the various modes of literary realism (13). Swales examines the relationship between Heinrich and his mother. This leads to a portrait of the mother, marked by social, economic, and cultural factors, which Swales believes has not been surpassed by any of the canonical European realists. Any thorough account of human behavior must include a narrative account of the psychological, spiritual, social and economic factors. Keller's portrayal of individual characters in *Der grüne Heinrich* assume a psychological and social dimension, which are traditional features of the narrative in European realism. Swales argues credibly that the significant dimension of reflectivity in Keller's novel provides the bridge between artistic medium and socio-economic reality (20).

The second essay, Hartmut Laufhütte's "Ein Seldwyler in Münsterberg — Gottfried Kellers Martin Salander und die Deutungstradition," offers a fresh look at Keller's last novel. Laufhütte suggests that we as readers do Keller an injustice when we read *Martin Salander* only as a *Zeitroman*, that is to say a fictional account of Zurich in the 1880s. Rather, Laufhütte suggests that we need to evaluate the elder Salander's views on society, politics, education, and in particular, his grip on reality. Laufhütte shows us with many examples just how tenuous and illusionary Martin's grip on reality is, particularly when compared to the worldly and rational wisdom of Marie Salander. Laufhütte believes that one must see beyond Martin's illusionary impressions of reality, to assess for ourselves the actual situation at hand (Laufhütte, 1990, 31). Both Martin's son, Arnold and particularly Martin's spouse, Marie provide the reader with a counterbalance that tempers, restrains and ameliorates Martin's own overzealous progressively-inclined attitude toward society, politics, pedagogy and economics. Marie becomes the measure against which the reader comes to judge Salander. Marie's worldly wisdom represents an alternative possibility to Martin's own illusionary orientation. Often she is able to temper, assuage and thereby to influence happenings without direct intervention (36). Laufhütte shows the continuity that Martin Salander and his illusionary visions have in common with a host of Keller's characters, as though they all hail from Seldwyla and are related to Heinrich Lee. Likewise, he cites Marie's role in this novel as part of a long tradition of Keller's female characters (Nettchen, Justine, Ursula, and Judith), who save the day for the disoriented hero. Thus Keller, Laufhütte contends, is more concerned with the individual and representative failure to grasp reality, than he is with depicting corruption in society. Keller's last novel hints at the dangers of illusionary reality at a time and in circumstances, when an accurate analysis of the current reality should form the foundation for future action. The implication of the novel, based largely on Martin's son Arnold's reflective steadfastness, enables the reader to draw a positive, open-ended and future oriented rather than a resigned conclusion. This revelation, Laufhütte suggests, could lead to a new understanding and a reevaluation of Keller's last novel.

Gerhard Kaiser's essay reveals Heinrich Lee as a character type that had already appeared on the stage during the era of the Sturm und Drang (Storm and Stress; 1767–1785). Kaiser is primarily concerned with the social construct of problems and conflict, which Heinrich Lee represents, specifically in his relationship to nature, in his concept of family, and in his utopian fantasy. In Kaiser's reading, both Goethe's Faust and Keller's Lee are imprisoned by their respective situations and both yearn for nature. Many of the nature-themes voiced in *Faust*, while altered by Keller's subjectivity, psychological frame of mind and shifting perceptions of reality in a rapidly changing society, are still recognizable in the Wald und Höhle scene in *Faust* and "Flucht zur Mutter Natur" in the story of Heinrich's youth (Kaiser, 1990, 49). Faust is of course a victim of his own actions, whereas Heinrich, while in part responsible for his decisions, is primarily a victim of circumstances beyond his control. Kaiser reminds us that the family depicted by Goethe was very much the patriarchal family. Keller's own family and Heinrich's family reflected the changing times. The father was now the intermediary between the public sphere (the work place and society) and the private sphere of the family. The mother's role thus takes on the additional burden of holding the family together; she becomes the emotional mainstay of the family. Heinrich grows up in a family in which the mother must fulfill not only her natural maternal role, but that of the father as well. Kaiser shows us how Heinrich, handicapped in this manner, turns to nature for solace and sustenance; he demonstrates how both Heinrich's career as a landscape artist and his experiences in love with Anna, Judith, and Dortchen) reflect this return to nature (52–3). Whereas Goethe saw in art the bearer of the ideal nature, Heinrich's attempts to paint were frustrated by his own lack of talent and by an age that had forsaken the importance of art in Goethe's sense, in favor of a solid bourgeois existence. Mother nature had lost her former strength. Indeed, the two different conclusions in the two versions of *Der grüne Heinrich* reflect these changing times. Kaiser's essay concludes by citing contemporary events that mirror Keller's views of nature.

In his essay, "Kellers Romane und Romanvorstellungen in europäischer Perspektive" Hartmut Steinecke examines Keller's novels in the European context. Steinecke explores the extent to which the topics, themes, and social circumstances of Keller's novels are Swiss and to what extent they are European. He investigates Keller's concept of the novel and his penchant for the episodic, the tangential, for infusing the plot with his own reflections, and suggests that Keller's novel is much closer to the epic than to drama. Keller's conception of the novel ran against the grain of his own time, for many critics viewed the strict dramatic structures in Freytag's *Soll und Haben* as the ideal form of the novel. Keller was a free spirit and he was not to be bound by the strictures imposed by critics. He was concerned with capturing the world with all its complexities in fiction without oversimplifying (Steinecke, 1990, 80). The Bildungsroman became the quintessential national genre of the Wilhelminian era. Freytag's *Soll und Haben* was considered to exemplify such a genre because the hero acquired the mindset of a respected German liberal. Likewise, *Der grüne Heinrich* in its revised edition was adopted by the Swiss as their national education epic; this,

Steinecke suggests, focused too much attention on the conclusion and far too little attention on the process of education. The confrontation in Keller's novel between the protagonist and the world often occurs according to the whims of fate. Steinecke argues that individualism and subjectivity do not have to stand in opposition to society or to reality. The significance of poetic realism was precisely that: to place the individual in the context of reality. Keller's works, Steinecke concludes, when seen in this light, are very close to the most significant European fiction of Keller's time. Reflection becomes in the autobiographical novel self-reflection; the attempt to objectify the self to a level of observation and commentary transforms the autobiography into an artwork (83). Keller stands at the end of his century and at the end of his possibilities for the novel as the nineteenth century had known it. Thomas Mann in his *Buddenbrooks* wrote perhaps the last German novel of the century, in which he pulled together all of the achievements of the nineteenth-century novel. Thereafter, Joyce, Proust, Musil and Kafka all sought to create new and different forms of artistic expression.

Erika Swales, in her essay, "Gottfried Kellers (un)schlüssiges Erzählen," focuses on the inadequacies and incongruities in Keller's fiction. Swales is concerned with discovering these textual flaws in the richly woven texture of Keller's works, and illuminating them. Keller's narrative mode, Swales suggests, is not so concerned with interpretation and portrayal as with the conditions and determinedness of the act of interpretation. Keller writes with reservations; his writing contains something of the Socratic method. Regularly, particularly in the cycles, he challenges the reader to pursue relationships, parallels, and contradictions, to pursue a narrative mode that refuses to provide closure. Keller does not cultivate or appease the wish of the modern reader to experience the kind of concordance of beginning, middle, and end that constitutes the essence of our explanatory fiction. Swales sees three contradictory philosophical strains in Keller: 1) Keller's sense of the ontological certainty of human existence and human achievement; 2) his extensive knowledge of the social, material, and spiritual-philosophical conditions in the nineteenth century; and 3) his despair over the incalculability of literary production in an era of change (E. Swales, 95). Keller depicts two versions of man: the first embodies the eighteenth-century belief in the potentially reasonable, rational actions of a competent human being, while the second is that of a man led by blind instinct. Heinrich Lee embodies these two contradictory concepts. In *Der grüne Heinrich* Keller emphasizes repeatedly that man's existence and his awareness are caught up in an unsurveyable net or web — particularly in a period of social and cultural transition. Either we avoid responsible action or we learn to accept it in the full consciousness that it cannot be completely explained (102). The superficial didacticism in Frau Regel Amrain is undermined by the fundamental discrepancy between the narrator's ideal and the narrative mode. The narrator's language is charged with a dynamism and energy that clashes with the flat narrative, a laundry list of linear corrective episodes that cannot possibly produce the dynamic character envisioned; rather free will is stifled by making the character a prisoner of education. Swales concludes that Keller's skeptical, questioning disposition is intellectually more honest than other writers of his day. Keller does not observe the world from some lofty perspective; rather he stands in the middle of the complex textuality of existence. Swales's examination of the inadequacies and incongruities in Keller's fiction has led her to interpret his fiction in a new and exciting way. The themes contained in this essay evolved into a book, *The Poetics of Scepticism*, published in 1994 and discussed in chapter five.

Peter von Matt's essay, "Gottfried Keller und der brachiale Zweikampf" confronts rumors and hearsay about Keller and his works perpetuated by the general public and by German literary historians. Von Matt examines Keller's temper, which, according to rumor and some hard evidence could reveal itself unsuspectingly in the most precarious of social situations. He questions whether this unpredictable temper is the outward manifestation of a desire for justice, but concludes based on substantial evidence that Keller seemed to strike out at others in order to relieve an inner burden. He reminds us that fist fighting is really a social regression, harkening back to a time when two suitors would face off or when unfulfilled erotic love has not yet given way to the mature ability to love. Turning to Keller's fiction, von Matt discovers that such battles produce no clear victors and usually end in a draw. Von Matt suggests the code of proper social behavior is both a burden and an escape. It liberates us by suppressing us. Breaking through this code results in choking fear and flighty relief. Keller's task as author, according to von Matt, was to derive nourishment from all of these incompatible paradoxes in the world, paradoxes that cannot be resolved rationally. In view of such irresolvable paradoxes, Keller employs symbols such as the fistfight between two bearded children to express the inexpressible. By questioning rumors perpetuated by scholarship von Matt has deepened our understanding of Keller.

Adolf Muschg's essay, "Der leere Spiegel — Bemerkungen zu Kellers Lyrik," similarly to von Matt's and Erika Swales's articles, focuses on the paradoxes and incongruities in Keller's work, but with a concentration on the poetry. Muschg leads us through a reading of one of his favorite Keller poems, "Jugendgedenken," which, not unlike many of Keller's poems, has a curious flaw (in this case in the fifth stanza) that seemingly diminishes to the degree of disparagement the message of the rest of the poem (here the first four stanzas). Muschg demonstrates that the paradox in Keller's poem that makes it flawed is precisely what makes it interesting. Muschg suggests that Keller's work often fails just where he has the most to say, where the attempt to mold the material at hand doesn't succeed (Muschg, 1990, 135). Muschg's investigation leads him to an unpublished poem, "Eine Nacht," which was written immediately after Keller's return from Munich and expresses his sentiments about life at that time. It contains a paradox that would seem to say "you haven't any life left, so use it"

(144). Muschg compares Keller's sentiments in the poem to those of Heinrich Lee, who learns to live with his past, and in the revised edition eventually comes to serve the community. Keller's wisdom arises from the underworld, from the realm of death, from his *Unleben*. Seldwyla is in Muschg's reading a realm of the dead in its own right (147–48). A fresh green grass grows over Heinrich's grave. While the walled cemetery affords the dead their well deserved rest, the cemetery also represents an open field for the living that may be sown and eventually harvested. Muschg's example encourages readers to examine the paradoxes in Keller's poetry. These incongruities, these disturbing paradoxes make Keller, at least for Muschg, a more significant poet than either Eduard Mörike or Theodor Storm (149).

Hans Wysling focuses on the use and application of fable and myth in his essay, "Und immer wieder kehrt Odysseus heim — Das Fabelhafte bei Gottfried Keller." Wysling compares Heinrich Lee's journey home to Zurich with the return of Odysseus to Ithaca. *Der grüne Heinrich* reveals a large number of these fables and archetypes that cross one another leading to an unusual blend of genres. One moment we are reading an artist's novel, the next a Bildungsroman, then suddenly a legend or myth; confession suffuses the whole (Wysling, 1990, 153). Wysling compares Heinrich with Don Quixote, then with Cid, the brave campeador and debtor. In the next instance Heinrich appears to be Robinson, trying to survive in his hostile environment. Wysling questions why Keller borrows so heavily from these myths; he believes that Keller freely applies these archetypes, myths, and fables as props to lend his novel resonance and his main character stability. Perhaps Keller wanted to demonstrate that he was well read, perhaps such a prolific use of myth and archetype was a sign that Keller wanted to join the ranks of the "corpus litterarum"; that he was a young ambitious author aspiring to become great. In a letter to Paul Heyse, Keller wrote that it was the task of the author to place these myths in a modern context, to embellish, to cloak them anew according to one's fantasy, one's poetic license, so as to make these images and archetypes, fables and myths applicable to the society and culture of the age and thereby ever informing and inextinguishable (*G.B.* III/1, 57). Wysling provides a fascinating list of Keller's characters and their archetypal counterparts.

My own contribution, "Gottfried Kellers Ethik im Zusammenhang mit ästhetischen, religiösen und historischen Aspekten seiner Kunst," focuses on Keller's conception of an individual ethic, as it reveals itself in his works. The social and economic transitions in the nineteenth century shattered many long-held ethical convictions and rent the social and religious fabric from which they came. Keller believed that each person must experience a uniquely individual process of ethical development, largely determined by individual situations and destiny. These strains of external influence will bring about self-reflection and introspection which enables the individual to fashion his own moral code; this introspection is an unending, lifelong process of refinement. Although each individual develops and refines his own ethical code, all of these codes, at least in theory, will be similar insofar as they will all be bound by the same natural law, to which all men are subject. Indeed, the young Keller kept a journal that enabled him to filter and reflect on his ideas, observations and beliefs. This self-reflection raised his self awareness and made him more critical of his own actions as well as of external events. Reflection and introspection humbles one and teaches one to search inwardly for truth. Both Jukundus and Justine in *Das verlorene Lachen* must find their way through introspection. Crisis often precipitates this introspection and leads to recovery, to intellectual freedom and ultimately to a better understanding of the self. Crisis and life's experience renew and refine individual moral principles in keeping with the natural law. In times of great social, political and economic upheaval, Keller would seem to suggest that the individual may have to rely on himself.[5] However, this process of ethical refinement through introspection is not a withdrawal from society; rather, it is an ephemeral stepping back, a moment of stock-taking. Keller believed firmly in the civic obligation of the individual to work with his fellow citizens for the betterment of the commonweal, but suggests that in difficult times of social and economic upheaval, one must rely on oneself to determine right from wrong, by refining one's personal moral code subject to the natural law.

The last two essays in the volume complement each other insofar as they discuss happiness (*Glück*) in Keller's work. Renate Böschenstein's essay, "Keller's Glück," endeavors to discover what Keller means by the term. Böschenstein cites the various places where *Glück*, embodied by Fortuna, manifests itself in Keller's works. Happiness seems to be a matter of chance and is occasioned by fortunate conditions; it may arise as a result of love, marriage, or friendship and is generally a condition or state of harmony and satisfaction which may even connote protection. Böschenstein then turns to Keller and to his formula: worth + misfortune = consciousness = happiness (*Wert + Unglück = Bewußtsein = Glück: S.W.* XIX, 355). Böschenstein shows how Keller, like all great authors, developed a coherent network of signs, which reveal an entire substructure. What we learn about Keller in Böschenstein's reading is that happiness stems not so much from success achieved by recognizing one's possibilities and limitations, but from favorable conditions that result from good fortune (178). The enduring happiness of the protagonists is dependent not only upon their inner maturity, but is also dependent upon pure chance. The force that directs destinies or fate remains unknown and perhaps unknowable. The all-pervasive fear that man will find himself in an incoherent, lawless universe guided by an uncontrollable chain of events is unsettling; so much so that it led Spielhagen to assert that it is the

---

[5] "Das Finden seiner selbst in dunklen Tagen ist meistens mehr Glückssache, als die Menschen gewöhnlich eingestehen wollen . . . " Gottfried Keller, *Sämtliche Werke.* Ed. Thomas Böning. Frankfurt/Main: Deutscher Klassiker Verlag, 1989, IV, 551.

task of the novelist to persuade the reader of a rational order in the cosmos through an all-encompassing cosmic closure in his fiction. Or to take Dortchen's perspective in *Der grüne Heinrich*, that Heinrich's chance encounter at the count's castle is not testimony to the abiding power of a holy ruling will, but rather the benevolent work of the gods of chance, to whom one must offer roses and coconut milk (180). Böschenstein concludes that Keller's concept of happiness would seem to fill out that empty void without completely sealing or covering it.

Taking up Böschenstein's topic of happiness, Karl Pestalozzi's essay "Sprachliche Glücksmomente bei Gottfried Keller" investigates how Keller conveys happiness in his fiction. Building upon a theoretical foundation composed of Staiger, Freude and Echo, Pestalozzi proceeds to exam in detail the narrative and linguistic structure of three examples of happy moments in Keller's work: the domestic farmyard scene following the passionate scene between Anna and Heinrich in the Heidestube following the Tell performance, the breakfast scene between Sali and Vrenchen in *Romeo und Julia auf dem Dorfe* and finally, the banquet in *Das Fähnlein der Sieben Aufrechten*. With these examples, Pestalozzi demonstrates three methods, namely the incorporation of the lyrical into the epic, the Homeric epic medium itself with changing narrative perspectives and humor, to illuminate the linguistic method and narrative techniques Keller employed to impart the experience of happiness depicted in his fiction to the reader.

Having just completed a discourse on happiness in Keller's fiction, it would seem fitting to conclude this overview of Keller scholarship by applauding the recently completed publication of a new historical-critical edition of Keller's works by Verlag der deutschen Klassiker. The standard 26 volume critical edition of Keller's works by Jonas Fränkel and Carl Helbling has been the mainstay of Keller scholars the world over. It has also been out of print for decades. The new historical-critical edition under the main editorship of Thomas Böning includes seven volumes, each of which contains a section on the history of the work or works contained in that volume, a section devoted to sources, replete also with annotations and commentary on the text and a host of relevant materials and documents.

The first volume, devoted entirely to Keller's poetry, is edited by Kai Kauffmann and was published in 1996. It includes all of the poems ever published during Keller's lifetime.

The second volume, edited by Thomas Böning and Gerhard Kaiser, contains *Der grüne Heinrich* in the original 1855 edition and furnishes several hundred pages of valuable annotation which includes Keller's private and public commentary on the novel drawn largely from his correspondence and public statements. This volume also offers a valuable reevaluation of the biographical material on Keller and valuable information regarding the political, social, and art history of Zurich. The editors have also supplied a useful register of the most important scholarly literature on *Der grüne Heinrich*. The editors have striven to correct errors in the original critical edition from Fränkel and Helbling, and have drawn upon Ermatinger's Studienausgabe, the Fränkel/Helbling critical edition, the Goldammer (Aufbau) edition and the Heselhaus (Hanser) edition in an effort to derive the most accurate text hitherto available.

The third volume, which appeared in 1996 under the editorship of Peter Villwock, is the companion piece to the second volume, and contains the revised 1880 edition of *Der grüne Heinrich*. Particularly beneficial to those who may wish to compare the two versions is a concordance that allows the reader to pinpoint particular events in each volume.

Die Leute von Seldwyla is housed in the fourth volume, edited by Thomas Böning and published in 1989. Böning, chief editor of the critical edition, has established specific guiding principles which are adhered to when editing and correcting mistakes made in earlier editions. To produce the most accurate text available, he has returned to the original manuscript of the collected Seldwyla stories published in 1874. Böning scrutinizes and accepts Keller's corrections on the type-setter's galleys (*Korrekturbogen*) and corrects only clear orthographic errors. One can conclude that Böning's painstaking work has produced the most accurate edition of *Die Leute von Seldwyla* available, because he has returned to the original manuscripts. Böning relies upon Fränkel's historical overview regarding the origins of these novellas, although he has corrected and augmented Fränkel's information according to need. For example, Böning has included a story, "Schneidergesellen, welcher den Herrn spielt," which was printed in the *Bündner-Kalender für das Jahr 1847* and is believed to have been written by Keller.

The fifth volume, which appeared in 1989, also edited by Böning, includes the *Züricher Novellen*, and is based on the 1883 edition, the last that Keller personally edited. In doing this, Böning has incorporated many of the mistakes that the typesetter made and Keller simply overlooked. Fränkel's sharp critique of Helbling's edition of the *Züricher Novellen*, which was also based on the 1883 edition, provides abundant evidence of these typesetter's errors. As Hans Zeller has suggested, Böning would have done better to base his text for this edition on the 1878 book edition. Also in the volume are two stories, "Der Wahltag" (1862) and "Verschiedene Freiheitskämpfer" (1863) which are thematically related to the *Züricher Novellen*, but which Keller chose not to include in his *Gesammelte Werke*.

Dominik Müller edited the sixth volume, which was published in 1991 and includes: *Sieben Legenden, Das Sinngedicht*, and *Martin Salander*. Müller based both *Das Sinngedicht* and *Martin Salander* on the canonical edition of Keller's *Gesammelte Werke* published in 1889. This is the first historical-critical edition of the novella cycle and of Keller's last novel. Especially valuable in this volume are the annotations regarding the social, economic, constitutional, and historical events that form the backdrop to *Martin Salander*. The *Sieben Legenden* are based largely upon the third edition from 1884, which Keller meticulously edited.

The seventh volume, published in 1996, was also edited by Dominik Müller and is perhaps the most exciting, because it incorporates all Keller's essays, articles and official publications. It also includes the entire dramatic oeuvre, and contains the unpublished essays, fragments, diaries and journals. This volume offers new material for the Keller scholar.

This new critical edition is long awaited and welcome. More significantly, it serves as a manifestation of Keller's continuing popularity. Keller's fiction and poetry are still read today by students, scholars, and the general reading public, a testimony to his versatility and virtuosity. May Keller continue to inspire readers, and may they in reading his fiction achieve or recapture that "state of innocence" he sought to impart.

Works Cited

Baumann, Walter. *Auf den Spuren Gottfried Kellers.* Zurich: Verlag Neue Zürcher Zeitung, 1984.

Böschenstein, Renate. "Kellers Glück." In *Gottfried Keller. Elf Essays zu seinem Werk*, ed.. Hans Wysling. 163–84. Zurich: Verlag Neue Zürcher Zeitung, 1990.

——. "Der Schatz unter den Schlangen. Ein Gespräch mit Gerhard Kaisers Buch *Gottfried Keller: Das gedichtete Leben*." *Euphorion* 77 (1983): 176–99.

Cowen, Roy. "Spiegel und Widerspiegelung: Zu Kellers Märchen 'Spiegel, das Kätzchen.'" In *Zu Gottfried Keller*, ed. H. Steinecke. 68–78. Stuttgart, Klett, 1984.

Fehr, Karl. *Gottfried Keller: Aufschlüsse und Deutungen.* Bern & Munich: Francke, 1972.

Hohendahl, Peter Uwe. *A History of German Literary Criticism, 1730–1980.* 179–276. Lincoln: U of Nebraska P, 1988.

Holub, Robert. *Reflections of Realism.* 101–32. Detroit: Wayne State UP, 1991.

Jennings, Lee B. "The Model of the Self in Gottfried Keller's Prose." *German Quarterly* 56 (March 1983): 196–230.

Kaiser, Gerhard. *Gottfried Keller. Das gedichtete Leben.* Frankfurt am Main: Insel, 1981.

——. "Grüne Heinriche— ein epochaler Typus." In *Gottfried Keller. Elf Essays zu seinem Werk*, ed. Hans Wysling. 44–60. Zurich: Verlag Neue Zürcher Zeitung, 1990.

——. *Gottfried Keller: Eine Einführung.* Munich: Artemis, 1985.

Laufhütte, Hartmut. "Ein Seldwyler in Münsterberg. Gottfried Kellers *Martin Salander* und die Deutungstradition." In *Gottfried Keller. Elf Essays zu seinem Werk*, ed. Hans Wysling. 22–44. Zurich: Verlag Neue Zürcher Zeitung, 1990.

Locher, Kaspar T. *Gottfried Keller: Welterfahrung, Wertstruktur und Stil.* Bern: Francke, 1985.

Luck, Rätus. *Gottfried Keller als Literaturkritiker.* Bern: Francke, 1970.

Martini, Fritz. "Gottfried Keller: 'Hadlaub' oder Falschklang der Kunst und Wahrhaftigkeit der Liebe." In *Zu Gottfried Keller,* ed. H. Steinecke. 122–38. Stuttgart: Klett, 1984.

Matt, Peter von. "Gottfried Keller und der brachiale Zweikampf." In *Gottfried Keller. Elf Essays zu seinem Werk,* ed. Hans Wysling. 109–32. Zurich: Verlag Neue Zürcher Zeitung, 1990.

Muschg, Adolf. *Gottfried Keller.* Munich: Kindler, 1977.

——. "Der leere Spiegel. Bemerkungen zu Kellers Lyrik." In *Gottfried Keller. Elf Essays zu seinem Werk,* ed. Hans Wysling. 133–50. Zurich: Verlag Neue Zürcher Zeitung, 1990.

Pestalozzi, Karl. "Sprachliche Glücksmomente bei Gottfried Keller." In *Gottfried Keller. Elf Essays zu seinem Werk,* ed. Hans Wysling. 185–202. Zurich: Verlag Neue Zürcher Zeitung, 1990.

Preisendanz, Wolfgang. "Gottfried Kellers 'Sinngedicht.'" In *Zu Gottfried Keller,* ed. H. Steinecke. 139–57. Stuttgart: Klett, 1984.

Richartz, Heinrich. *Literatur als Gesellschaftskritik: Darstellungsweise und politisch-didaktische Intention in Gottfried Kellers Erzählkunst.* Bonn: Bouvier, 1975.

Ruppel, Richard R. "Gottfried Kellers Ethik im Zusammenhang mit ästhetischen, religiösen und historischen Aspekten seiner Kunst." In *Gottfried Keller. Elf Essays zu seinem Werk,* ed. Hans Wysling. 61–76. Zurich: Verlag Neue Zürcher Zeitung, 1990.

Steinecke, Hartmut. "Der Erzähler Gottfried Keller." In *Zu Gottfried Keller,* ed. H. Steinecke. 5–17. Stuttgart: Klett, 1984.

——. "Kellers Romane und Romanvorstellungen in europäischen Perspektive." In *Gottfried Keller. Elf Essays zu seinem Werk,* ed. Hans Wysling. 77–90. Zurich: Verlag Neue Zürcher Zeitung, 1990.

Swales, Erika. "Gottfried Kellers (un)schlüssiges Erzählen." In *Gottfried Keller. Elf Essays zu seinem Werk,* ed. Hans Wysling. 91–108. Zurich: Verlag Neue Zürcher Zeitung, 1990.

Swales, Martin. "Das realistische Reflexionsniveau: Bemerkungen zu Gottfried Kellers *Der grüne Heinrich.*" In *Gottfried Keller. Elf Essays zu seinem Werk,* ed. Hans Wysling. 9–22. Zurich: Verlag Neue Zürcher Zeitung, 1990.

——. "Gottfried Kellers *Romeo und Julia auf dem Dorfe.*" In *Zu Gottfried Keller,* ed. H. Steinecke. 54–67. Stuttgart: Klett, 1984.

Weber, Bruno. *Gottfried Keller. Landschaftmaler Zürich.* Zurich: Verlag Neue Zürcher Zeitung, 1990.

Wenger, Kurt. *Gottfried Kellers Auseinandersetzung mit dem Christentum*. Bern: Francke, 1971.

Wysling, Hans. *Gottfried Keller 1819–1890*. Zurich: Artemis, 1990

Wysling, Hans, ed. *Gottfried Keller: Elf Essays zu seinem Werk*. Zurich: Verlag Neue Zürcher Zeitung, 1990.

——. "Und immer wieder kehrt Odysseus heim: Das Fabelhafte bei Gottfried Keller." In *Elf Essays*, ed. Wysling. 151–62. Zurich: Verlag Neuer Zürcher Zeitung, 1990.

Zäch, Alfred. *Gottfried Keller im Spiegel seiner Zeit*. Zurich: Sientia, 1952.

Zierleyn, Jörg. *Gottfried Keller und das klassische Erbe: Untersuchungen zur Goetherezeption eines Poetischen Realisten*. Frankfurt am Main: Peter Lang, 1989.

Conclusion

IN THE PRECEDING STUDY OF GOTTFRIED Keller's scholarly reception over the past one hundred and fifty years, careful consideration has been given to the selection of representative works that exemplify criticism and scholarship of a given period, reflect a particular critical approach, or are simply profoundly original interpretations in their own right. Every effort has been made to illuminate as broadly as possible the wealth and diversity of scholarly investigation that Keller's works have enjoyed. While selecting representative interpretations is a subjective act, a genuine effort has been made to discuss them as objectively as possible. Recent scholarly interpretations of Keller's works and the 1996 completion of the new historical critical edition serve as testimony to his enduring popularity and to the relevance of his fiction among scholars of literature and among lay readers as we approach the end of the millennium.

While Keller has not become a household name in the English-speaking world despite a number of English translations available, teachers of German continue to assign his works, particularly *Romeo und Julia auf dem Dorfe* and *Kleider Machen Leute* in their survey courses of the novella and academics continue to include his fiction and poetry in surveys of nineteenth-century German literature and in courses on Realism. Keller helps the modern reader to negotiate his way in a transitional world; contemporary readers find in his fiction, particularly in Seldwyla, a set of enduring values, traits, and characters that provide comfort, solace and sustenance they need to render contemporary life comprehensible. Keller's language is humane, and his belief that art can engender a better humanity and a more humane sense of community is an inspiration and an aspiration that transcends both time and space. The collapse of the old social and economic order as a result of advances in science and technology, new philosophical and sociological orientations, and industrialization have had substantial ramifications for our own century. It is therefore not surprising that Keller's works, which recorded and interpreted the changes he witnessed, still intrigue us today because we live in an advanced stage of the society of Keller's day, and because we understand (or are still seeking to understand) the manifestations of the social, economic, and political ferment that inspired his fiction.

The sesquicentennial of Keller scholarship is marked by a surprisingly harmonious and continuous development. Such continuity of reception has not been the norm for many authors. Keller scholars have never had to correct the misinterpretation or misappropriation of the past. Keller scholarship, as exemplified in the work of Hitschmannn, Muschg, G. Kaiser, Jennings, and Pascal, and M. Kaiser, Richartz, and Erika Swales, can be seen as a further development and enrichment of earlier efforts. Erika Swales's perceptive examination of the incongruities and paradoxes in Keller's fiction has begun to change the way we read the Seldwyla stories. We are beginning to comprehend the degree to which Keller was cognizant of the historical events of his day and to realize how well he understood the implications of the social, historical, and economic changes affecting his century.

It is through these multifarious interpretations that we have come to broaden and to deepen our understanding of Keller's works. Our evaluation, our understanding, our critique of a text changes with every critical reading of that text. Each subsequent examination is therefore rewardingly new. Through multiple investigations of a single text we refine our perceptions; with recurrent encounters we bring our increased experience with life and with other texts to bear on that most recent reading and thereby deepen our understanding of it. Some would even suggest that through the very act of reading, we become co-authors in the literary enterprise, that we bring our increasing experience to that text and in effect rewrite the text anew with each reading. As book lovers, scholars, and critics we share our individual interpretations with one another and learn thereby to refine our understanding of a particular author or text through these exchanges with fellow readers in a process Wayne Booth has called "Co-duction" (Booth, 70–75). I would like to think of all the voices we have heard in this book as our "co-ductions" on Meister Gottfried.

Keller sought through his art to inspire his readers to create an ever better humanity. This eighteenth-century concept was already difficult to fulfill in the nineteenth century and has become progressively more difficult (the cynic would say "impossible") to fulfill in our own time. Yet Keller's successful attempt to create dynamic fiction that reflected what he referred to as the dialectics of the cultural movement or the eternally evolving society, is perhaps what speaks to many readers today. In Keller's works one detects shades of contemporary society in the existential quandaries of Heinrich Lee and in Arnold Salander, two characters that mark the beginning and the end of Keller's literary career. It is our task and our challenge as readers and as teachers to make Gottfried Keller's fiction comprehensible and relevant to fellow readers and to our students so that they too, may wander along the verdant paths of memory that were once traversed by Heinrich Lee, share his thoughts and reflect upon the relevance of those thoughts for our time.

Gottfried Keller's Works

1845 "Lieder eines Autodidakten." *Deutsches Taschenbuch* 1, 167–236. Zürich and Winterthur: Verlag des literarischen Comptoirs.

1846a. "Einundzwanzig Liebeslieder. Feueridylle, eine Allegorie." *Deutsches Taschenbuch.* 2, 75–141. Zürich: Julius Fröbel and Comptoirs.

1846b. *Gedichte von Gottfried Keller.* Heidelberg: C. F. Winter.

1847a. "Nachtgesänge." *Lyrische Blätter.* Ed. H. Rollet.

1847b. "Ave Maria auf dem Vierwaldstättersee" ("Fuhr ein Schifflein gegen Flüelen"). *Europa* 49: 807.

1847c. "Morgenlied" ("So oft die Sonne aufersteht"), "Sommer" ("Das ist doch eine uppige Zeit"), "Warnung" ("Ja, du bist frei, mein Volk"),"Pietistenwalzer," "Loyolas wilde verwegene Jagd," "Apostatenmarsch," "Für Gott, König und Vaterland." In *Die politischen Lyriker unserer Zeit*, 305f. Leipzig: Arnold Ruge.

1847d. "Der Schneidergeselle, welcher den Herrn spielt." *Bündner-Kalender für das Jahr 1847* (Chur: Braun). (Thought to be from Gottfried Keller. See Jakob Baechtold, 3, 37).

1847e. "Literarische Briefe aus der Schweiz." *Blätter für literarische Unterhaltung* 215, 36–39 (Reprinted in Baechtold, Jakob, *Gottfried Kellers Leben. Seine Briefe und Tagebücher*, vol. 1., 446. Berlin, Besser: 1894–97 [4th ed.: 453].)

1847g. "Goethes Reineke Fuchs von Kaulbach." *Neue Zürcher-Zeitung* 61, March 2.

1847h. "Wieder hat der jung Mai Seine Alte Kraft bewährt." *Neue Zürcher-Zeitung*, 125.

1848a. "Kunstbericht über Boßhard's 'Waldmann.'" *Neue Zürcher-Zeitung* 42/43 (February 11, 12).

1851 *Neuere Gedichte.* Braunschweig: Vieweg.

1852b. *Berliner Gedichte. Deutsches Museum* 1: 881ff.

1854a. "Ehescheidung," "Jung gewohnt, alt gethan," "Liebeslied" ("Weise nicht von dir mein schlichtes Herz"), "Trochäen" ("Wohl, ich faß im Eichenbaume"). In *Deutscher Musenalmanach*, ed. Christian Schad, 40, 37, 187, 41.

1854b. "Sinngedichte von G. Keller" (12 epigrams; five were reprinted in the *Gesammelte Gedichte*, 1883). In *Deutsches Museum* 11.

1854c. *Neuere Gedichte.* 2nd expanded edition. Braunschweig: Vieweg.

1854d. *Der grüne Heinrich.* Vols. 1–3. Braunschweig: Vieweg.

1855a. *Der grüne Heinrich.* Vol. 4. Braunschweig: Vieweg.

1855b. Review of Jeremias Gotthelf's "Erlebnisse eines Schuldenbauers." *Blätter für literaturische Unterhaltung* 9.

1856a. *Die Leute von Seldwyla.* Braunschweig: Vieweg.

1856b. "Lieder zum Kadettenfest in Zürich and Winterthur." Zurich: Züricher und Furrer.

1858b. "Auf lasset uns singen, Es ist uns ein Hort" and "Auf der Ufenau." (Poems composed for the commemorative celebration [Jubiläumsfeier] at the University of Zurich and set to music by W. Baumgartner. No publication information.)

1858c. "Sängergruss auf das Eidgenössische Sängerfest in Zürich." (Poems composed by Gottfried Keller for the all-male choir and set to music by W. Baumgartner.) Zurich: Gebrüder Hug.

"Da nun die Eichen wieder grün Und licht die Lande stehn."(Composed as a greeting to the marksmen of Bremen who were attending the Eidgenössischen Schützenfest in Zurich. No publication information.)

1860a. "An die Wahlmänner des Kantons Zürich." (A political appeal to the people for an open meeting in Uster on October 7. No publication information.)

1860b. "Becherlied." (Song composed for the all-male choir in remembrance of the federal Sängerfest in Chur.) Schaffhausen: Brodtmann'sche Buchhandlung.

1863a. "Bettagsproklamation." (An annual appeal on behalf of the government of Zurich addressed to its citizens on the annual day of prayer and repentance. No publication information.)

1863b. "Das provisorische Komitee zur Unterstützung der Polen an die Bewohner Zürich's." (Political leaflet dated 18 March: Keller was secretary of the committee.)

1864. "Antiquarische Buss- und Opferhymne auf den Berchtoldstag." (Reprinted in the *Liederchronik der Antiquarischen Gesellschaft*, Zürich.)

1867a. "Zum Gedächtnis an Wilhelm Baumgartner." (Composed for the federal music festival in Zurich. No publication information.)

1867b. "Bettungsmandat für den auf Sonntag den 15. Herbstmonat festgesetzten Bettag." (Annual appeal to the people of Zurich on the day of prayer and repentance. No publication information.)

1867c. "Eine autobiographische Skizze" In: *Die poetische Nationalliteratur der deutschen Schweiz,* ed. Robert Weber, vol. 3, 1–16. Glarus: Verlagsbuchhandlung J. Vogel.

1870. "Prolog zur Feier von Beethovens Hundertjährigem Geburtstage in Zürich." Special edition. (Published in *Gesammelte Gedichte,* [1883], 222.)

1871 "Bettungsmandat für den auf Sonntag den 17. Herbstmonat festgesetzten Bettag." (Partially reprinted in *Nachgelassene Schriften*, 344.)

1872a. "Bettungsmandat für den auf Sonntag den 15. Herbstmonat festgelegten Bettag."

1872b. *Sieben Legenden.* Stuttgart: Göschen.

1873a. "Der Parteigänger" ("Gefallen sind die Hiebe"), "Kleine Passion." *Über Land und Meer* 29: 218, 227. Stuttgart: Hallberger. (Reprinted in *Gesammelte Gedichte*, 371, 367.)

1873b. "Schließt auf den Ring, drin wir im Frieden tagten." (Festival song for the folk festival in Solothurn, June 15. Reprinted in *Gesammelte Gedichte*, 211.)

1873c. "Nacht im Zeughaus." In *Die Illustrierte Schweiz*. Bern: n. p., 232. (Reprinted in *Gesammelte Gedichte*, 269.)

1874a. *Die Leute von Seldwyla*. 2d ed., 4 vols. Stuttgart: Göschen. New editions appeared in 1876, 1883, and 1887.

1874b. "Krötenfrage," "Revolution" (Es wird schon geh'n"). In *Das Schweizerhaus. Ein vaterländisches Taschenbuch*, vol. 3: 1, 89. Bern: Fent und Reinert. (Reprinted in *Gesammelte Gedichte*, 369, 324.)

1876a. "Die Johannisnacht." Zurich: Friedrich Schultheß. (Becherweihe der Zunftgesellschaft zur Schmieden in Zürich [Poem to dedicate a chalice for a guild]. Reprinted in *Gesammelte Gedichte*, 240.)

1876b. *Romeo und Julia auf dem Dorfe*. (Special edition). Stuttgart: Cotta.

1876–77 "Züricher Novellen." *Deutsche Rundschau*, ed. Julius Rodenberg, November/April.

1876–77 "Autobiographisches von G. Keller." *Die Gegenwart*, 10, no. 51 and 11, no. 1.

1877a *Schweizerischer Miniaturalmanach*. Bern: Rudolf Buri. (Twelve already-published poems by Keller.)

1877b. "Ein Festzug in Zürich." In *Kunst und Leben. Ein Neuer Almanach für das deutsche Haus von Fr. Bodenstedt*. Stuttgart: Spemann. (Reprinted in *Gesammelte Gedichte*, 226.)

1877c. *Der Schweizerische Bildungsfreund, ein republikanisches Lesebuch*. Ed. Dr. Thomas Scherr. Poetry Section, 7th edition. Revised by Gottfried Keller. Zurich: Orell, Füßli and Co., 1877.

1878a. *Züricher Novellen*. Stuttgart: Göschen. 2 vols. (New editions appeared in 1879, 1883, and 1886.)

1878b. "Heinrich Leutholds Gedichte." *Neue Zürcher-Zeitung* 583, Dec. 12.

1878c. "Tafelgüter," "Das Weinjahr," "Am Rhein." *Deutsche Rundschau* 16, 288.

1879a. "Ein Schwurgericht," "Stutzenbart," "Abendlied" ("Augen, meine lieben Fensterlein"), "Tod und Dichter." *Deutsche Rundschau* 20, 451.

1879b. "Die Weihnachtsfeier im Irrenhaus." *Neue Zürcher-Zeitung*, 16, Jan. 11.

1879c. "Niklaus Manuel." *Neue Zürcher-Zeitung* 78/80, Feb. 17/18.

1879d. "Ludwig Vogel." *Neue Zürcher-Zeitung* 396, August 25.

1879e. "Ein nachhaltiger Rachekrieg." *Neue Zürcher-Zeitung*, 457, Sept. 30.

1879f. *Der grüne Heinrich*. New edition: vols 1–3. Stuttgart: Göschen.

1880a. *Der grüne Heinrich*. New edition: vol. 4.

1880b. "Herbstlandschaft" ("Ich sah ein holdes Weib im Traum"), "Ein Berittener" ("Ein Häuptling ritt geehrt durchs Land"), "Auf ein Gesangfest im Frühling" ("Nun ist des Winters grimmer Frost"). *Kunst und Leben* 3. Stuttgart: Spemann, 146.

1881a. "Parabel." In *Sturm und Noth*. Berlin: Selbstschriften-Album des deutschen Reiches.

1881b. "Das Sinngedicht." *Deutsche Rundschau* 26/27 (Jan./May)

1882a. "Ein bescheidenes Kunstreischen." *Neue Zürcher-Zeitung*, 81/82 (Mar. 22/23).

1882b. "Was heißt bei uns: aus dem Volke? " *Neue Zürcher-Zeitung*, July 31.

1882c. "Der Apotheker von Chamounix." *Nord und Süd* 20 (March): 277–85.

1982d. *Das Sinngedicht*. Berlin: W. Hertz.

1883a. "Der Kranz." *Zürcher Taschenbuch* 6: 158. Zürich: Orell Füßli. (Also in *Gesammelte Gedichte*, 397.)

1883c. Cantata zur fünfzigjährigen Stiftungsfeier der Hochschule Zürich. (Reprinted in *Gesammelte Werke*, vol. 9, 267 [1889].)

1883d. *Gesammelte Gedichte*. Berlin: Verlag von Wilhelm Hertz.

1884a. "Escher-Denkmal." *Neue Zürcher-Zeitung* 197, July 15.

1884b. "Kleider machen Leute" In *Novellen, Humoresken und Skizzen* (Collection Schick 20). Chicago: L. Schick.

1885a. *Das Fähnlein der sieben Aufrechten*. Wetzikon bei Zürich: Stenographische Bibliothek des allgemeinen schweizerischen Stenographenvereins. Vol. 1. (Reprinted in 1889 by Wetzikon and in Leipzig by Robolsky.)

1885b. "Ein Brief Gottfried Kellers über falschen Goethe-Kultus." *Goethe-Jahrbuch*. ed. Ludwig Geiger.(Letter dated March 11, 1884.)

1886a. *Martin Salander. Deutsche Rundschau* 46/48 (Jan./Sept.).

1886b. *Martin Salander*. Berlin: Wilhelm Hertz.

1887. "Zu Friedrich Th. Vischers achtzigstem Geburtstage." Special to *Allgemeine Zeitung* (Munich) 179, June 30.

1889a. "Zu Alfred Eschers Denkmalweihe." *Neue Zürcher-Zeitung*, June 22.

1889b. "Gottfried Keller. Selbstbiographie." In *Chronik der Kirchgemeinde Neumünster*, 430.

1904a. "Der Briefwechsel zwischen Theodor Storm und Gottfried Keller." Ed. A. Köster. *Deutsche Rundschau* 117, October-December. (Reprinted by Peter Goldammer, 1960.)

1904b. "Emil Kuhs Briefe an Gottfried Keller." Ed. A. Schaer. *Zürcher Taschenbuch* 28, 189–252.

1905a. "Der Briefwechsel zwischen Friedrich Nietzsche und Gottfried Keller." In *Nietzsches gesammelte Briefe*, ed. Elisabeth Förster-Nietzsche and Peter Gast, vol. 3, 207–217. Berlin: Schuster & Löffler.

1919. *Paul Heyse und Gottfried Keller Briefwechsel*. Ed. Max Kalbeck. Braunschweig: Westermann.

1922. *Gottfried Keller und Josef Viktor Widmann: Briefwechsel*. Ed. Max Widmann. Zurich: Art Institut Orell Füßli.

1924. "Gottfried Kellers Briefe an Adolf Stern." *Euphorion* 25: 11–113.

1927. *Aus Gottfried Kellers glücklicher Zeit. Der Dichter im Briefwechsel mit Marie und Adolf Exner*. Ed. Hans Frisch. Vienna: F. G. Speidel.

Editions of Keller's Collected Works

1889. *Gesammelte Werke*. 10 vols. Berlin: Wilhelm Hertz, 1889. (The first collected edition, with which Keller was also associated.)

1921. *Gottfried Kellers Werke*. Kritisch-historische und erläuterte Ausgabe. 8 vols. Ed. Max Nußberger. Leipzig: Bibliographisches Institut.

1921–1923. *Gottfried Kellers Werke*. 6 vols. Ed. Harry Maync. Berlin: Propyläen-Verlag.

1936. *Gottfried Kellers Werke*. 10 vols. Ed. Max Zollinger. Berlin: Deutsches Verlagshaus Bong & Co.

1926–1948. *Sämtliche Werke*. 24 vols. Based upon Keller's literary estate and edited and annotated by Jonas Fränkel (17 vols.) and from 1944 on by Carl Helbling (7 vols.). Vols. 3–8 and 16–19 were published by Eugen Rentsch, Erlebach-Zürich, 1926–27. All other volumes were published by Benteli in Bern. Cited in the text as *S.W.*

Vol. 1: *Gesammelte Gedichte, Teil 1* (Collected Poems, Part 1). 1931–1938.

Vol. 2/1: *Gesammelte Gedichte, Teil 2* (Collected Poems, Part 2). 1931–1938.

Vol. 2/2: *Kommentar zu den Gedichten* (Commentary to the poems). 1931–1938.

Vol. 3–6: *Der grüne Heinrich*. 1926.

Vol. 7–8: *Die Leute von Seldwyla*. 1927.

Vol. 9: *Züricher Novellen*. Vol. 1 (*Hadlaub, Der Narr auf Manegg, Der Landvogt von Greifensee*). 1944.

Vol. 10: *Züricher Novellen*. Vol. 2 (*Das Fähnlein der sieben Aufrechten, Ursula, Sieben Legenden.*) 1945.

Vol. 11: *Das Sinngedicht*. 1934.

Vol. 12: *Martin Salander*. 1943.

Vol. 13: *Frühe Gedichte* (until 1846). 1939.

Vol. 14: *Gedichte* (1846). 1936.

Vol. 15/1: *Neuere Gedichte* (1851 and 1854) and *Der Apotheker von Charmounix oder: Der kleine Romanzero.* 1932.

Vol. 15/2: *Nachgelassene Gedichte seit 1846. Entwürfe zu Gedichten, Fragmente, Gesamtregister zu den Gedichten* (Unpublished poems since 1846. Poem fragments, fragments, register of the poems). 1949.

Vol. 16–19.*Der grüne Heinrich.* First edition (1855). 1926.

Vol. 20: *Nachgelassene Erzählungen, dramatischer Nachlaß* (Unpublished stories, dramatic fragments). 1946.

Vol. 21: *Autobiographien, Tagebücher* (Autobiographies, journals [including the Dream-Book], essays on Politics and current topics, including the *Bettagsmandate* 1–5). 1947

Vol. 22: *Aufsätze zur Literatur und Kunst* (Essays on literature and art [Börne, Ruge, Gotthelf, among others]; "Am Mythenstein"; book reviews; also miscellaneous, reflections, etc.). 1948.

Keller, Gottfried. *Sämtliche Werke und ausgewählte Briefe.* 3 vols. Ed. Clemens Heselhaus. Munich: C. Hanser: 1956–58.

Vol. 1: *Der grüne Heinrich* (first edition); *Der grüne Heinrich* (revised edition) from the end of the "Jugendgeschichte."

Vol. 2: *Die Leute von Seldwyla; Sieben Legenden; Züricher Novellen; Das Sinngedicht;* Nachgelassene Erzählungen; Unvollendetes.

Vol. 3. *Gedichte* (*Frühe Gedichte; Gedichte* (1846); *Neuere Gedichte* 1851–54; Späte Gedichte; nachgelassene Gedichte); *Der Apotheker von Chamounix; Martin Salander;* Dramatische Versuche; Autobiographien und Tagebücher, Traumbuch; Aufsätze über Literatur, Kunst und Politik; Ausgewählte Briefe 1857–1889; Anhang (Commentary, annotations); Afterword and chronological table.

Keller, Gottfried. *Sämtliche Werke.* Eds. Thomas Böning, Gerhard Kaiser, Kai Kaufmann, Dominik Müller, and Peter Villwock. Frankfurt am Main: Deutscher Klassiker Verlag, 1985–1996.

Vol. 1: *Gedichte,* ed. Kai Kauffmann, 1995.

Vol. 2: *Der grüne Heinrich* (original edition), ed. Thomas Böning and Gerhard Kaiser (1985).

Vol. 3: *Der grüne Heinrich* (revised edition), ed. Peter Villwock (1996).

Vol. 4: *Die Leute von Seldwyla,* ed. Thomas Böning (1989).

Vol. 5: *Züricher Novellen,* Thomas Böning (1989).

Vol. 6: *Sieben Legenden, Das Sinngedicht, Martin Salander,* ed. Dominik Müller (1991).

Vol. 7: Nachgelassene Erzählungen; Dramatischer Nachlaß; Aufsätze zu Literatur, Kunst und Politik; Autobiographisches; Tagebücher, ed. Dominik Müller (1996).

Gottfried Keller: Gesammelte Briefe. 4 vols. Ed. Carl Helbling. Bern: Beneteli Verlag, 1950–1954. (The critical edition of Keller's correspondence, cited in text as *G.B.*)

English Translations of Keller's Works available 1998

Green Henry. Trans. A. M. Holt. New York: Riverrun, 1986.

Legends of Long Ago. Trans. Charles H. Handschin. 1911; reprint, Stratford, NH: Ayer, 1977.

Martin Salander. Trans. Kenneth Halwas. New York: Riverrun, 1981.

People of Seldwyla & Seven Legends. Trans. M. D. Hottinger. 1929; reprint, Stratford, NH: Ayer, 1977.

Seldwyla Folks: Three Singular Tales by the Swiss Poet. Trans. Wolf Von Schierbrand. 1919; reprint, Stratford, NH: Ayer, 1977.

Stories. Ed. Frank Ryder. The German Library. New York: Continuum, 1982.

Includes:
   The Three Righteous Combmakers. Trans. Robert M. Browning
   A Village Romeo and Juliet. Trans. Paul Bernard Thomas,. adapted by F. Ryder
   Mirror, the Cat. Trans. Robert M. Browning
   Clothes Make the Man. Trans. Harry Steinhauer
   The Lost Smile. Trans. Frank Ryder
   The Banner of the Upright Seven. Trans. B. Q. Morgan

From the *Seven Legends:*
   Eugenia. Trans. Martin Wyness.
   The Virgin and the Devil. Trans. Martin Wyness.
   The Virgin as Knight. Trans. Robert M. Browning
   The Virgin and the Nun. Trans. Robert M. Browning.

Chronological List of Works Cited

Hettner, Hermann. 1852 *Das moderne Drama.* Braunschweig: F. Vieweg. 177.

Gervinus, Georg Gottfried. 1853. *Geschichte der deutschen Dichtung.* 4th rev. ed., 5 vols. Leipzig: W. Engelmann.

Hettner, Hermann. 1854. Review of *Der Grüne Heinrich,* vols. 1–3. *National-Zeitung* (Berlin) May 5.

Varnhagen von Ense, Karl August. 1855. Review of *Der grüne Heinrich. Vossische Zeitung,* June 14, 6.

Schmidt, Julian. 1856. "Rezension der Newcomers." *Grenzboten* 15: 1, 405–409

Grosse, Julius. 1857. "Der grüne Heinrich." 3 parts. *Abendblatt zur Neuen Münchener Zeitung,* May 2, 9, 19, 1857.

Prutz, Robert. 1859. *Die deutsche Literatur der Gegenwart 1848–1858.* Vol. 1. Leipzig: Voigt & Günther.

Schmidt, Julian. 1866–1869. *Geschichte der Deutschen Literatur seit Lessing's Tod.* 3 vols. Leipzig: F. W. Grunow.

Hillebrand, Karl. 1873. "G. G. Gervinus." *Preußische Jahrbücher* 32: 379–428.

Schmidt, Julian. 1873. *Neue Bilder aus dem geistigen Leben unserer Zeit.* 4 vols. Leipzig: Duncker & Humblot.

Kuh, Emil. 1874. "Die Leute von Seldwyla." *Wiener Abendpost,* Dec. 28.

Auerbach, Berthold. 1875. "Gottfried Kellers Neue Schweizergestalten." *Deutsche Rundschau* 4 (July–September): 34.

Kürnberger, Ferdinand. 1877. "Gottfried Kellers *Sieben Legenden.*" In: F. K.: *Literarische Herzenssachen.* 239–254. Reprinted in *Meisterwerke deutscher Literaturkritik,* ed. Hans Mayer, vol. 2, 1956. 713–725.

Scherer, Wilhelm. 1878. "Gottfried Kellers *Züricher Novellen.*" *Deutsche Rundschau* 17 (Oct.–Dec.): 324.

Brahm, Otto. 1880. "Gottfried Kellers 'Grüner Heinrich.'" *Deutsche Rundschau* 25 (Oct.–Dec.): 466.

Zimmern, Helen. 1880. "A Swiss Novelist." *Fraser's Magazine,* April 21: 459–76; reprinted in *Appelton's Journal,* June 1880 and *Littwell's Living Age,* May 1880.

Vischer, Friedrich Theodor. 1881. "Gottfried Keller, eine Studie." In Friedrich Theodor von Vischer: *Altes und Neues,* vol. 2. 135–216. Stuttgart: Bonz & Co., 1881.

Engel, Eduard. 1882. "Gottfried Keller: Sinngedicht." *Das Magazin für Literatur des In- und Auslands,* 4 February.

Spielhagen, Friedrich. 1882. *Westermanns Monatsheften* 52 (June): 309.

Brahm, Otto. 1883. *Gottfried Keller. Ein literarisches Essay.* Berlin: Auerbach.

——. 1883. "Gottfried Kellers Gedichte." *Deutsche Rundschau* 32 (Oct.–Dec.).

Schmidt, Erich. 1886. "Wege und Ziele der deutschen Literaturgeschichte." In Schmidt, *Charakteristiken,* 480–98. Berlin: Weidmann.

Schlenther, Paul. 1887. Review of *Martin Salander. Deutsche Rundschau* 51 (April–June).

Frey, Adolf. 1890. "Gottfried Keller — Das Letzte Jahr." *Deutsche Rundschau* 65 (Oct.–Dec.).

Rodenberg, Julius. 1890. "Gottfried Keller." *Deutsche Rundschau* 64 (July–September).

Stiefel, Julius. 1890. "Rede bei der Bestattung von Gottfried Keller am 18. Juli 1890." In *Reden und Vorträge,* 46–53.

Frey, Adolf. 1892. *Erinnerungen an Gottfried Keller.* Leipzig: Haessel. (Reprinted 1893, 1919.)

Baechtold, Jakob. 1894–97. *Gottfried Kellers Leben. Seine Briefe und Tagebücher.* 3 vols. Berlin: Besser.

Baechtold, Jakob. 1897. *Gottfried Keller Bibliographie (1844–1897).* Berlin: Wilhelm Hertz.

Köster, Albert. 1900. *Gottfried Keller. Sieben Vorlesungen.* Leipzig: B. G. Teubner. (Reprinted 1907, 1917, 1923.)

Freytag, Gustav. 1901–03. *Vermischte Aufsätze aus Jahren 1848 bis 1894.* Ed. Ernst Elster. 2 vols. Leipzig: S. Hirzel.

Coar, John F. 1903. *Studies in German Literature in the Nineteenth Century.* New York: MacMillan, 270–302.

Haym, Rudolf. 1903. *Gesammelte Aufsätze von Rudolf Haym.* Ed. Wilhelm Schrader. Berlin: Weidmann.

Huch Ricarda. 1904. *Gottfried Keller.* Berlin: Schuster & Löffler. (Subsequent editions appeared with Insel Verlag.)

Hugo von Hoffmannsthal, 1905. "Unterhaltungen über die Schriften von G. Keller." In Hofmannsthal, *Gesammelte Werke,* vol. 7, 510. Frankfurt: Fischer, 1979.

Thomas, Calvin. 1909. *A History of German Literature.* Reprint: 1970, Port Washington, NY: Kennikat Press.

Kuh, Emil. 1910. "Die Leute von Seldwyla." In Kuh, *Kritische und literarische Aufsätze,* 361–75. Vienna: Literarische Verein in Wien.

Korrodi, Eduard. 1911. *Gottfried Keller. Ein Deutscher Lyriker.* Leipzig: Hesse und Becker.

Wüst, Paul. 1911. *Gottfried Keller und Conrad Ferdinand Meyer in ihrem persönlichen und literarischen Verhältnis.* Leipzig: H. Haessel.

Faulkner, William H. 1912. "Der grüne Heinrich. Anna and Judith and their Predecessors in Rousseau's Confessions." *Virginia University Philosophical Society Bulletin,* Humanistic Series 1, no. 2 (February). 51–57.

Dünnebier, Hans. 1913. *Gottfried Keller und Ludwig Feuerbach.* Zurich: Ketner.

Hitschmann, E. 1913. "Über Träume Gottfried Kellers." *Zeitschrift für ärtzliche Psychoanalyse* 1.

Ermatinger, E. 1914. *Der Grüne Heinrich.* (Critical edition of the first version of 1854–55 With introduction and notes.) Stuttgart: J. G. Cotta.

Ermatinger, Emil. 1915–1919. *Gottfried Kellers Leben, Briefe und Tagebücher.* 3 vols. Stuttgart & Berlin: J. G. Cotta. (Based upon the biography of Jakob Baechtold.)

Hauch, Edward F. 1916. *Gottfried Keller as a Democratic Idealist.* New York: Columbia UP.

Kriesi, Hans Max. 1918. *Gottfried Keller als Politiker.* Frauenfeld & Leipzig: Huber.

Vischer, Friedrich Theodor. 1918. *Friedrich Theodor Vischers Ausgewählte Werke.* Ed. Gustav Keyßner. Vol. 3, 342–408. Stuttgart & Berlin: Deutsche Verlags-Anstalt.

Hitschmann, Eduard. 1919. *Gottfried Keller: Psychoanalyse des Dichters, seiner Gestalten und Motive.* Leipzig: Internationaler Psychoanalytischer Verlag.

Hesse, Hermann. 1919. "Seldwyla im Abendrot: Zu G. K. s 100. Geburtstag am 19. Juli." *Vossische Zeitung,* July 19.

Hochdorf, Max. 1919a. *Gottfried Keller im europäischen Gedanken.* Zurich: Rascher.

——. 1919b. *Zum geistigen Bilde Gottfried Kellers.* Vienna: Amalthea.

Kalbeck, M. 1919. *Paul Heyse und Gottfried Keller im Briefwechsel.* Braunschweig: G. Westermann.

Maync, H. 1919. "Gottfried Keller, 1819–1890." Bern: K. J. Wysse Erben. (Commemorative lecture at the University of Bern on July 19, 1919 as part of the Keller Centennial celebration. Reprinted in 1928 by Huber & Co.)

Schaffner, Paul. 1919. *Der grüne Heinrich als Künstlerroman.* Stuttgart: J. G. Cotta.

Spitteler, Carl. 1919. "Gottfried Keller-Rede in Luzern." Lucerne: Otto Wicke.

Hay, M. 1920. *The Story of a Swiss Poet. A Study of Gottfried Keller's Life and Works.* Bern: F. Wyss.

Gleichen-Russwurm, A. F. v. 1921. *Gottfried Kellers Weltanschauung.* Philosophische Reihe, vol. 23. Munich: Rösl & Cie.

Meyer, Richard M. 1921. *Die Deutsche Literatur des 19. und 20. Jahrhunderts.* 364–87. Berlin: George Bondi. (Earlier editions appeared in 1906 and 1912.)

Maync, Harry. 1923. *Gottfried Keller. Sein Leben und seine Werke.* Leipzig Frauenfeld: Huber & Co.

Schaffner, Paul. 1923. *Gottfried Keller als Maler.* Stuttgart: J. G. Cotta.

Hofmannsthal, Hugo von. 1924. "Unterhaltung über die Schriften von Gottfried Keller." In Hoffmannsthal, *Gesammelte Werke*, vol. 2., 266–275. Berlin: Fischer.

Widmann, M. 1925. *Gottfried Keller and J. V. Widmann Briefwechsel.* Zurich: Art Institut Orell Füßli.

Frisch, H. 1927. *Aus Gottfried Kellers glücklicher Zeit. Der Dichter im Briefwechsel mit Marie u. Adolf Exner.* Vienna: F. G. Speidel.

Hettner, Hermann. 1928. *Geschichte der deutschen Literatur im 18. Jahrhundert.* Ed. by Georg Witkowski. Leipzig: P. List.

Roffler, Thomas. 1931. *Gottfried Keller. Ein Bildnis.* Frauenfeld: Huber.

Hunziker, Fritz. 1932. "Gottfried Keller und Zürich." *Jahresbericht der Gottfried Keller-Gesellschaft.* Zurich: Gottfried Keller-Gesellschaft. (Cited in text as *Jb. GKG.*)

Robertson, John G. 1935. *Essays and Addresses on Literature.* London: Routledge.

Zippermann, Charles C. 1935. *Gottfried Keller Bibliographie 1844–1934.* Zurich: Rascher & Cie.

Schaffner, Paul. 1936. "Gottfried Keller als Malerdichter." *Jahresbericht der Gottfried Keller-Gesellschaft.* Zurich: Gottfried Keller-Gesellschaft.

Ackerknecht, Erwin. 1937. *Gottfried Keller.* Berlin-Lichterfelde: Widukind.

Staiger, Emil. 1937. "Gottfried Keller und die Romantik." *Jahresbericht der Gottfried Keller-Gesellschaft.* Zurich: Gottfried Keller-Gesellschaft.

Demeter, Hildegard. 1938. *Gottfried Kellers Humor.* Berlin: Ebering, 1938.

Helbling, Carl. 1938. "Gottfried Keller in seinen Briefen." *Jahresbericht der Gottfried Keller-Gesellschaft.* Zurich: Gottfried Keller-Gesellschaft.

Ackerknecht, Erwin. 1939. *Gottfried Keller. Geschichte seines Lebens.* Berlin and Leipzig: Insel.

Fränkel, Jonas. 1939. *Gottfried Kellers politische Sendung.* Zurich: Oprecht.

Kramer, Priscilla M. 1939. *The Cyclical Method of Composition in Gottfried Kellers Sinngedicht.* New York: Ottendorfer.

Staiger, Emil. 1939. "Die ruhende Zeit." In *Die Zeit als Einbildungskraft des Dichters. Untersuchungen zu Gedichten von Brentano, Goethe und Keller.* 159–210. Zurich: Atlantis. (2nd edition, 1953: 161–221).

Ackert, Ernst. 1942. *Gottfried Kellers Weltanschauung.* Bern: Mettler & Salz.

Faesi, Robert. 1942. *Gottfried Keller.* Zurich: Atlantis.

Hauptmann, Gerhard. 1942. "Gottfried Keller." In *Gesammelte Werke*, vol. 17, 331. Berlin: S. Fischer.

Schaffner, Paul. 1942. "Gottfried Keller als Maler." Zurich: Atlantis.

Rilla, Paul. 1943. *Gottfried Keller. Sein Leben in Selbstzeugnissen, Briefe und Berichten.* (Reprint: Zurich: Diogenes Verlag, 1978.)

Lukács, Georg. 1946. "Gottfried Keller." In Lukács, *Deutsche Realisten des 19. Jahrhunderts*, 147–230. Reprint, Berlin: Aufbau, 1952.

Boeschenstein, Hermann. 1948. *Gottfried Keller: Grundzüge seines Lebens und Werkes.* Bern: Paul Haupt.

Ackerknecht, Erwin. 1949. *Heidelberg im Leben Gottfried Kellers.* Heidelberg: Wunderhorn.

Reichert, Herbert W. 1949. *Basic Concepts in the Philosophy of Gottfried Keller.* Chapel Hill, NC: U of North Carolina P.

Ermatinger, Emil. 1950. *Gottfried Kellers Leben.* Zurich: Artemis. (Based upon Jakob Baechtolds biography, reduced to one volume.)

Zäch, Alfred. 1952. *Gottfried Keller im Spiegel seiner Zeit. Urteile und Berichte über den Menschen und Dichter.* Zurich: Sientia.

Fränkel, Jonas. 1954. *Dichtung und Wissenschaft.* Heidelberg: Lambert Schneider, 84–194.

Silz, Walter. 1954. "Romeo und Julia." In Silz, *Realism and Reality*, 79–93. Chapel Hill, NC: U of North Carolina P.

Zollinger-Wells, W. 1954. *Gottfried Kellers Religiosität.* Zurich: Artemis.

Benjamin, Walter. 1955. *Schriften.* Vol. 2, 284–296. Frankfurt am Main: Suhrkamp.

Wiese, Benno von. 1956. "Gottfried Keller — Kleider Machen Leute" In *Die Deutsche Novelle*, vol. 1, 238–49. Düsseldorf: August Bagel.

Lemke, Victor J. 1956. "The Deification of Gottfried Keller." *Monatshefte* 48: 119–26.

Pascal, Roy. 1956. *The German Novel.* Manchester: Manchester UP, 30–51.

Brinkmann, Richard. 1957. *Wirklichkeit und Illusion.* Tübingen: Niemeyer.

Frye, Northrup. 1957. *Anatomy of Criticism.* Princeton: Princeton UP.

Höllerer, Walter. 1957. "Gottfried Keller: Die Zeit geht nicht." In *Die deutsche Lyrik*, ed. Benno von Wiese, vol. 2, 201–06. Düsseldorf: August Bagel.

Preisendanz, Wolfgang. 1958. "Die Keller-Forschung der Jahre 1939–1957." *Germanisch-Romanische Monatschrift* 39: 144–78.

Hauser, Albert. 1959. *Gottfried Kellers Geburt und Zerfall der dichterischen Welt.* Zurich: Atlantis.

Mann, Thomas. 1960. "Ein Wort über Gottfried Keller," In Keller, *Gesammelte Werke*, vol. 9, 23–24. Frankfurt am Main: S. Fischer.

Martini, Fritz. 1962. *Deutsche Literatur im bürgerlichen Realismus.* 557–610. Stuttgart: Metzler.

Martini, Fritz. 1962. *Forschungsbericht zur deutschen Literatur in der Zeit des Realismus.* 43–56.

McCormack, E. Allan. 1962. "The Idylls in Keller's 'Romeo und Julia.' A Study in Ambivalence." *German Quarterly* 35: 265–79.

Wiese, Benno von. 1962. "Gottfried Keller: Der Landvogt von Greifensee." In von Wiese, *Die Deutsche Novelle*, vol. 2, 149–75.

Theodor Fontane. 1963. *Sämtliche Werke*. Vol. 21/1: 262. Munich: Nymphenburger.

Hauser, Albert. 1963. "Über das wirtschaftliche und soziale Denkens Gottfried Kellers." *Jahrbuch der Gottfried Keller Gesellschaft.*

Heselhaus, Clemens. 1963. Afterword, *Gottfried Keller Sämtliche Werke und Ausgewählte Briefe*, vol. 3, 1315–41. Darmstadt: Wissenschaftliche Buchgesellschaft.

Pestalozzi, Heinrich. 1963. *Lebendiges Werk*. Ed. Adolf Haller. 4 vols. Basel & Stuttgart: Birkhäuser.

Preisendanz, Wolfgang. 1963. "Keller: Der grüne Heinrich." In *Der Deutsche Roman*, vol. 2, ed. Benno von Wiese, 76–127. Düsseldorf: August Basel.

———. 1963. *Humor als dichterische Einbildungskraft. Studien zur Erzählkunst des poetischen Realismus*. Munich: Eidos. 143.

Reichert, Karl. 1963. "Die Entstehung der Sieben Legenden von Gottfried Keller." *Euphorion* 57: 97–131.

Reichert, Karl. 1963. "Die Entstehung der Züricher Novellen von Gottfried Keller." *Zeitschrift für deutsche Philologie* 82: 471–500.

Auerbach, Erich. 1964. *Mimesis. Dargestellte Wirklichkeit in der abendländischen Literatur*. 3d ed. Bern & Munich: Francke.

Brahm, Otto. 1964. *Kritiken und Essays*. Edited, introduced, and annotated by Fritz Martini. Zurich & Stuttgart: Artemis, 1964.

Stern, J. P. 1964. *Re-Interpretations: Seven Studies in Nineteenth Century German Literature*. 301–47. New York: Basic Books.

Wildbolz, Rudolf. 1964. *Gottfried Kellers Menschenbild*. Bern: Francke, 1964.

Guggenheim, Kurt. 1965. *Das Ende von Seldwyla. Ein Gottfried Keller-Buch*. Zurich: Artemis.

Kaiser, Michael. 1965. *Literatursoziologische Studien zu Gottfried Kellers Dichtung*. Bonn: Bouvier.

Kohlschmidt, Werner. 1965. "Theodor Storm und die Zürcher Dichter." In *Dichter Tradition und Zeitgeist*, 349–62. Bern: Francke.

Wehrli, Max. 1965. *Gottfried Kellers Verhältnis zum eigenen Schaffen*. Bern: Francke.

Benjamin, Walter. 1966. "Gottfried Keller. Zu Ehren einer kritischen Gesamtausgabe seiner Werke." In: *Angelus Novus*. Ausgewählte Schriften, vol. 2. Frankfurt am Main: Suhrkamp. 384–95.

Reichert, Herbert W. 1966. *Basic Concepts in the Philosophy of Gottfried Keller*. 2nd ed. New York: AMS Press.

Robertson, John George. 1966. *A History of German Literature*. 5th revised edition. London: William Blackwood & Sons Ltd. (Originally published 1902).

Becker, Eva D. 1967. "Das Literaturgespräch zwischen 1848 und 1870 in Robert Prutz' Zeitschrift 'Deutsches Museum.'" *Publizistik* 12: 14–36.

Demetz, Peter. 1967. "Zur Definition des Realismus." *Literatur und Kritik* 16/17: 333–45.

Breitenbruch, Bernd. 1968. *Gottfried Keller*. Reinbek bei Hamburg: Rowohlt.

Lindsay, J. M. 1968. *Gottfried Keller. Life and Works*. London: Oswald Wolff.

Gerhard, Melitta. 1968. *Der deutsche Entwicklungsroman bis zu Goethes "Wilhelm Meister."* Bern/Munich: Francke. (Originally published 1926.)

Auerbach, Erich. *Mimesis. The Representation of Reality in Western Literature*. Trans. Willard R. Trask. Princeton: Princeton UP, 1969.

Boeschenstein, Hermann. 1969. *Gottfried Keller*. Stuttgart: Metzler.

Jeziorkowski, Klaus, ed. 1969. *Gottfried Keller: Dichter über ihre Dichtung*. Munich: Ernst Heimeran.

Laufhütte, Hartmut. 1969. *Wirklichkeit und Kunst in Gottfried Kellers Roman "Der Grüne Heinrich."* Bonn: Bouvier.

Locher, Kaspar T. 1969. *Gottfried Keller — Der Weg zur Reife*. Bern: Francke.

Preisendanz, Wolfgang. 1969. "Gottfried Keller." In *Deutsche Dichter des 19. Jahrhunderts*, ed. Benno von Wiese, 440–62. Berlin: Erich Schmidt.

Luck, Rätus. 1970. *Gottfried Keller als Literaturkritiker*. Bern: Francke.

Scherer, Wilhelm. 1971. *A History of German Literature*. Trans. F. C. Conybeare, ed. F. Max Müller. New York: Haskell House.

Wenger, Kurt. 1971. *Gottfried Kellers Auseinandersetzung mit dem Christentum*. Bern: Francke.

Fehr, Karl. 1972. *Gottfried Keller: Aufschlüsse und Deutungen*. Bern & Munich: Francke.

Hesse, Hermann. 1972. *Eine Literaturgeschichte in Rezensionen und Aufsätzen*. Vol. 2, ed. Volker Michels, 293–302. Frankfurt: Suhrkamp.

Tremmer, Mark J. 1973. *Art And Influence of Jean-Jacques Rousseau: The Pastoral, Goethe, Gottfried Keller, And Other Essays*. Chapel Hill, NC: U of North Carolina P, 69–91.

Ellis, John M. 1974. "Die drei gerechten Kammacher." In *Narration in the German Novelle*, 136–54. Cambridge (UK): Cambridge UP.

Richartz, Heinrich. 1975. *Literaturkritik als Gesellschaftskritik: Darstellungsweise und politisch-didaktische Intention in Gottfried Kellers Erzählkunst*. Bonn: Bouvier.

Zöckler, Chistofer. 1975. *Dilthey und die Hermeneutik*. Stuttgart: J. B. Metzler.

Demetz, Peter. 1977. "Über die Fiktionen des Realismus." *Neue Rundschau* 4: 554–67.

Martino, Albert, Günter Häntzel, & Georg Jäger, eds. 1977. *Die deutsche Leihbibliothek und ihr Publikum*. In *Aufsätze und Forschungsberichte zum 19. Jahrhundert*. 1–26. Tübingen: Niemeyer.

Muschg, Adolf. 1977. *Gottfried Keller*. Munich: Kindler.

Preisendanz, Wolfgang. 1977. *Wege des Realismus.* 104–203. Munich: Fink.

Muschg, Adolf. 1978. "Professor Gottfried Keller?" *Jahresbuch der Gottfried Keller-Gesellschaft.*

Swales, Martin. 1978. *The German Bildungsroman from Wieland to Hesse.* 86–104. Princeton: Princeton UP.

Passavant, Rudolf von. 1978. *Zeitdarstellung und Zeitkritik in Gottfried Kellers Martin Salander.* Bern: Francke.

Frey, Adolf. 1979. *Erinnerungen an Gottfried Keller.* Reprint, originally published 1891. Zurich: Rotapfel-Verlag.

Jäger, Georg and Jörg Schönert, eds. 1980. *Die Leihbibliothek als Institution des literarischen Lebens im 18. und 19. Jahrhundert. Organisationsformen, Bestände, und Publikum.* Hamburg: Hauswedell.

Sautermeister, Gert. 1980. "Gottfried Keller: 'Der Grüne Heinrich' (1854–55; 2. Fassung 1879–80) Gesellschaftsroman, Seelendrama, Romankunst." In *Romane und Erzählungen des Bürgerlichen Realismus. Neue Interpretationen,* ed. Horst Denkler. 80–123. Stuttgart: Reclam.

Tompkins, Jane P. 1980. "The Reader in History. The Changing Shape of Literary Response." In *Reader-Response Criticism. From Formalism to Post-Structuralism,* ed. J. Tompkins. 201–32. Baltimore, London: Johns Hopkins UP.

Kaiser, Gerhard. 1981. *Gottfried Keller. Das gedichtete Leben.* Frankfurt am Main: Insel.

Menninghaus, Winfried. 1982. *Artistische Schrift.* (Studien zur Kompositionskunst Gottfried Kellers.) Frankfurt am Main: Suhrkamp.

Neumann, Bernd. 1982. *Gottfried Keller: Eine Einführung in sein Werk.* Königstein: Athenäum.

Schiller, Friedrich. 1982. *On the Aesthetic Education of Man.* Edited by Elizabeth M. Wilkinson and L. A. Willoughby. Oxford, Clarendon Press.

Böschenstein, Renate. 1983. "Der Schatz unter den Schlangen. Ein Gespräch mit Gerhard Kaisers Buch *Gottfried Keller: Das gedichtete Leben.*" *Euphorion* 77: 176–99.

Jennings, Lee B. 1983. "The Model of the Self in Gottfried Keller's Prose. *German Quarterly* 56 (March): 196–230.

Baumann, Walter. 1984. *Auf den Spuren Gottfried Kellers.* Zurich: Verlag Neue Zürcher Zeitung.

Steinecke, Hartmut. 1984. *Zu Gottfried Keller.* Stuttgart: Klett.

Includes:

Cowen, Roy C. "Spiegel und Widerspiegelung: Zu Kellers Märchen 'Spiegel, das Kätzchen.'" 68–78.

Henkel, Arthur. Gottfried Kellers "Tanzlegendchen." 108–21.

Kunz, Josef. "Gottfried Kellers 'Die Leute von Seldwyla.'" 40–53.

Laufhütte, Hartmut. "Gottfried Keller: 'Der grüne Heinrich.'" 18–39.

Martini, Fritz. "Gottfried Keller: 'Hadlaub' oder Falschklang der Kunst und Wahrhaftigkeit der Liebe." 122–38.

Muschg, Adolf. "Gottfried Keller: 'Martin Salander.'" 158–66.

Preisendanz, Wolfgang. "Gottfried Kellers 'Sinngedicht.'" 139–57.

Sautermeister, Gert. "Erziehung und Gesellschaft in Gottfried Kellers Novelle 'Kleider Machen Leute.'" 88–107.

Steinecke, Hartmut. "Der Erzähler Gottfried Keller." 5–17.

Swales, Martin. "Gottfried Kellers 'Romeo und Julia auf dem Dorfe.'" 54–67

Wiese, Benno von. "Gottfried Keller: 'Kleider Machen Leute.'" 79–87.

Hohendahl, Peter Uwe. 1985. *Literarische Kultur im Zeitalter des Liberalismus 1830–1870.* Munich: C. H. Beck.

Holub, Robert C. 1985. "Realism, Repetition, Repression: The Nature of Desire in Romeo und Julia auf dem Dorfe." *Modern Language Notes* 100 (April): 461–97.

Cowen, Roy C. 1985. *Der Poetische Realismus.* Munich: Winkler.

Kaiser, Gerhard. 1985. *Gottfried Keller: Eine Einführung.* Munich: Artemis.

Locher, Kaspar T. 1985. *Gottfried Keller: Welterfahrung, Wertstruktur und Stil.* Bern: Francke.

Meyer, C. F. 1985. "Erinnerungen an Gottfried Keller." In: *Sämtliche Werke Conrad Ferdinand Meyers,* vol. 15, ed. Hans Zeller and Alfred Zäch, 179–85. Bern: Benteli.

Whalley, George. *Studies in Literature and the Humanities: Innocence of Intent.* Kingston and Montreal: McGill-Queens UP, 1985.

Boeschenstein, Hermann. 1986. "Gotthelf oder Keller? " In *Zur deutschen Literatur und Philosophie,* ed. Rodney Symington. 30–38. Bern/New York: Peter Lang.

Booth, Wayne. 1988. *The Company We Keep — An Ethics Of Fiction.* Los Angeles: U of California P.

Godwin-Jones, Robert, and Peischl, Margaret T. 1988. *Three Swiss Realists: Gotthelf, Keller, and Meyer.* 81–153. Lanham, New York: UP of America.

Hohendahl, Peter Uwe, ed. 1988. *A History of German Literary Criticism, 1730–1980.* 179–276. Lincoln & London: U of Nebraska P. (Originally published in Germany in 1985 as *Geschichte der deutschen Literaturkritik.*)

Mullen, Inga E. 1988. *German Realism in the United States.* 31–56. New York & Bern: Peter Lang.

Ruppel, Richard R. 1988. *Gottfried Keller: Poet, Pedagogue and Humanist.* New York & Bern: Peter Lang.

Smidt, Irmgard & Streitfeld, Erwin. 1988. *Gottfried Keller — Emil Kuh Briefwechsel.* Stäfa (Zurich): Th. Gut.

Hart, Gail K. 1989. *Readers and Their Fictions in the Novels and Novellas of Gottfried Keller.* Chapel Hill: U of North Carolina P.

Zierleyn, Jörg. 1989. *Gottfried Keller und das klassische Erbe: Untersuchungen zur Goethere-zeption eines Poetischen Realisten.* Frankfurt am Main: Peter Lang.

Eagleton, Terry. 1990. *The Ideology of the Aesthetic.* Oxford: Oxford UP.

Stähli, Fridolin. 1990. *Gottfried Keller im Briefwechsel mit Paul Heyse.* Stäfa (Zurich): Th. Gut.

Weber, Bruno. 1990. *Gottfried Keller: Landschaftmaler Zürich.* Zurich: Verlag Neue Zürcher Zeitung.

Wysling, Hans, ed. 1990. *Gottfried Keller 1819–1890.* Zurich: Artemis.

Wysling, Hans, ed. 1990. *Gottfried Keller. Elf Essays zu seinem Werk.* Zurich: Verlag Neue Zürcher Zeitung.

Includes:

Böschenstein, Renate. "Kellers Glück." 163–84.

Kaiser, Gerhard. "Grüne Heinriche — ein epochaler Typus." 44–60.

Laufhütte, Hartmut. "Ein Seldwyler in Münsterburg. Gottfried Kellers *Martin Salander* und die Deutungstradition." 23–44.

Muschg, Adolf. "Der leere Spiegel. Bemerkungen zu Kellers Lyrik." 133–50.

Pestalozzi, Karl. "Sprachliche Glücksmomente bei Gottfried Keller." 185–202.

Ruppel, Richard R. "Gottfried Kellers Ethik im Zusammenhang mit ästhetischen, religiösen und historischen Aspekten seiner Kunst." 61–76.

Steinecke, Hartmut. "Kellers Romane und Romanvorstellungen in europäischen Perspektive." 77–90.

Swales, Erika. "Gottfried Kellers (un)schlüssiges Erzählen." 91–108.

Swales, Martin. "Das realistische Reflexionsniveau: Bemerkungen zu Gottfried Kellers *Der grüne Heinrich.*" 9–22.

Von Matt, Peter. "Gottfried Keller und der brachiale Zweikampf." 109–32.

Wysling, Hans. "Und immer wieder kehrt Odysseus heim: Das Fabelhafte bei Gottfried Keller." 151–62.

Holub, Robert. 1991. *Reflections of Realism.* Detroit: Wayne State UP. 101–32.

Swales, Martin & Flood, John. 1991. *1990 London Symposium: Gottfried Keller 1819–1890.* Stuttgart: Heinz.

Includes:

Adey, Louise. "'Göttlicher Unsinn und unbeschränkter Mutwillen': Keller and the Concept of Comedy." 109–26.

Holmes, T. M. "*Romeo und Julia auf dem Dorfe:* the Idyll of Possessive Individualism." 67–80.

Jacobs, Margaret. "The Art of Allusion in Keller's Fiction." 97–108.

Jackson, David. "*Kleider machen Leute*: Literary Outfitters by Appointment to the Muses or to the Paying Public?" 81–96.

Mason, Eve. "Two Views on Bürgerlichkeit in Gottfried Keller's *Die Leute von Seldwyla*." 127–44.

Minden, Michael. "*Der grüne Heinrich* and the Legacy of *Wilhelm Meister*." 29–40.

Pestalozzi, Karl. "Kellers Gedicht 'Rosenglaube'" 11–28

Rowley, Brian A. "Views of Society Implied in *Die Leute von Seldwyla*." 53–66.

Swales, Erika. "Dead End(ing)s in Keller." 145–61.

Swales, Martin. "Reflectivity and Realism. On Keller's *Der grüne Heinrich*." 41–52.

Graef, Eva. 1992. *Martin Salander*. Königshausen & Neumann.

Kolb, Waltraud. 1992. *Die Rezeption Gottfried Kellers im englischen Sprachraum bis 1920*. Bern: Peter Lang.

Sammons, Jeffrey L. 1992. *The Shifting Fortunes of Wilhelm Raabe*. Columbia, SC: Camden House.

Rohe, Wolfgang. 1993. *Roman aus Diskursen*. Munich: Wilhelm Fink.

Swales, Erika. 1994. *The Poetics of Scepticism: Gottfried Keller and Die Leute von Seldwyla*. Providence, RI & Oxford: Berg Publishers.

Index